BRIEF CONTENTS

MW01195176

ЈE TO SAMPLE STUDENT WORK

.out this book, you will find examples of a student's work as she composes
lemic research paper. You can read the examples in order, to follow the
ͺpment of her paper; you can also read them individually to help you think
about your writing as you make decisions about your work at a particular stage in
your writing process.

The Little DK Handbook

SECOND EDITION

ANNE FRANCES WYSOCKI
University of Wisconsin, Milwaukee

DENNIS A. LYNCH
University of Wisconsin, Milwaukee

New!
2016
MLA
Updates

PEARSON

Boston   Columbus   Hoboken   Indianapolis   New York   San Francisco
Amsterdam   Cape Town   Dubai   London   Madrid   Milan   Munich   Paris   Montréal   Toronto
Delhi   Mexico City   São Paulo   Sydney   Hong Kong   Seoul   Singapore   Taipei   Tokyo

Vice President and Editor-in-Chief: Joseph Terry
Program Manager: Eric Jorgensen
Product Marketing Manager: Allison Arnold
Field Marketing Manager: Mark Robinson
Project Manager: Shannon Kobran
Project Coordination: Cenveo® Publisher Services
Design Lead: Beth Paquin
Information Design and Page Layout: Stuart Jackman, DK, and Anne Frances Wysocki
Cover Photos: *Clockwise from top left:* Kongsak/Shutterstock, MPF Photographer/Shutterstock, Anders Photo/Shutterstock, Tuulijumala/Shutterstock, Tischenko Irina/Shutterstock, Studio Vin/Shutterstock
Senior Manufacturing Buyer: Roy L. Pickering, Jr.
Printer and Binder: R. R. Donnelley and Sons Company–Crawfordsville
Cover Printer: Lehigh-Phoenix Color Corporation–Hagerstown

Part 1: Pressmaster/Fotolia. Part 2: Lolo Stock/Fotolia; Fotosmile777/Fotolia; Portland State University. Used with permission. Part 3: Michael Jung/Fotolia; Edward Strickland, *Minimalism: Origins*, Bloomington: Indiana University Press, 2000. Courtesy of Indiana University Press; Juliet B. Schor, "In Defense of Consumer Critique: Revisiting the Consumption Debates of the Twentieth Century." *Annals of the American Academy of Political and Social Science.* 611 (2007): 16-30. JSTOR. Web. 12 Feb. 2014. ©2000-2014 ITHAKA. JSTOR and the JSTOR logo are registered trademarks of ITHAKA; Joshua Becker, "The 10 Most Important Things to Simplify in Your Life," *becomingminimalist.com*, February 17, 2014. Used with permission; Helen Merrick, "Promoting Sustainability and Simple Living Online and Off-line: An Australian Case Study," *First Monday*, November 12 - 3 December 2012. Copyright © 2012 by First Monday. Used with permission; "Get Slimmer at Dinner," *OnHealth, Consumer Reports*, Volume 26, Number 2, February 2014. Used with permission; Katherine Martinko/Treehugger.com, "5 steps toward going 'zero waste' in the kitchen," March 13, 2014. Used with permission; Mimohe/Fotolia. Part 4: Berc/Fotolia; David Evans, "Thrifty, Green, or Frugal: Reflections on Sustainable Consumption in a Changing Environmental Climate," *Geoforum* 42 (2011): 550–557; Jessica Dang, "Why Minimalism Brings Happiness," *Minimal Student Blog* http://www.minimal student.com/. Used with permission; "UNICEF Bring Back the Child campaign" from "'Bring Back the Child' UNICEF and Sri Lanka launch media campaign on child soldiers." Copyright by UNICEF. Used by permission of UNICEF. http://www.unicef.org/infobycountry/sri_lanka_48286.html. Part 5: Monkey Business/Fotolia; Laurence Gonzales, *Deep Survival*, W. W. Norton & Company, October 17, 2004; Louis Menand, *The Metaphysical Club: A Story of Ideas in America*, Macmillan, 2002; Michael Pollan, *The Omnivore's Dilemma*, Penguin Group (USA) Inc, 2006; Excerpt from Paul Bloom, "Is God an Accident?" *The Atlantic Online*, December 1, 2005; "The Boys are Back in Town," Christian Hoard, *Rolling Stone*, 10/5/2006, Issue 1010; Excerpt from Emily Bazelon, "Death Nap," *Slate*, September 7, 2007; Excerpt from Leo Babauta, "Minimalist FAQs," *mnlist.com*. Part 6: Lolo Stock/Fotolia; Barbara Wallraff, "The Web in My Own Language," November 2000, *The Atlantic.com*. Part 7: Yanmingzhang/Fotolia. Part 8: Wave Break Media Micro/Fotolia. Part 9: Angelo.gi/Fotolia; W.B. Yeats, "Maid Quiet."

PEARSON and ALWAYS LEARNING are exclusive trademarks, in the United States and/or other countries, of Pearson Education, Inc., or its affiliates.

Unless otherwise indicated herein, any third-party trademarks that may appear in this work are the property of their respective owners and any references to third-party trademarks, logos, or other trade dress are for demonstrative or descriptive purposes only. Such references are not intended to imply any sponsorship, endorsement, authorization, or promotion of Pearson's products by the owners of such marks, or any relationship between the owner and Pearson Education, Inc., or its affiliates, authors, licensees, or distributors.

Library of Congress Control Number: 2014046002

3   17

www.pearsonhighered.com

Student Edition
ISBN-13: 978-0-13-458653-3
ISBN-10: 0-13-458653-0
A la Carte Edition
ISBN-13: 978-0-13-458265-8
ISBN-10: 0-13-458265-9

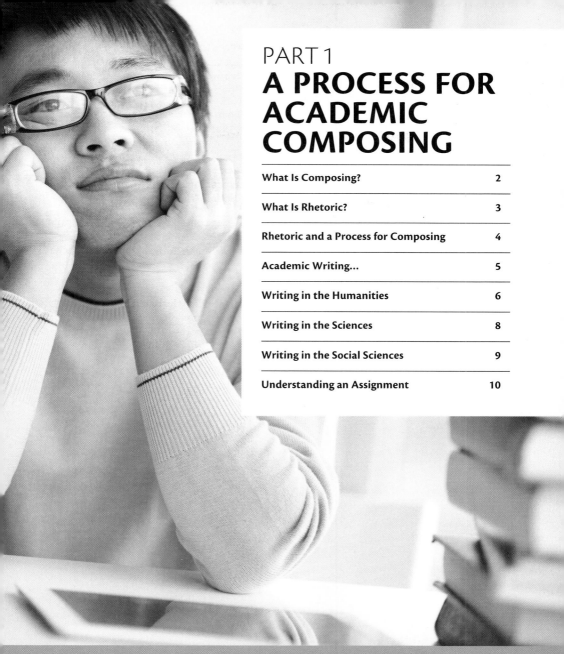

PART 1
A PROCESS FOR ACADEMIC COMPOSING

WHAT IS COMPOSING?

Composing a paper, you arrange words into sentences and then sentences into paragraphs, hoping that the arrangement will engage your readers. Composing a poster, you arrange words, photographs, and colors so that viewers will want to look and heed the poster's purposes. Composing a podcast, you arrange voices and other sounds so that others want to listen. In other words, composing—as we use the word in this book—refers to written, visual, oral, and mixed-media texts that you create.

The New London Group—British and American teachers who research how we learn to communicate—argues that composing requires three steps:

1 No matter the medium—written, visual, oral, or a mix—we compose with elements and arrangements already familiar to others. These existing elements and arrangements are called **available designs** by the New London Group.

2 As we compose our texts out of available designs, we are **designing**, trying out new shapes and combinations of what is available.

3 When we finish composing, we have made the **redesigned**, something new out of past possibilities. The redesigned, in turn, becomes a new available design for our or others' future composing.

This process shapes what we offer in this handbook.

If you are to be an effective and satisfied composer, you need to learn the designs that are available to you—the conventions, grammars, and expectations—so you can make what audiences can understand, but also so that you can compose for your own purposes, which might be new and unexpected.

WHAT IS RHETORIC?

Rhetoric is a method for understanding how communication works.

Rhetoric developed in the western Mediterranean area more than 2,000 years ago as political systems became democratic and as legal institutions came into being. People saw that audiences were moved by some speeches and writings more than by others—and they noticed that some speeches and writings failed, achieving the opposite of their composers' purposes.

Some people started systematically studying why some speeches and writing were more effective than others. The result of these studies is rhetoric.

AUDIENCES

Rhetoric begins with the understanding that writers (and composers of any text) address audiences. Audiences are not mindlessly and automatically under a composer's sway; instead, audiences come to texts with beliefs, values, and ideas. Using rhetoric, composers consider the relationships they can build with audiences so that audiences will want to listen and engage with the issues at hand.

CONTEXT

Where and when do composer and audience meet? Is it face to face or through an essay? Late Saturday night or early Monday? How will recent events influence an audience's attitudes? Rhetoricians recognize that composers need to consider the contexts of communication because the contexts shape how audiences respond.

PURPOSE

The earliest rhetoricians realized that composers need purposes: If composers cannot articulate their purposes in detail, then they cannot decide how to shape compositions. (As when one young woman went to court to appeal a ticket for driving through a red light: it was only after her appeal was denied that she realized her purpose was not to tell the judge how a truck hid the traffic light but rather how she did not even know there was a traffic light.)

STRATEGIES

Once composers have a sense of audience, purpose, and context, they can begin making the particular decisions—big and small—that shape a composition. Composers need to consider how choosing a particular word, just like choosing how the parts of a composition are ordered, is likely to affect an audience's attitude toward a purpose.

■ ■ ■

RHETORICAL SITUATIONS

The combination of audience, purpose, and context make up what rhetoricians (starting in the twentieth century) call **the rhetorical situation**. This term helps us keep in mind that communication is not a simple transfer of information but is rather an interaction among real, complicated people within the real, complex events of lives and cultures.

Even classrooms are rhetorical situations, where writing an essay involves people with different cultural and educational backgrounds: students and teachers. How do you use the audiences, purposes, and contexts of classrooms—and the strategies available to you—to learn to communicate as you hope?

RHETORIC AND A PROCESS FOR COMPOSING

People who study writers and writing have learned that all effective writers have processes they follow to develop writing. These processes differ in their particulars from writer to writer, but generally—when it comes to composing a research paper—the processes contain the steps below. (Keep in mind that, although the process looks linear, writers move back and forth through the steps as they produce several drafts of their work.)

Understanding your project	*At this step, you develop your first tentative ideas of your audience, context, and purpose.*
Getting started	*Mulling over different ways of understanding audience, context, and purpose helps you determine what and where you need to research.*
Asking questions	*How does your research help you understand how your audience, context, and purpose relate to each other—and vice versa?*
Shaping your project for others	*Here, you focus on audience and how their understandings and expectations shape what and how you will compose.*
Drafting a paper	*Given your understanding of audience, context, and purpose, what strategies might help you compose most effectively?*
Getting feedback	*Once you have a draft, listen to how your audience reads and understands: What worked in your composition, and what didn't?*
Revising	*In response to feedback, how can you refine your strategies better to fit your audience, context, and purpose?*
Polishing	*Now you know your audience, context, purpose, and strategies, so you can polish them into a solid, shining, finished composition.*

ACADEMIC WRITING...

IS ABOUT BUILDING KNOWLEDGE.

Academic audiences expect you to approach writing seriously because through writing you add to our understandings of the world and each other. You have to take already existing arguments seriously, research and gather evidence methodically and honestly, give careful and full acknowledgment any time you use the ideas of others, and make only those arguments you can support with credible evidence and careful reasoning.

ALWAYS HAS AN ELEMENT OF DOUBT.

Academic writers accept that there are very few thoughts and ideas that apply to everyone, everywhere, at all times. Instead, academic writers consider a range of reasons and opinions. To this end, academic writers often use phrases like *These facts suggest…* or *Given the available evidence, it would seem that…*.

IS EXPLICIT AND GETS TO AND STAYS ON THE POINT.

Academic writers say what their writing is about—and so a paper's introduction also states what the paper is about. Academic writers give full definitions of any terms they use because they understand that many readers have differing understandings of terms. The writer ought to be able to explain how each and every sentence helps move a reader to the conclusion, without digressions.

USES LOGICAL DEVELOPMENT OF IDEAS AND TRIES TO BE OBJECTIVE AND UNBIASED.

Logic is about ideas that relate to each other because of their structure or form. Thesis statements help writers create such relations among ideas.

→ See pages 68–69 for an introduction to thesis statements and pages 81–82 on using a thesis statement to organize a paper.

The point of view of academic writing is rarely personal. Instead, the emphasis is on the argument being made and on ideas that benefit as many people as possible.

IS FORMAL.

Academic writers strive for a thoughtful tone of voice and rarely tell jokes or use emotional language or colloquialisms. In some disciplines, writers use *I* and their own experiences as evidence or examples; reading examples of writing in a discipline will help you learn the particulars of the discipline. (For help with writing assignments in disciplines that are new to you, ask your teacher.)

→ See pages 113–117 for more on creating a formal tone.

Academic writing usually uses longer words and sentences, a broader vocabulary, and more complex grammar than spoken language. Some of the more complex grammatical forms that academic writing uses are

→ dependent clauses, described on page 217.

→ complex, compound, and complex-compound sentences, described on pages 254–259.

WRITING IN THE HUMANITIES

Writing in the humanities can be creative, theoretic, or analytic. We focus on analytic writing, for you will be asked to produce such writing in literature, film, rhetoric, modern languages, art, philosophy, history, and gender studies classes.

When you write analytically, you focus on a text—such as a short story or film—or on a topic, as we describe in Part 2. Whether you analyze a text or a topic, you analyze to understand **how** and **why** the text or topic is presented as it is.

ANALYZING TEXTS

When you analyze a text, you can focus on the text by itself, describing its parts and arguing how the parts create an overall effect: You might show how a poem's line lengths and soft vowel sounds encourage a reader's reflections. You might also analyze a text by comparing it with other texts or by explaining how it embodies cultural values and structures: You might compare contemporary graphic novels and short stories to show how both use quick, pictorial description and go on to argue that this echoes the timing of fast food and video edits.

ANALYZING TOPICS

When you analyze a topic, you do the work we describe in Parts 2, 3, and 4 of this book. You look to texts—books, journals, films, interviews—to help you learn about the topic. Then, using what you have learned from those other texts as evidence, you develop an argument focused on the values, ideas, or effects associated with the topic.

ORGANIZING ANALYTIC PAPERS

1 **TITLE.** Examples: "Counterfeit Motion: The Animated Films of Eadweard Muybridge" or "'To Protect and Serve': African American Female Literacies."

2 **INTRODUCTION.** In humanities papers, an introduction can begin with a relevant quotation or example to pique interest, but the introduction's purpose is to draw readers' attention to the question or problem being discussed and to make clear why it should matter to them.

ARGUMENT. The main argument is usually explicitly stated in the introduction and is probably also repeated in the conclusion. Writers rarely leave readers to infer the argument. Subsequent ideas and information are related to the argument; nothing is put into the text that doesn't support or further the argument.

3 **BODY.** This contains the writer's analysis of the text or topic. Evidence supports the analysis: In the analysis of a text, the evidence is drawn from the text itself, through quotation; in the analysis of topics, evidence comes from a range of sources.

→ See pages 76–77 on the kinds of evidence used in humanities writing.

ARRANGEMENT OF IDEAS. Writers state the main argument in the beginning of the paper and then provide evidence for it.

→ Page 78 explains some aspects of the logic used in academic writing.

Each paragraph usually picks up on and develops a point from the preceding paragraph, moving readers forward with little repetition.

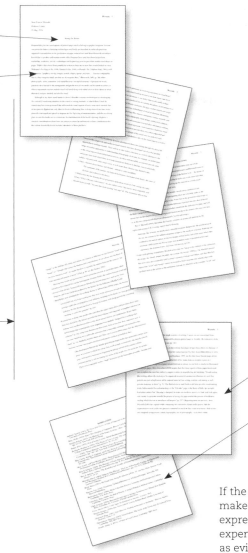

Writers consolidate or group related issues to make their writing less repetitive. They also develop their ideas by taking advantage of the different possible structures of paragraphs.

→ See page 87 to learn about development in paragraphs. (Pages 83–86 discuss how to build coherence within paragraphs.)

→ See page 111 to learn about writing transitions between paragraphs.

EVIDENCE IN SUPPORT OF THE ARGUMENT. Evidence is given to support the main argument. Different disciplines will value different types of support and will use it in specific ways; in general, academic writers tend to avoid using only stories or examples as evidence.

→ See pages 76–77 for the types of evidence used in academic and technical writing.

The body of the writing is composed almost exclusively of evidence. Statistics, examples, and facts support any generalizations used in the argument.

4 CONCLUSION. The conclusion summarizes the paper's argument while offering no new information.

5 WORKS-CITED LIST. At the end of the paper, list any works by other writers that are cited in the paper.

→ See pages 124–165 to learn MLA style, most often used in the humanities.

If the writer's purpose and the context of the writing make it appropriate, writing in the humanities can be expressive: Writers can use *I*, draw on their personal experiences or those of others, and use narratives as evidence. Check with your teacher if you are considering doing any of this for a class assignment.

WRITING IN THE SCIENCES

Research reports by scientists and engineers usually follow a specific arrangement. The arrangement directs readers' attention to how an experiment was performed; readers can then judge the results and perhaps replicate the experiment.

The arrangement that scientists and engineers have developed to support communication about experiments asks that any report be separated into the following parts, labelled with the names shown here:

1 **TITLE,** which describes the experiment. One example: *The Physiological Effects of Pallidal Deep Brain Stimulation in Dystonia.*

2 **ABSTRACT,** which is a short and concise overview of the paper; abstracts help readers see quickly if a paper is relevant to their work.

3 **INTRODUCTION.** The introduction states why the research was done, what was being tested, and the predicted results— the hypothesis. There might also be a review of earlier relevant research.

4 **METHODS.** Researchers describe the procedures they undertook to perform their experiments, including the materials and equipment used.

5 **RESULTS.** Researchers describe what they learned from the experiment.

6 **DISCUSSION.** Researchers discuss their understanding of the results. *Did the results support the hypothesis? Why—or why not?*

7 **CONCLUSION.** The researchers describe possible implications of their experiment as well as possible further research.

8 **REFERENCE LIST.** Any works by other researchers that are cited in the report—or any related reports written at an earlier time by the authors—are listed in CSE style (see below).

In addition, scientific writing usually has the following features:

- Because experiments are supposed to be repeatable anywhere by anyone, the experiment is emphasized, not the experimenter. Scientific writers therefore rarely use the first person *I* or *we* in writing; instead, they often use passive voice.

  → See page 112 on passive voice.

- Because scientific and engineering evidence is often quantifiable, writers display it in charts, graphs, and tables. Photographs of objects used in experiments are also used as evidence.

- Because science and engineering research is most often carried out in labs where many people work, or across labs, research reports often have multiple authors.

CSE STYLE

The Council of Science Editors (CSE) established the publishing and citation conventions used in the sciences.

→ See pages 192–196 to learn about CSE style.

TIP: CLASS ASSIGNMENTS

If you write a report in a science or social science class, your teacher will probably expect you to include several of the parts described here. If the organization or features are not described in the assignment, ask what your teacher's expectations are.

WRITING IN THE SOCIAL SCIENCES

As the term **social sciences** suggests, the disciplines under this name apply scientific methods to studying people as social groups and as individuals within social groups. The social sciences include anthropology, economics, education, geography, linguistics, political science, psychology, sociology, and speech communication. (Some schools consider history and gender studies as social sciences, if those fields use primarily scientific approaches to support their research.)

In writing for the social sciences, the arrangements that have developed over time follow the overall pattern of science writing as described on the facing page, but within the steps are some differences:

1 **TITLE,** describing the study reported in the paper. One example: *Black Women's Hair and Questions of Freedom.*

2 **ABSTRACT** of 100–200 words that summarizes the purpose of the study, its methods, and its results.

3 **INTRODUCTION.** This defines the problem that was studied, reviews previous writing on the problem, notes the gaps in the previous writing that the current study addresses, and gives an overview of the methods used. Writers also tell readers why the research matters.

4 **METHODS.** Evidence used in the social sciences is usually observational, because social scientists are making and testing claims about human behavior. Methods for gathering such evidence include surveys and questionnaires, observations, interviews, and fieldwork. In a paper's methods section, the writer describes the methods used as well as the details of how the method was carried out (for example, how many people were interviewed and what questions were asked).

5 **RESULTS.** A description of what can be learned from the research.

6 **DISCUSSION.** The researchers argue how the results of the study do (or do not) help with the problem described in the introduction.

7 **CONCLUSION,** which summarizes the problem, the research carried out, and what was learned.

8 **REFERENCE LIST.** Any works by other researchers that are cited in the writing are listed at the end of the paper, in APA style (see below).

If the social science paper is longer than about five pages, the above sections are labeled by the names listed.

Because the social sciences seek as much objectivity as possible, further features of social science writing echo what we have described for science writing:

• use of passive voice

• use of charts, graphs, tables, and photographs as evidence

• multiple authors

APA STYLE

The American Psychological Association (APA) established the publishing and citation conventions used in the social sciences.

→ See pages 166–191 for a sample paper in APA style and to learn APA citation conventions.

UNDERSTANDING AN ASSIGNMENT

WHAT IS THE PURPOSE?

Three levels of purpose shape assignments:

- **Your own learning purposes**: How can you use the assignment to focus on skills you wish to build (transitions, research, analysis, or complex paragraphs)?

- **Your rhetorical purpose in writing**: For example, *I would like to persuade people to write to their congressional representatives about providing more funding for education.*

- **The teacher's purposes**: Examine assignments for explicit statements of what the teacher hopes you will learn; if they are not there, ask.

To understand what a teacher hopes you will achieve, look for these terms in an assignment:

summarize: to describe as concisely as possible the main points of a text

define: to explain a term or concept

inform: to tell others about an issue, with supporting examples and data

analyze: to break a process or object into its conceptual parts while showing how the parts relate to make a whole

persuade: to present your opinions on a topic using evidence, so that others might come to agreement with you

WHO IS YOUR AUDIENCE?

If an assignment does not specify the audience for whom you should write, ask your teacher who the audience is and how you are to learn about the audience.

WHAT IS THE CONTEXT?

Where and in what circumstances will your paper be read? How are the values of your campus or of the surrounding community, or current national and international events, likely to shape how your audience will read? What has happened recently in the audience members' individual and shared lives that shapes how they think and feel in general as well as about your specific topic?

■ ■ ■

WRITING TO LEARN

To prepare, reflect on the assignment in writing, asking any questions that come up, as the person who wrote the following did:

> The assignment: write a persuasive research paper on a topic I choose. I am supposed to provide evidence, and the audience is the others in class. I've written research papers before, but I don't know what "persuasive" means with a research paper—and that sounds like the overall purpose for the teacher, so I have to ask. (I'm also not sure what counts as evidence; I'll have to ask about that, too.) And I don't really know anyone in class yet, but they seem to be just like everyone else on campus, so I can ask my friends to help me. The context? Well, it's this writing class—so I guess that means I have to be careful about how I write.

PART 2
FINDING IDEAS

A RESEARCH PROCESS

FOR EXAMPLE:

GENERAL TOPIC
By doing initial broad research into their area of interest, writers learn what aspects of the topic might be of concern to their audiences.

file sharing

RESEARCH using general and popular sources

NARROWED TOPIC
General topics must be narrowed—toward particular times, places, or actions—to enable deeper research and more focused writing.

file sharing and the success of new bands

RESEARCH using general and popular sources

QUESTIONS TO GUIDE RESEARCH
Developing questions from different perspectives around their narrowed topic helps writers learn what focused research they need to undertake.

What is file sharing? Who shares files? What kinds of files are shared? Who decides whether file sharing is good or bad? ...

RESEARCH using academic journals and other specialized sources

THESIS STATEMENT
A thesis statement logically arranges your argument about the topic and offers reasons for your position that will be persuasive to your audience.

Musicians who share their music freely online sell more of their music; therefore, sharing music helps bands become more successful.
→ See pages 68–69 and 81–82 for more.

RESEARCH using academic journals and other specialized sources

STATEMENT OF PURPOSE
A statement of purpose uses a thesis statement and a writer's knowledge about an audience and context to work out the strategies that help the writer reach the audience.

→ Because a statement of purpose is usually several paragraphs long, we cannot show one here; see pages 92–94 for examples.

RESEARCH using academic journals and other specialized sources

FINISHED WRITING

→ You can see a sample finished paper on pages 126–135.

FINDING A TOPIC

WHAT A TOPIC IS

A topic is a general area of interest. It's often just a name or a word or two ideas together:

- computer game violence
- the cost of a college education
- automobiles
- racism
- women's rights
- sports and advertising
- health and aging

A topic is a place to start but is too broad for a paper; you have to narrow it by doing research to shape it for a particular audience in a particular context.

CHOOSING A TOPIC

In writing classes, you are often asked to write a research paper on a topic you choose. If a topic does not come immediately to your mind, try:

- **Asking yourself some questions.** What current issues matter to you—or are affecting a friend or someone in your family? What current events or issues do you not understand?

- **Talking to others.** Ask friends and family what matters to them now and why.

- **Going online.** Some library and writing center websites provide lists of current topics that are rich with possibilities for research. Do a Google search for **research topics**, checking out .edu websites.

STARTING TO DEVELOP A TOPIC FURTHER

- **Write a little bit on each possible topic.** Use the following questions to help you explore directions you might take with a topic.

  Audience questions: *Why might my audience care about this topic? What might they already know about it?*

  Purpose questions: *How does this topic help me address the assignment's purposes? Will this topic expand my learning? How can I shape this topic into a purpose that will interest my audience?*

  Context questions: *Does this topic seem rich enough to help me write a paper of the length specified by the assignment? Does it seem complex enough for the assignment? What is happening locally/nationally/internationally around this topic that might be affecting how my audience thinks or feels or acts?*

  → See page 3 to review the concepts of audience, purpose, and context.

- **Do a Google search on the topic.** The following questions will help you determine the strength of your topic and possible directions you might explore: *Does it look like there's lots of interest in the topic? What are people's different positions on the topic? Do the webpages you visit suggest other related topics or other directions for research?*

NARROWING A TOPIC

You can start narrowing a topic by researching it using general and popular research sources—as one writer, Jamie, does below.

TOPIC:
living with less stuff to have a minimalist lifestyle

TALKING TO OTHERS
Jamie learns about *the minimalist lifestyle* by talking with a neighbor in her apartment building; when she asks him why he is giving away almost all his possessions, he explains that he wants to own less and to feel more free and happy.

USING A GOOGLE SEARCH
A Google search for minimalism links to blogs written by people trying to simplify their lives; the search also helps Jamie find other search terms such as *frugality, the simple life,* and *lightweight living.* A Google Scholar search for minimalist lifestyle also helps her see that enough scholarly writing exists on her topic for her to write a paper for class.

READING NEWSPAPERS
Articles in the *New York Times* show that a minimalist lifestyle can be pursued for art or for economic reasons.

CHECKING THE REDDIT WEBSITE
Jamie reads the Reddit website, which contains many different discussion forums. She searches for *minimalism* and finds a forum specifically on the minimalist lifestyle. In the forum, *minimalism* is defined as "decluttering of possessions & thoughts" and people like Jamie discuss how and why they seek this lifestyle.

After such initial research, Jamie could narrow the possibilities to:

- How minimalism became a lifestyle
- Why many young people think owning fewer possessions helps them be more free and happy
- How art, economics, and a desire to be more free combine in a minimalist lifestyle

NARROWED TOPICS

Narrowed topics usually relate a general topic to specific places, times, actions, or groups of people.

GENERAL TOPIC		NARROWED TOPIC
women in the workforce	→	the number of women in politics in the United States during the last 50 years
advertising	→	advertising and democratic participation in the United States
water as a resource	→	water management in the Middle East
the Internet	→	how corporations shape Internet social networking sites
poetry	→	poetry written by people rooted in two cultures
racial profiling	→	racial profiling and law-enforcement policies
global warming	→	global warming education in elementary schools
sports	→	college sports training and men's body images
religion	→	the tax-exempt status of churches and their role in political races
technology	→	the development of the compass, gunpowder, and papermaking in China
the civil rights movement	→	organizational strategies of the civil rights movement

TIP: USE GOOGLE TO TEST YOUR TOPIC

There are two ways Google can tell you if your topic is narrow enough:

- If the first websites that Google suggests come from academic sources or respected organizations, your topic is narrow enough to be worth further research. (→ Pages 18 and 22–27 can help you determine if the sources are academic.)
- If Google responds with hundreds of millions of possible links, your topic is not yet focused enough.

QUESTIONS TO GUIDE RESEARCH

CATEGORIES OF QUESTIONS TO GUIDE RESEARCH

The categories of questions below can help you invent questions to shape your research; they can also help you determine which questions are likely to lead to rich research.

QUESTIONS OF FACT

- What happened?
- Who was involved?
- Where did it happen?
- When did it happen?

QUESTIONS OF DEFINITION

- What is the thing or issue under discussion? What is it made of?
- What is the expected way (in the particular context) of using the thing, word, title, or expression?

QUESTIONS OF INTERPRETATION

- How do we understand and make sense of what happened?
- How are we to incorporate facts and definitions into a story that makes sense?

QUESTIONS OF CONSEQUENCE

- What caused what happened? What changes—to which persons, processes, or objects—led to the issue at hand?
- What are the effects of what happened? Who is affected? What changes might result from what happened?

QUESTIONS OF VALUE

- Is what is at stake good, useful, worthy of praise, or worthy of blame?
- What audiences will value the matter at hand? What do people say about the issue?
- Which of our (or our audience's) values are called upon as we make judgments about what happened?

QUESTIONS OF POLICY

- Given the circumstances, what should we do?
- Given the circumstances, what rules or policies should we make or enforce?
- Given the circumstances, what laws should we write or enforce?

USING THE QUESTION CATEGORIES

Use the categories to generate as many questions on your narrowed topic as you can. Doing this can help you see

- areas of research you might not have considered otherwise
- possible ways for shaping your purposes
- questions your audience might have that you need to address in your writing
- the specific research directions you need to take
- whether your opinion on the topic is well informed

You may not need to address all the questions you develop, but you won't know for sure until you start using them to dig into sources with focus.

When you use the research questions to help you generate more questions, just let the questions come: Don't judge them, but let one question lead to another. The more questions you can generate, the more you will have a sense of what further research you need to do.

DEVELOPING SEARCH TERMS FOR ONLINE AND DATABASE SEARCHES

From your questions, use the words and phrases directly related to your topic to perform online searches for sources.

Here are terms coming from all the questions Jamie generated to the right: minimalism, frugality, the simple life, living with less, anticonsumerism, a plain life, freedom from stuff, a spartan life

USING THE RESEARCH QUESTIONS

Jamie chose the topic of a minimalist lifestyle, and narrowed her topic to why people choose this lifestyle of trying to own as little as possible. Using the question categories, she brainstormed these questions:

QUESTIONS OF FACT
How long has the notion of "minimalism" existed? How did the notion get started?

QUESTIONS OF DEFINITION
How do different people define "minimalism"? What do people mean by "free" and "happy" when they say a minimalist lifestyle helps them be more free and happy?

QUESTIONS OF INTERPRETATION
Why do people choose to own fewer things? Why do people believe that a minimalist lifestyle helps them be more free?

QUESTIONS OF CONSEQUENCE
What happens when people own fewer things? What can they do that they couldn't do before? What can't they do? Who benefits from a minimalist lifestyle?

QUESTIONS OF VALUE
When people choose to own fewer things, what do they value instead of stuff?

QUESTIONS OF POLICY
What policies encourage us to own many things? Are there policies that get in the way of living a minimalist lifestyle? If everyone lived a minimalist lifestyle, how might policies change?

KINDS OF SOURCES

1 PRIMARY AND SECONDARY SOURCES

To determine whether a source is primary or secondary, ask yourself if you are reading someone's original words or reading about the person. In a paper about Ida B. Wells, for example, speeches and books by Wells are primary sources; commentaries about Wells by other writers are secondary sources.

Examples of primary sources:

- novels, poems, autobiographies, speeches, letters, diaries, blogs, e-mails
- eyewitness accounts of events, including written, filmed, and photographed accounts
- field research (surveys, observations, and interviews) that *you* conduct

Examples of secondary sources:

- biographies
- encyclopedias
- news articles about events
- reviews of novels, poems, autobiographies, speeches, letters, diaries, e-mails, blogs
- academic articles (which can be written about primary sources)

Knowing the distinction between primary and secondary sources helps you seek out both kinds and develop a credible set of sources for supporting your writing.

2 ACADEMIC AND POPULAR SOURCES

This distinction depends on the authority and reliability of a source.

In academic sources:

- Authors have academic credentials: They have studied the topic in depth and know how to weigh and present different sides of the topic.
- The sources used by the writer are listed so readers can check that the sources have been used fairly.
- Topics are examined at length.
- The purpose is to spread knowledge: These sources are usually found in libraries; they contain little or no advertising.

In popular sources:

- Authors are journalists or reporters, usually without academic study in the topic.
- The sources are not listed.
- Topics are addressed briefly.
- The purpose is to be quickly informative or entertaining: You find these sources at newsstands and stores, and they contain advertising.

Starting research with a range of popular sources can help you quickly get an overview of available perspectives on a topic. But the expectation for an authoritative research paper is that most of its sources are academic.

KINDS OF RESEARCH

With most research projects you will mix several of these kinds of research.

ONLINE RESEARCH

Not everything is online—nor does Google link to all that is online.

- **Unspecialized search engines**—like Google and Yahoo!—are useful for the following, usually early in research:
  - developing a sense of popular opinion on topics
  - finding popular sources on topics, in both popular magazines and in blogs
  - finding person-on-the-street quotations
  - finding links or references to academic sources
- **Specialized search engines** (such as The Internet Public Library 2, Google Scholar, or INFOMINE) provide access to material to which popular search engines often don't have access.

FIELD RESEARCH

Interviews, observations, and surveys are all forms of research. To carry them out, you usually have to go out of your classroom or library to talk with people **in the field**—which could be a suburban strip mall, urban nonprofit organization, other classroom, or rural farm. Those carrying out field research work systematically by using prepared interview questions or surveys when they talk with others.

LIBRARY RESEARCH

Get to know, in person, a reference librarian at your school's library: Talking with a librarian about a topic can help you find new approaches. A reference librarian can help you with both in-library and online uses of the library's resources.

In-library resources include the obvious books, journals, and reference materials.

Online library resources can include catalogs of the library's holdings and databases of newspapers and journals from across disciplines. (Later we discuss how to use such databases.)

Finally, libraries usually give you access to interlibrary loans: If your library does not have a book or journal you need, a librarian can order it for you from another library.

RESEARCH IN ARCHIVES AND SPECIAL LIBRARY COLLECTIONS

Physical archives include local history associations or museums that have collections of old manuscripts, photographs, clothing, or other items. Such archives are usually private or provide limited access; contact the archive to learn their policies. To find archives that might be close to you, do an online search using *archive* or *museum* as a keyword along with the kind of information you seek, look in the phone book under *museum*, or ask a librarian.

Virtual archives are online collections of digitized materials such as letters, posters, photographs, or speeches. Online searches can help you find these.

Many libraries also have special collections of paintings and prints, films and video, and sound recordings—often not digitized. If you are writing on a topic that has a historical dimension or are just curious, such special collections can be fascinating.

DETERMINING WHERE TO RESEARCH

WHAT SOURCES AND RESEARCH WILL HELP?

Almost all research writing starts by grounding its readers in definitions and facts; the writing often then focuses on interpretation to show a consequence of an event or to argue for certain policies. Once you have research questions, use this chart to choose kinds of sources and research.

	primary source	secondary source	academic source	popular source	online research	library research	archival research	field research
QUESTIONS OF FACT								
encyclopedias, atlases, and other reference works		✓	✓	✓	✓	✓		
statistics	✓				✓	✓		
government or organizational documents	✓				✓	✓	✓	
firsthand accounts (interviews, autobiographies)	✓				✓	✓	✓	✓
photographs of events	✓				✓	✓	✓	
trial transcripts	✓				✓	✓	✓	
surveys and polls	✓			✓	✓	✓		✓
QUESTIONS OF DEFINITION								
dictionaries (general as well as specialized)		✓	✓	✓	✓	✓		
academic journal articles		✓	✓		✓	✓		
QUESTIONS OF INTERPRETATION								
editorials and opinion pieces	✓	✓		✓	✓	✓		
partisan news sources	✓			✓	✓	✓		
people's stories	✓				✓		✓	✓
artwork (movies, novels, short stories, documentary photography)	✓			✓	✓	✓	✓	
position statements	✓			✓	✓	✓		
biographies	✓	✓		✓	✓	✓	✓	
academic journal articles		✓	✓		✓	✓	✓	

As you develop your research project and a thesis statement, you will know which of these question categories most guides your work. Knowing the most important question categories allows you to focus your research efforts as you gather evidence to support your work.

→ To develop a thesis statement, see pages 68–69 and 81–82.

→ To see how a thesis statement can help you shape a paper, see pages 81–82.

	primary source	secondary source	academic source	popular source	online research	library research	archival research	field research
QUESTIONS OF CONSEQUENCE								
statistics	✓		✓	✓	✓	✓		
historical accounts	✓		✓	✓	✓	✓	✓	
photographs of the aftermaths of events	✓			✓	✓		✓	
academic journal articles		✓	✓		✓	✓		
Also see the items listed under QUESTIONS OF INTERPRETATION								
QUESTIONS OF VALUE								
organizational mission statements	✓			✓	✓		✓	✓
voting results	✓			✓	✓		✓	✓
surveys and polls	✓			✓	✓	✓	✓	✓
position statements	✓			✓	✓		✓	✓
academic journal articles		✓	✓		✓	✓		
Also see the items listed under QUESTIONS OF INTERPRETATION								
QUESTIONS OF POLICY								
government decisions	✓				✓	✓	✓	
organizational policy statements and decisions	✓			✓	✓		✓	✓
business records	✓			✓	✓		✓	✓
trial decisions	✓			✓	✓		✓	✓
academic journal articles		✓	✓		✓	✓		

CHOOSING SOURCES

Compositions that audiences take seriously offer as much support as possible from a range of sources. The kinds of sources appropriate for your argument depend on the argument you are making, the audience for the argument, and your context.

→ Pages 24–27 provide more detail on the characteristics of these categories of sources.

CATEGORIES OF SOURCES

PERIODICALS
They are called *periodicals* because they are published periodically: daily, weekly, monthly, quarterly.
- **DAILY NEWSPAPERS**
- **POPULAR MAGAZINES**
- **ACADEMIC JOURNALS**

BOOKS
- **NONFICTION BOOKS**
- **REFERENCE BOOKS** provide factual information such as definitions or statistics or may contain records of different documents.
- **EDITED COLLECTIONS** contain essays written by multiple authors bound into one book.
- **CORPORATE AUTHOR.** Companies publish annual reports on their finances and accomplishments; they also might publish books or pamphlets relevant to their products or services.

- **GOVERNMENT AUTHOR.** The U.S. government, at both federal and state levels, publishes a range of books, pamphlets, guides, and reports on health, agriculture, statistics, education, and other issues.

ONLINE SOURCES
- **PERSONAL WEBSITES & BLOGS** present the personal opinions of individuals who may or may not have the credentials to write on a particular topic.
- **GROUP BLOGS** bring together people who care about similar issues, each of whom contributes individual entries.
- **CORPORATE WEBSITES & BLOGS** present information about and opinions of companies.
- **WEBSITES FOR NONPROFIT ORGANIZATIONS.** According to the Internal Revenue Service, an organization is a nonprofit if its income does not go to stockholders, directors, or anyone else connected with the organization; instead, its income supports only the work the organization does. A nonprofit's URL usually ends in *.org*.
- **GOVERNMENT WEBSITES.** U.S. government websites usually end in *.gov*. State websites end with the two-letter abbreviation for the state followed by *.gov*.
- **ONLINE PERIODICALS.** Distinguish among online periodicals just as you do among print periodicals.
- **ONLINE REFERENCE WORKS** can be online versions of print reference works or reference works created to be only online.
- **DATABASES OF JOURNALS** are like search engines into collections of periodicals.
- **WIKIPEDIA**

CHARACTERISTICS THAT DISTINGUISH SOURCES

On the next pages, we describe often-used source categories so you can judge their appropriateness for your purposes. We use the following criteria:

- **WHEN TO USE**

  We make suggestions for using sources in ways readers will trust—but keep in mind that you always need to consider *your* readers, *your* purposes, and *your* contexts in making choices about what sources to use and how to use them. If you have any questions about a source, ask people from your intended audience how they would respond to your use of the source.

- **AUDIENCE**

  If a source is aimed at a general audience, its information will tend to be broad but shallow. Sources for academic or other specialized audiences will usually be more developed and better supported.

- **WRITERS**

  When writers are paid by the company or organization for which they write, they might offer opinions and information that are in line only with the goals of the company or organization.

- **REVIEW**

  When reviewed by people who are not paid by and have no connection with a publisher, sources hold more authority for readers.

- **BIBLIOGRAPHY**

  Your readers will consider as most authoritative those sources that provide information that allows them to check the sources—information such as a works-cited list or other kind of bibliography.

OTHER KINDS OF SOURCES

Almost any text can be a source: You can cite song lyrics to show how hip-hop artists interpret current events differently from mainstream media, use a computer game screenshot to discuss representations of women, or interview a neighbor about local development.

We cannot list all the sources you might use because what you use is limited only by what supports your purposes, given your audience. The characteristics we consider on these pages can help you decide whether and how to use sources we have not listed.

TIPS: **CHOOSING WISELY**

- MOST IMPORTANT: Teachers want you to compare and make judgments about a range of positions on your topic. Such thinking helps you contribute to community and civic discussion. When you research, seek out the widest range of others' positions.

- Sometimes teachers give you guidelines for how many sources to use. If you have not been given guidelines, ten or more sources are reasonable in a seven- to ten-page research paper.

- Not just any ten or more sources will do. Generally, use only one or two popular sources, perhaps to present others' opinions to show how and why an issue matters. The rest of your sources should be academic.

- Avoid using only one kind of source. Having all your citations come from reference books (whether in print or online) indicates you have not done thorough research.

PRINT

	WHEN TO USE	AUDIENCE	WRITERS
PERIODICALS			
DAILY NEWSPAPERS	Examples and evidence from newspapers can be appropriate if you write for a general audience.	General public	Newspaper writers are paid; their credentials are rarely given, so you don't know their background.
POPULAR MAGAZINES	Examples and evidence from popular magazines can be appropriate if you write for a general audience.	General public	Employees of the magazines or freelancers are paid to write; their credentials may or may not be given.
ACADEMIC JOURNALS	Evidence from academic journals can help make your arguments as well-informed as possible.	Researchers, scholars, specialists	Experts or specialists write for no pay; their credentials are usually provided.
BOOKS			
NONFICTION BOOKS	Because of the publishing review process, such books tend to have authority for readers.	General public or specialists	Publishing companies solicit writers or accept proposals and choose what to publish.
REFERENCE BOOKS	Use these books to provide definitions of words or terms unfamiliar to an audience.	General public or specialists	Authorities on a topic usually write entries in reference books.
EDITED COLLECTIONS	Because of the publishing review process, such books tend to have authority for readers.	General public; specialists; scholars	Publishing companies solicit writers or accept proposals and choose what to publish.
CORPORATE AUTHOR	A company's reputation on the publication topic will shape its authority with your readers.	General public or specialists	Company employees, or people hired specifically for a project, produce these texts.
GOVERNMENT AUTHOR	Use such texts when your audience will accept the government's authority on your topic.	General public or specialists	Writers can be government employees or people hired because of their expertise.

→ See pages 22–23 if you want to learn more about these kinds of sources.

REVIEW	BIBLIOGRAPHY	EXAMPLES
Articles are assigned to writers and reviewed for content and mechanics by editors.	References might be mentioned, but there are few ways for readers to check sources.	*New York Times* *Chicago Tribune* *Kansas City Star* *Los Angeles Times*
Articles are assigned to writers and reviewed for content and mechanics by editors.	References might be mentioned, but there are few ways for readers to check sources.	*Newsweek* *Rolling Stone* *Harper's* *Sports Illustrated*
Reviewers who are recognized experts in the field review articles for no pay.	Articles end with lists of references (and/or contain footnotes or endnotes) so readers can check the sources.	*College English* *Computer Graphics Forum* *World Journal of Microbiology and Biotechnology* *European Journal of Public Health*
Publishers approve the writing and may arrange for fact-checking.	References are usually mentioned.	*The Mind's Eye* *Where Good Ideas Come From: The Natural History of Innovation* *Central Works in Technical Communication*
Publishers approve the writing and may arrange for fact-checking.	References are usually mentioned.	*World Book* *Longman Dictionary of Contemporary English* *Encyclopedia of China*
Publishers approve the writing and may arrange for fact-checking.	References are usually mentioned.	*The Best American Nonrequired Reading 2015* *Comics as Philosophy* *Learning from the Histories of Rhetoric: Essays in Honor of Winifred Bryan Horner*
Companies *may* set up reviews.	References *may* be mentioned.	*Mountains to Marshes: The Nature Conservancy Preserves in Maryland* *Publication Manual of the American Psychological Association*
The writing can be reviewed in the same or other government agencies.	References *may* be mentioned.	*Washington State Building Code* *Digest of Supreme Court Decisions Interpreting the National Prohibition Act and Willis-Campbell Act*

WEBPAGES AND OTHER ONLINE SOURCES

	WHEN TO USE	AUDIENCE	WRITERS
PERSONAL WEBPAGES AND BLOGS	If the writer is an expert on the topic, you can use the writing to support your points.	General public or readers interested in the particular topic of the pages.	Such pages can be produced by anyone.
GROUP BLOGS	If the writers are respected in their fields, citing their opinions can support your writing.	Group blogs usually focus on a shared set of interests; the audience will be drawn to those interests.	These writers want to be read; they tend to choose each other carefully on the quality of their writing.
CORPORATE WEBSITES AND BLOGS	These blogs are usually promotional; their words can be used to inform about the company.	General public, consumers, people interested in the topics covered.	Employees of the company or freelancers.
WEBSITES FOR NONPROFIT ORGANIZATIONS	Organizations present information that supports their causes.	Anyone interested in the work of the organization; organizations want to inform and attract donors.	Employees of the organization or freelancers.
GOVERNMENT WEBSITES	Use government websites for statistics or wording of policies.	General public; specialists looking for information the government compiles.	Government employees or freelancers.
ONLINE PERIODICALS	Use online periodicals as you would use their print counterparts, as described on pages 24–25.	The audience can be general or technical, depending on the periodical.	Writers can be paid employees, freelancers, or volunteers.
ONLINE NEWSPAPERS	Examples and evidence from newspapers can be appropriate if you write for a general audience.	General public	Newspaper writers are paid; their credentials are rarely given, so you don't know their background.
DATABASES OF JOURNALS	Any time you want to find a generally credible range of articles to help you narrow your topic or develop your arguments, use these databases, which should be available through your school library.		
WIKIPEDIA	Wikipedia is a particular kind of online reference work, developed by volunteers who write and edit on topics of interest to them. Teachers consider Wikipedia controversial because the entries can be shaped by nonspecialists and because there are no easy ways to check the authority of entries.		

→ See pages 22–23 to learn more about these categories of sources.

REVIEW	BIBLIOGRAPHY	EXAMPLES
No one reviews the materials except the writer.	Writings may be accompanied by source links or links to supporting webpages.	*www.stevenberlinjohnson.com* *www.camillaengman.com* *digbysblog.blogspot.com*
The writers on such blogs can run their writing by each other.	Writings may be accompanied by source links or links to supporting webpages.	*crookedtimber.org* *www.boingboing.net* *www.metafilter.com*
Company websites may be reviewed by lawyers to protect the company from lawsuits.	Writings may be accompanied by source links or links to supporting webpages.	*www.apple.com* *googleblog.blogspot.com* *panelfly.com*
The organization approves what is on the website.	Writings may be accompanied by source links or links to supporting webpages.	*www.anacostiaws.org* *www.commongoodradio.org* *standnow.org*
Government websites adhere to governmental accessibility and writing policies.	Writings may be accompanied by source links or links to supporting webpages.	*www.ca.gov* *www.nyc.gov/apps/311* *www.whitehouse.gov*
Such websites might have review policies, which will vary.	Academic periodicals will provide sources; others may or may not.	*www.time.com/time/* *www.americanscientist.org* *www.utne.com/daily.aspx*
Articles are assigned to writers and reviewed for content and mechanics by editors.	References might be mentioned, but there are few ways for readers to check sources.	*www.nytimes.com* *www.chicagotribune.com* *www.mininggazette.com*

Unless you are writing about databases, you are not going to cite them; you will instead use them to find periodical articles—and so their authority is not at issue.

→ See pages 30–31 to learn more about using databases to find journals.

Wikipedia can be useful in the early stages of research, when you seek quick and preliminary information. You can learn how others think on a topic and might find links to more authoritative sources. Citing *Wikipedia* in a works-cited or reference list, however, shows readers that you have only done quick and shallow research.

FINDING SOURCES

The two-step process here can help you find popular and academic sources. For this process to work well, have your initial search terms and some sense of the kinds of sources you need.

1 SEARCH ONLINE

THEN

Enter your search terms and their variations (see page 17) in popular search engines to find:

- **Popular (online) sources**
    newspapers
    magazines
    blogs
    organizational reports
    government websites
    videos
    photographs and illustrations

- **Titles of academic sources**
    (You will rarely find the sources themselves on the public Internet):
    journal articles
    books
    If you find source references this way, be sure to record all the information you can about the source so you can find it in your library.

2 SEARCH USING YOUR LIBRARY'S RESOURCES

Go to your library's webpage and follow each step below to search using the library's resources.

> **Search in the library's catalog for any books whose titles you found in your online search—and search for books that might not have come up in your online search.**
> → Page 29 describes how to use a library's online catalog.

> **Use the library's advanced database search features to look for the journal articles whose titles you found in your online search.**
> → Pages 30–31 describe what databases are and how to use them.

> **Use the library's database subject search features to look for journal articles (and other academic and popular sources) that didn't show up in your online search.**

> **Search using specific databases if you still need more sources.**

AS YOU FIND SOURCES...

KEEP TRACK OF THEM
→ Pages 42–51 describe how to do this.

EVALUATE THEM
→ Pages 34–39 describe how to do this.

USING LIBRARY CATALOGS

If you have narrowed search terms and questions, look for a **Catalog** or **Advanced Search** option on your library website's first page, which will lead you to a page with features similar to the one below. The features may show up in different places on screen or in checkboxes instead of pop-up menus—but they will work in the same way. To prepare to use such a catalog, be sure you have a focused set of search terms.

What search terms?

Using these pop-up menus, you can search using a keyword or phrase or just the subject; you can combine searches, looking for a periodical title along with a word or phrase. Choose an option, then enter your terms in the boxes on the right.

Peer-reviewed or not?

If you seek sources that have authority because they have been reviewed by authorities and found to be well-argued, use this option if it is available.

Where to search?

Sometimes a university system will contain multiple or specialized libraries; such an option allows you to search any of them—or, sometimes, to search libraries all over the world.

What dates are most useful for your sources?

This option helps you search for sources published within a particular time frame, helpful if you need only very recent sources— or sources from years ago.

Portland State
UNIVERSITY

Enter search terms in at least one of the fields below

Keyword:

Title:

Author:

Popular Limits (optional)

Only return peer-reviewed articles

Narrow your search (optional)

Limit to: Libraries Worldwide

Year: to:
e.g. 1971   e.g. 1977

Format: All Formats
Return only items in the format

Search   Clear

What format?

If you know you want to search only for books, or for journals, or for video— or from a large range of other text formats, look for an option like this.

USING LIBRARY JOURNAL DATABASES

Most scholarly journals are now online—and not accessible through Google. To get to articles from these journals, you need to use online databases provided by your college library.

These databases sometimes provide only bibliographic information for a source—the article title, author name(s), date and place of publication, and journal or periodical name—and an abstract giving a brief description. Once you find this information, you have to determine whether your library has a subscription to the journal so that you can see the full article.

Often, though, these databases provide **full-text** versions of journal articles and periodicals you can read online, without ever having to leave the computer. (*Full-text* means that you can read entire articles online and not just their bibliographic information.)

FINDING YOUR COLLEGE LIBRARY'S DATABASES

On the main page of your school library's webpage will be some sort of link to the databases. There may be an option labeled *Resources for Research*, *Indexes and Databases*, or *E-Resources*.

Clicking such a link will take you to a screen where you can choose the database to search.

TIP: GET TO KNOW A REFERENCE LIBRARIAN

Reference librarians know a tremendous amount about different kinds of sources and how to find them, in print and online. Whenever you have research questions, ask your librarian.

You can help your librarian help you if you have specific questions. "I need some statistics about how many manufacturing jobs have been lost in the U.S. in the past ten years. What are the best places you can suggest for finding that information?" will help the librarian find you useful and specific information. "I want to learn something about job loss in the U.S." is less likely to do so.

WHAT IS A JOURNAL DATABASE?

When you have lots of data—such as collections of many articles from many journals—it must be organized if it is to be searchable. In a computer database, journal articles can be organized by tags—records—such as title, author, keywords, and so on; the database software can then use your search terms to find records that match your terms.

1 CHOOSE A DATABASE TO SEARCH

CHOOSE A DATABASE BASED ON WHAT YOU ARE RESEARCHING

Databases are usually specialized: There are databases for popular periodicals and for scholarly journals; there are databases for specific academic disciplines. Most library websites will provide descriptions of the databases to which they subscribe. Look for databases most focused in your area of interest.

CHOOSE A DATABASE WITH FULL-TEXT ACCESS

Full-text means that you can read whole articles online and not just their bibliographic information. If databases do not have full-text access, use the bibliographic information to see if your library has the journal you seek; you might need to order it through interlibrary loan.

2 USE THE DATABASE'S SEARCH FEATURES

ENTER YOUR SEARCH TERMS

Enter your search terms into the text entry box and then click "Search" to do the most basic search.

USE THE SEARCH TIPS

Most databases offer tips on how to use the database so that you find what you want most directly. An "advanced search" can usually help you find the most focused and useful results.

EXPLORE THE DATABASE'S FEATURES

Database search screens can be visually daunting because they offer so many possible ways to research. As you become more at ease with these sorts of searches, you will make your research richer if you take time to explore the features of the databases most linked to your interests.

3 CHOOSE THE MOST RELEVANT SOURCES

DON'T JUST CLICK TO SEE THE FIRST RESULT

When a search is complete, you will see a list of possible sources. Not all will fulfill your needs. Read the short description of each source first: Does the source look as though it might answer your research questions? Is the source academic?

Not all the results will be appropriate, and sometimes scanning the results shows that your search terms are too broad or need fine-tuning. As you look at the list, ask yourself why you are getting these results from your search terms to determine whether other terms might be more useful.

TRY DIFFERENT SEARCH OPTIONS

Sometimes it takes two or three (or even four) attempts to find a list of relevant and useful sources.

STARTING A PAPER

GENERAL TOPIC AND INITIAL RESEARCH

Jamie, the writer considering why young people choose a minimalist lifestyle (→ See page 14), has done exploratory research and learned that many young people want fewer possessions for many different reasons.

NARROWING THE TOPIC

Jamie decided to narrow her concerns to *why* some people believe that owning fewer possessions brings them freedom and happiness.

QUESTIONS FOR FURTHER RESEARCH

Based on her initial research, Jamie brainstormed questions to guide her further research (→ See page 17). Brainstorming the questions helped her understand that she needs to define *minimalism* in her writing, since not many people know what it is. She also realized that she needs to define *freedom* and *happiness* because so many of the blog writers use these terms without defining them, as though everyone understands these concepts in the same way.

Jamie's lists of questions also helped her see that her curiosity about why people believe minimalism is connected to happiness and freedom involves questions of interpretation, consequence, and value, and so she needs to find sources to help her answer those questions.

CHOOSING SOURCES

1 All the personal blogs that Jamie found through her first Google searches helped her learn how people define *minimalism* for themselves. Because Jamie is writing about individual belief, and because there is so much overlap in the definitions she found on the blogs, she knows these popular, primary sources do the work she needs in her paper to define this term.

2 To define *happiness* and *freedom*, Jamie checks dictionaries, but their definitions don't really help her understand why people would choose a minimalist lifestyle—and so she does a Google Scholar search for sources on *minimalism*, *happiness*, and *freedom*, and she finds references for a book and several academic articles that look like they might help. Jamie uses her library catalog to find these sources.

3 As Jamie read the sources she found in the library to find definitions that linked *minimalism*, *happiness*, and *freedom*, Jamie also read carefully to see how her questions of interpretation, consequence, and value were addressed.

→ Jamie didn't find any one source that answered all her questions, but she found enough to develop a thesis statement for her own argument—as you can see in Part 5, on page 82.

PART 3
EVALUATING AND TRACKING SOURCES ETHICALLY

EVALUATING SOURCES for RELEVANCE

Once you have found some sources using the strategies we described in Part 2, you need to evaluate them to be sure they do indeed work for your purposes and audience.

When you are evaluating the relevance of a source, you are evaluating how likely most readers will believe that what is presented in the source is appropriate to your arguments.

Finding sources that meet all the criteria below does not guarantee that they will end up in the works-cited list at the end of your paper—but sources that meet all the criteria are much more likely to help you write a solid, strong, and persuasive argument.

IS A PARTICULAR SOURCE RELEVANT TO YOUR ARGUMENT?

❏ Is the source on topic?

❏ **Does the source have a publication date appropriate to your research?**
If you are writing about the current state of a rapidly changing topic—such as AIDS research—you need sources dated close to the moment you are writing; if you are writing about a past event or about past situations that have led to a current event, then you need sources from those time periods as well as from the present.

❏ **Does the source bring in perspectives other than those of the sources you have already collected?**
You do not want to collect sources that all take the same position, for two reasons. First, if all you can find are sources that take the same perspective on your topic, then your topic is probably not controversial or interesting enough to be the subject of a paper. Second, your audience is not likely to be persuaded by writing that does not consider multiple perspectives on a topic.

❏ **Does the source bring in data or other information different from the sources you have already collected?**
While similar to the preceding criterion, this asks you to consider how much data or other information is useful for you to collect in order to construct a persuasive position in your writing.

❏ **Does the source suggest other possible directions your research could take?**
We do want you to stay on track in your research given that you have a deadline—but we also want you to stay open to the possibilities of reshaping or retouching your research question and purpose as you discover potentially new and exciting approaches.

> **TIP: APPLY THE CRITERIA ON THESE PAGES IN ORDER**
> Although the criteria of relevance and credibility are equally important, use the steps in order. Determining credibility often takes more effort than determining relevance, so save yourself time by checking relevance first.

EVALUATING SAMPLE SOURCES

Below are sources Jamie found as she researched why people believe minimalism connects with happiness and freedom, showing how these sources are—or are not—relevant for Jamie's purposes and audience.

Strickland, Edward. *Minimalism: Origins.* Indiana UP, 2000.

Because this source discusses minimalism in the arts of painting, sculpture, and music, it is **NOT RELEVANT** for Jamie, given the questions she is exploring in her paper. By finding this source and reading about it, Jamie learned the existence of the art movement named Minimalism. Learning about this art movement helped Jamie realize that she needed to include *lifestyle* as one of her search terms so that the results would not include sources about art, which are not relevant to her research.

(Jamie found this source through a Google search using the search term *minimalism*.)

Schor, Juliet B. "In Defense of Consumer Critique: Revisiting the Consumption Debates of the Twentieth Century." *Annals of the American Academy of Political and Social Science*, vol. 611, 2007, pp. 16–30. *JSTOR*, www.jstor.org /stable/25097906.

In this academic article, the author reviews influential writing about consumers and the forces that make them desire to own more things. In addition, the author describes how buying things is linked to "notions of individuality, community, and social relations" (29). Because these ideas help Jamie answer her questions about how owning less connects with values such as community and how we get along with others, the article is **RELEVANT** to Jamie's research.

(Jamie found this source through Google Scholar, using the search terms *consumer* and *value*.)

EVALUATING SOURCES for CREDIBILITY

When you evaluate the credibility of a source, you evaluate whether your audience will trust the source and hence be likely to be persuaded by its arguments.

DETERMINING THE CREDIBILITY OF A **PRINT** SOURCE

❏ **Who published the source?**
Look at pages 18 and 22–27, on kinds of sources, to read about different kinds of publishers. A publisher's motivations can help you decide the credibility the source will have for your audience.

❏ **Does the author have sufficient qualifications for writing on the topic?**
Most print publications will tell you something about the author so that you can judge the author's qualifications.

❏ **What evidence is presented?**
Does the evidence fit the claims? What evidence would be stronger?

❏ **Does the evidence seem accurate?**

❏ **Do the author's claims seem adequately supported by the offered evidence?**

❏ **Does the source try to cover all the relevant facts and opinions?**
If you are at the beginning of your research, this might be hard to answer. As you dig deeper into your topic, you'll have a sense of the range of perspectives one can take on your topic, and you'll be able to judge how widely a source engages with the issues at stake.

❏ **What is the genre of the source?**
Is the source an advertisement or contain advertisements? Advertisers sometimes try to influence what is published near their advertisements to keep their appeal strong.
But it also matters if the source is an opinion piece, a thought-experiment or essay, or a piece of scholarship: Writers and readers have different expectations for different genres regarding how much (unsupported) opinion is appropriate.

❏ **Does the source make its position, perspective, and biases clear?**
When writers do not make their own biases clear, they often do not want readers to think about how those biases affect the writers' arguments.

❏ **Does the source make a point of seeking out different perspectives?**
If so, this is an indication that a writer is trying to understand a topic fully and not just giving a narrow view.

❏ **Does the writing seek to sound reasonable and thoughtful?**
Inflammatory language is a sign that the writer is trying to move you solely through your emotional responses without engaging your thoughtfulness.

EVALUATING SAMPLE **PRINT** SOURCES FOR CREDIBILITY

Below are sources Jamie found as she researched why people believe minimalism connects with happiness and freedom, with information about how these sources are—or are not—credible for Jamie's readers.

Kyung, Emma Sofia. *Simply Minimal.* Elated Publishing, 2014.

This book receives four-and-one-half stars on its Amazon page, with 253 reviews—which makes it look like perhaps a useful source. When she researches the publisher, however, Jamie learns the publisher has printed only two books: the book above and another by the same author on how to be frugal. Jamie can find no information on the author, and so she cannot judge whether the author has qualifications for writing academically on minimalism. This book will therefore be **NOT CREDIBLE** to Jamie's academic audience. Jamie could perhaps use the book for anecdotes about a popular understanding of minimalism (mentioning maybe how much its readers find it useful)—but Jamie cannot use this book to support her main work of carefully considering how and why minimalism might connect with freedom and happiness.

Schor, Juliet B. "In Defense of Consumer Critique: Revisiting the Consumption Debates of the Twentieth Century." *Annals of the American Academy of Political and Social Science*, vol. 611, 2007, pp. 16–30. *JSTOR*, www.jstor.org /stable/25097906.

Because Jamie found this article in a peer-reviewed academic journal, and because she is writing a paper for the academic audience of her class, this article provides her with **CREDIBLE** ideas and evidence to use in her writing.

DETERMINING THE CREDIBILITY OF AN ONLINE SOURCE

When you evaluate an online source, use all the criteria you would use to evaluate a print source, but also ask the following:

❏ **Does the author have qualifications for writing on the topic?**
With some websites you will not be able to answer this because you will not be able to determine the author, either because no name is given or a pseudonym is used.

If you cannot find the name of an author or sponsoring agency, perhaps no one wants to take responsibility or someone is worried about the consequences of publishing the information. If you are writing on a controversial topic, you could use information from such a site to describe the controversy and support the fact that there is a controversy— but you should not use the site to offer factual support for anything else.

❏ **What evidence is offered?**
In the most credible print sources, authors list the sources of their evidence; the same holds true for websites. If you cannot find the source of the evidence used, the site is not as credible as a site that does list sources.

❏ **Does the source make its position, perspective, and biases clear?**
Approach websites just as you approach print pages with this question, except that with websites you can also check where links on the site take you. A website may give the appearance of holding a middle line on a position, but if the websites to which it links support only one position, then question the credibility of the original site.

❏ **What is the genre of the source?**
Some online genres, such as newspapers and magazines, mimic print genres; approach them with the same questions as you would their print equivalents.

But websites can easily be made to look like any genre. For example, some look like the informational material you pick up in a doctor's office. Just as when you receive such material in a doctor's office, however, you need to look carefully: Is the website actually advertising a company's services or products?

Also keep in mind that blogs are a tricky genre to use as sources. There are many well-respected blogs published by experts; if you want to cite such a blog, you will need to give evidence of why that particular blog is respected by other experts. On the other hand, if you are citing words from a blog solely to show a range of opinions on a topic, the blog's credibility will not be an issue.

ALSO:

❏ **How well designed is the website or webpage?**
A site that looks professionally designed, is straightforward to navigate, and loads quickly suggests that its creators put time and resources into all the other aspects of the site; these characteristics could also indicate that the site was published by an organization rather than an individual. Do any of these factors matter for your purpose and audience?

EVALUATING SAMPLE **ONLINE** SOURCES FOR CREDIBILITY

Below are sources Jamie found as she researched why people believe minimalism connects with happiness and freedom; we tell these sources are—or are not—credible for her readers.

Becker, Joshua. "The 10 Most Important Things to Simplify in Your Life." *Becomingminimalist*, www.becomingminimalistcom/the-10-most-important-things-to-simplify-in-your-life. Accessed 15 Feb. 2016.

If you click the "About us" link on this website, you learn that Joshua Becker, the site's author, describes himself as part of "just your typical middle-class family . . . minus the dog and physical possessions." Becker's blog is "about our journey towards a rational approach to minimalism"; Becker has appeared on national news shows and published a popular book on the minimalist lifestyle. Becker can therefore speak about his own experiences with minimalism, and Jamie can draw on those experiences as anecdotes, but—unlike the essay discussed on the right—Becker does not do systematic research into minimalism and so cannot offer any evidence other than his own experiences. For making logical claims about minimalism, then, this website will be **NOT CREDIBLE** to Jamie's audience.

Merrick, Helen. "Promoting Sustainability and Simple Living Online and Off-line: An Australian Case Study." *First Monday*, vol. 17, no. 12, 2012, doi: http://dx.doi.org/10.5210/fm.v17i12.4234.

If you click the "About" link on this website, you will learn that the site's editorial board consists of a global range of respected academics. The writing on the site is peer-reviewed, and the site is sponsored by the University of Illinois at Chicago, a respected academic insitution. Those qualities will persuade Jamie's readers that essays published on this website come from a **CREDIBLE** source.

WHY CITE AND DOCUMENT SOURCES?
PLAGIARISM—AND HOW TO AVOID IT

WHAT IS PLAGIARISM?

Plagiarism is using the ideas or words of others without acknowledgment.

Whether plagiarism is inadvertent or purposeful, it is considered wrong in the United States. It can cause you to have to redo an assignment, fail an assignment or a class, or be expelled. It stops you from developing your own ideas and learning.

WHAT WORDS AND IDEAS DON'T NEED TO BE CITED

- **Common and shared knowledge.** If your audience will know a fact about which you write, you need not cite a source. If you're unsure, find and cite a source.

- **Facts that are available in a wide range of sources.** If a fact is in every encyclopedia you check, you can include it without citing any source.

WHAT WORDS AND IDEAS ALWAYS NEED TO BE CITED

- **Someone else's exact words** that you copy from a book, website, or interview.

- **Your paraphrase or summary of someone else's words or ideas.** (→ Pages 56–57 address paraphrasing and summarizing.)

- **Facts not known or accepted by everyone in your audience.**

- **Photographs, charts, graphs, or illustrations.** Give the source—and permission from the text's copyright holder—for any visual object you use in your writing.

TIPS FOR AVOIDING PLAGIARISM

The best way to avoid plagiarism is to have integrity toward your sources and toward yourself as a researcher: *Respect the words and ideas of others as you would like your own words and ideas respected.*

- Keep a working bibliography as you write.
  - → See pages 50–51 on working bibliographies.

- If you record someone else's words because you might use them later, mark that they are someone else's words.

  If you copy words from any source, color-code the notes or put quotation marks around them; always record the information you need for citing the words.

- If you work online, take advantage of websites like *diigo.com* or *citeulike.com*, or of software like Zotero, to track your sources.

- Understand how to quote, summarize, and paraphrase.
  - → See pages 55–59.

- Understand how to cite the words of others in your text.
  - → For MLA in-text citations, see pages 136–139; for APA, see pages 171–173; for CSE, see page 194 for CMS, see page 197

- Understand how to build an appropriate and accurate works-cited list.
  - → For sample MLA works-cited lists, see pages 101 and 134–135; for a sample APA reference list, see page 170.

There are four facets to
CITING AND DOCUMENTING

1 QUOTING, SUMMARIZING, OR PARAPHRASING
Quoting is using others' exact words; summarizing is reporting the main idea of others' words, without details; paraphrasing is putting others' ideas into your own words.

→ To learn more about quoting, summarizing, and paraphrasing, go to pages 55–59.

2 COLLECTING THE CITATION INFORMATION YOU NEED
Any time you quote, summarize, paraphrase, or otherwise use any source (including photographs, drawings, charts, and graphs), you need to give readers information about the source. For different sources you need to collect different information.

→ To learn the information to collect, see pages 42–49.

→ To determine the kinds of sources you have, see pages 42–49.

→ For help figuring out if the sources you have are right for your arguments, see pages 34–39.

3 CREATING IN-TEXT CITATIONS FOR YOUR SOURCES
When you use the words or ideas of others, provide information to help readers find those words themselves. Each style provides ways to give this information.

MLA STYLE
Monroe reminds us that there is no generic access to computers: Access at home is not the same as access at work or school (19–20, 26–27).

APA STYLE
Whalen (1995) analyzed how the talk of operators responding to emergency 911 calls was organized in part by the task of filling in required information on a computer screen with a specific visual organization.

4 CREATING WORKS-CITED, REFERENCE LISTS, AND BIBLIOGRAPHIES
Each style has its own name for the list of sources at the end of a piece of writing, but all of them require writers to list all the sources used in their writing.

APA STYLE
Panofsky, E. (1970). *Meaning in the visual arts*. Harmondsworth, England: Penguin.

CSE STYLE
20. Latchman DS. From genetics to gene therapy: the molecular pathology of human disease. London: Bios Scientific Publishers; 1994. 362 p. (UCL molecular pathology series).

COLLECTING CITATION INFORMATION
FROM PRINTED BOOKS

Whether a book is print or digital, you usually find a book's citation information in two places:

- on the title page, which is usually the second or third page of a book and has the title, the author's name, and the name and location of the publisher

- on the copyright page, which usually is the back of the title page but which may be on the very last page.

No matter your citation style, record the four pieces of information described on the next page. All the styles require this information; they just use it differently.

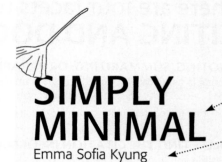

TITLE PAGE

SIMPLY
MINIMAL
Emma Sofia Kyung

ELATED PUBLISHING
Torrance, California

COPYRIGHT PAGE

Copyright © 2017
by Emma Sofia Kyung.
Elated Publishing.
All Rights Reserved.

No part of this publication may be reproduced, stored in a retrieval system, or transmitted, in any form or by any means—electronic, mechanical, photocopying, recording, or otherwise—without prior written permission from the publisher, except for the inclusion of brief quotations in review.

ELATED PUBLISHING
Torrance, California

ISBN: 978–0–98980888–0–7

Cover Design: David Kyung

RECORD:

❑ **BOOK'S TITLE**

Record the book's title exactly as it appears on the title page, including punctuation and any subtitle. If the title is not in English, copy it exactly, including any punctuation.

❑ **AUTHOR'S NAME(S)**

Record the author's name(s) exactly as on the book's title page. → For MLA style, see pages 149–151 for what to record in cases of no or multiple authors, if a company or organization is listed, or if the author is described as an editor. → For APA style on these issues, see pages 180–181.

❑ **PUBLISHER'S NAME**

Record the publisher's name exactly as it appears on either the title or the copyright page. (For the example, you would record *Elated Publishing*.)

❑ **DATE OF PUBLICATION**

Record the year listed on the copyright page (sometimes it is also on the title page). If no year is listed, record that there is no date. Record the latest date if more than one is listed.

WHAT IF?

- **If you cannot find an author's name,** make a note that you cannot find a name.

- **If there is not a person's name but instead the name of a government organization,** record the organization's name exactly as it appears.

- **If there are two or more author names listed,** record them all exactly as they appear, in the order they appear. Each citation style lists multiple authors' names differently, so check the style you are using when you make your citations.

- **If instead of a person's name there is the name of an organization or business,** you have *a corporate author*. Record the name exactly as it appears on the title page.

- **If the person listed on the title page is described as an editor,** record the person's name and that the person is the editor. (If more than one name is listed, record the names as you would record multiple authors' names, as above.)

- **If the book has an author listed as well as the name of someone who revised that person's work,** record both names.

- **If the book is a collection of essays or articles written by different authors and you are citing one article,** record all the information listed here, but also record the name of the person who wrote the article you are citing, the title of the article, and its page numbers.

THE MLA CITATION FOR THIS SOURCE

Kyung, Emma Sofia. *Simply Minimal*. Elated Publishing, 2014.

THE APA CITATION FOR THIS SOURCE

Kyung, Emma Sofia. (2014). *Simply minimal*. Torrance, CA: Elated Publishing.

COLLECTING CITATION INFORMATION
FROM PRINTED PERIODICALS

Periodicals are published periodically: daily, weekly, monthly, or quarterly. For sources that are printed periodicals, collect the seven pieces of information listed to the right so that you will be prepared for any citation style.

ConsumerReports

onHealth®

Volume 26 Number 2

FEBRUARY 2014

The safest ways to stop pain

Worried about new warnings on pain drugs? What you need to know to get relief

6
SPECIAL REPORT
5 steps to prevent heart disease

2
FROM OUR EXPERTS
Safer hip implants

3
HEALTH WIRE
Internet recipes • Eat Greek

8
GETTING PERSONAL
A better night's sleep

9
MEDICAL MATTERS
Vaccines you need now

10
FOOD SENSE
Alternatives to butter

11
OFFICE VISIT
Fixes for sore feet

12
ON YOUR MIND
Hearing aids • Itchiness

Get health advice online
For more information you can trust on health products, drugs, supplements, doctors and hospitals, and more, go to:
ConsumerReports.org

Open your medicine cabinet, your purse, your briefcase—chances are you'll find at least one type of pain reliever there. From over-the-counter drugs for headaches and muscle strains to powerful pills prescribed to control pain after surgery, those drugs are everywhere. In fact, almost 80 percent of adults say that they take some kind of pain medication at least once a week.

But determining which pain drug we actually need, and how to use it, has become increasingly fraught. We've seen frightening headlines about many pain relievers, including some that you may have considered harmless. In 2012 the Food and Drug Administration proposed that labels on products containing acetaminophen, the active ingredient in *Tylenol*, carry stronger warnings saying that the drug could cause severe liver damage if users exceed the recommended daily maximum dose. Even before that announcement, the maker of *Tylenol* reduced the maximum daily dose on *Extra Strength Tylenol* to 3,000 milligrams from 4,000 milligrams, and increased the dose interval from 4 to 6 hours, amid reports of increases in accidental overdoses.

The news on prescription pain pills is even more worrisome. As prescriptions for power-

Americans spend more than $2 billion a year on over-the-counter painkillers and nine times that on prescription drugs for pain.

ful painkillers such as hydrocodone and oxy-codone (*Percocet, Vicodin, OxyContin,* and generics) have shot up in recent years, there has been an increase in emergency-room visits and deaths from the illicit use of those drugs, known as opioids. Three-quarters of prescription drug overdoses (from which the death rate has more than tripled since 1990) are now attributed to painkillers. And there's growing evidence that those drugs are being prescribed when they're not necessarily warranted, including for such conditions as acute infections and heart problems.

In spite of all this, the need for pain relief is real. When should you self-treat with OTC drugs? When are prescription pills warranted? And how do you balance the need

Continued on page 4

RECORD:

❏ TITLE OF ARTICLE

Record the title exactly. If the title is not in English, copy it exactly, with its punctuation.

❏ AUTHOR'S NAME(S)

Record this exactly. In some periodicals, the author's name is at the end of the writing—or sometimes there will be no author, as here.

❏ PERIODICAL NAME

Record the name exactly as it appears on the periodical's cover, table of contents, or page header or footer.

❏ VOLUME AND ISSUE NUMBER

Record the volume and issue number from the table of contents. Sometimes this information is at the top of the page, but it might be at the bottom or on a second page. Look carefully— but know that some periodicals do not include this information. Record what you can find.

❏ DATE OF PUBLICATION

Record the exact date: It may be a month and year, two months, or a specific day. The date can appear in a page header or footer, but it is always on the table of contents. In this example, the date is 2014.

❏ PAGE NUMBERS

Record the numbers for all the article's pages, even if the article is not on sequential pages. The example to the left is on page 3 only, but you might have an article on pages 45–48 or that starts on pages 72–75 and continues on 122–124; record all this page information.

WHAT IF?

- If you are citing a letter to the editor, an editorial, a published interview, a review (of a book, movie, CD, performance, or anything else), or a microfilm, record the genre (that is, record *letter to the editor* or *review*).

- If you are citing a daily newspaper, collect the following in addition to the information shown to the left:
  - Newspaper name; if a local (not national) newspaper does not include the city name in its title, record the city name as well.
  - Date (day, month, and year)
  - Page number(s), including any letters that designate the section of the newspaper. If the article is on multiple pages, record all of its pages, even if they are not sequential.

- If you are citing a periodical that is published every week or every other week, collect all the information shown to the left, but you will need to collect the date as:
  - Date (day, month, and year)

- If you are citing a periodical that is published every month or once a season, collect all the information shown to the left, but you will need to collect the date as:
  - Date (month and year)

THE MLA CITATION FOR THIS SOURCE

"Get Slimmer at Dinner." *Consumer Reports On Health*, vol. 26, no. 2, 2014, p. 3.

THE APA CITATION FOR THIS SOURCE

Get slimmer at dinner. (2014). *Consumer Reports On Health*, 26(2), 3.

COLLECTING CITATION INFORMATION
FROM WEBPAGES

For the purposes of citation, there are two kinds of websites:

- databases of journals
- all others

We start with all others because this category requires collecting less information than when you cite articles found through databases.

On the facing page we list the seven pieces of information you should try to collect for webpages you cite.

→ To determine the kind of webpage you are using, see pages 26–27.

5 steps toward going 'zero waste' in the kitchen

Katherine Martinko (@feistyredhair)
Living / Green Home
March 13, 2014

CC BY 2.0 Ross Catrow

I've written a few times about my ongoing quest for a zero-waste household. While I don't have much hope of reaching Bea Johnson's level, whose family produces only one quart of waste annually, I have certainly learned a lot by paying close attention to how much garbage and recycling my household generates on a daily and weekly basis.

One happy discovery I've made is that the zero waste movement is much more popular and widespread than I thought. Recently I spoke with Shawn Williamson, who lives with his family just outside of Toronto and runs an environmental sustainability consultation firm called the Baleen Group. He hasn't taken a bag of garbage out to the curb since August 2011!

While Johnson's tips from her book, "Zero Waste Home," vary from easy to somewhat extreme (i.e. pulling silk thread from cloth to substitute for dental floss, planning drives in the car with priority given to right-hand turns), Williamson describes his zero-waste lifestyle as much more practical. He believes it's most important to focus on the big things that do a lot to divert waste from landfills, i.e. composting, rather than getting caught up in small details like dental floss.

If you're looking to go zero waste, or at least 'minimal waste', the kitchen is a great place to start. Here is a list of the most useful tips I've encountered, gathered from my conversation with Williamson, Johnson's book, and personal experience.

1. Shop with reusable containers

Prevent waste from entering your home, and then you won't have to deal with it.

RECORD:

❏ **URL**

Record the whole URL. (But if you are getting information for an article from a database, → see pages 48–49.)

❏ **WEBSITE NAME**

If there is a name for the overall webpage or website, record it exactly.

❏ **TITLE OF ARTICLE YOU ARE CITING / TITLE OF WEBPAGE**

Record the title exactly as it appears on the webpage, with its punctuation.

❏ **AUTHOR'S NAME**

Record this exactly.

❏ **PUBLICATION DATE**

The publication date can be near the author's name, or at the end of the text, or at page bottom. If you find only a year, record that. If you find nothing, note that, too.

❏ **PUBSLISHER**

If there is a company or organization that publishes or otherwise sponsors the information on the page, copy the name exactly. Sometimes, as in the example on the facing page, the publisher will be listed at the very bottom of the webpage. (In this case, the name of the pubslisher has a copyright symbol in front of it.) If you cannot find any sort of publisher, note that you cannot.

❏ **DATE ACCESSED**

Record the date on which *you* visited the webpage. If the webpage does not have a listed publication date, you will need to use your date accessed in your citation; this can also be useful information to readers if you cite a webpage that changes frequently.

TIP: LOOK EVERYWHERE!

With the exception of the URL, the information listed above can be anywhere on a webpage. If some of this information is not included on a webpage, leave it out of your final citation.

THE MLA CITATION FOR THIS SOURCE

Martinko, Katherine. "5 Steps Toward Going 'Zero Waste' in the Kitchen." *TreeHugger*, MNN Holding Company, 13 Mar. 2014, www.treehugger.com/green-home/5-steps-toward-going-zero-waste-kitchen.html.

THE APA CITATION FOR THIS SOURCE

Martinko, K. (2014, March 13). 5 steps toward going 'zero waste' in the kitchen. TreeHugger. Retrieved from http://www.treehugger.com/green-home/5-steps-toward-going-zero-waste-kitchen.html

COLLECTING CITATION INFORMATION
FROM AN ARTICLE YOU FIND IN A DATABASE OF JOURNALS

When you cite an article that you found through an online database, you need to collect the same information you would for a print article—but you also need to collect information about the database, as we show on the facing page.

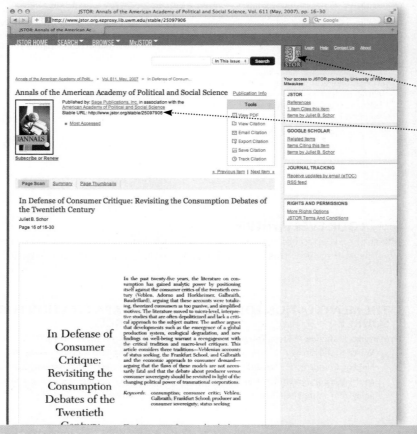

FIRST RECORD:

Record the same information as you would for a print article, all of which you should be able to find on the database's webpage for the article:

- ❏ **NAME(S) OF AUTHOR(S)**
- ❏ **TITLE OF ARTICLE**
- ❏ **NAME OF PERIODICAL**
- ❏ **PUBLICATION DATE**
- ❏ **VOLUME AND ISSUE NUMBERS**
- ❏ **ARTICLE'S PAGE NUMBERS**

THEN RECORD:

Record information about the database and your use of it, being aware that MLA style requires information in addition to what APA style requires:

- ❏ **MLA: THE NAME OF THE DATABASE**

- ❏ **MLA AND APA: THE DOI—OR THE STABLE URL**
  The digital object identifier (➔ see pages 162 or 188) is usually listed somewhere on the webpage; if you cannot find it, look for *a stable url*, which this website offers.

TIP: USE DATABASES WHENEVER YOU CAN

Using databases well requires your time and patience, but databases help you most easily find relevant and credible sources.

➔ See pages 30–31 to learn how to use online databases.

THE MLA CITATION FOR THIS SOURCE

Schor, Juliet B. "In Defense of Consumer Critique: Revisiting the Consumption Debates of the Twentieth Century." *Annals of the American Academy of Political and Social Science*, vol. 611, 2007, pp. 16–30. *JSTOR*, www.jstor.org /stable/25097906.

THE APA CITATION FOR THIS SOURCE

Schor, J. B. (2007). In defense of consumer critique: Revisiting the consumption debates of the twentieth century. *Annals of the American Academy of Political and Social Science, 611*, 16–30. Retrieved from http://www.jstor.org.ezproxy.lib.uwm.edu/ stable/25097906

KEEPING TRACK OF SOURCES: Starting a working bibliography

As you find sources that are useful to you or that contain phrases or sentences that will attract your readers' attention, keep track of both the sources and the quotations. You can do this on paper or online.

Keep all this information in order to produce writing that meets current academic expectations. In the academic world, writers acknowledge the sources from which they draw their ideas and by doing so make it easy for readers to check their sources. There are standard forms for showing this information in a research paper.

→ For information on the forms for documenting sources, see Part 7, pages 123–200.

WHEN YOU FIND A SOURCE YOU MIGHT USE . . .

Enter any source you might use into a working list—like the sample on the facing page—recording the information you need for that kind of source:

→ For a book or part of a book, see pages 42–43 for the information you will need.

→ For a newspaper, magazine, or journal article, see pages 44–45.

→ For a webpage or website, see pages 46–47.

→ For an article you find in a database, see pages 48–49.

IF YOU THINK YOU MIGHT QUOTE WORDS FROM ANY SOURCE . . .

In addition to the information listed above, record the words exactly, along with the page numbers on which the words appear or any webpage information that might help others find the words.

→ See pages 58–59 for how to format quotations.

HELPING YOURSELF AVOID PLAGIARISM

Because respecting the work of others and therefore acknowledging when you use their work is so important in academic writing, find strategies to keep track of when you copy the words of others. Whenever you copy words off a website into your notes or into a paper, color-code or otherwise mark those words.

→ See page 40 to learn more about plagiarism and how to avoid it.

EXAMPLE OF A WORKING BIBLIOGRAPHY

February 20, 2016.

"Get Slimmer at Dinner." Consumer Reports OnHealth. vol. 26, no. 2, 2014, p.3.

Merrick, Helen. "Promoting Sustainability and Simple Living Online and Off-Line: An Australian Case Study." First Monday, vol. 17, no. 12, 3 Dec. 2012, doi: http://dx.doi.org/10.5210/fm.v17i12.4234.

Skidelsky, Robert, and Edward Skidelsky. How Much is Enough?: Money and the Good Life. Other Press, 2012.

Toohey, Peter. "The Thrill of Boredom." New York Times, 6. Aug. 2011. www.nytimes.com/2011/08/07/opinion/sunday/the-thrill-of-boredom.html.

TIP: KEEP A PAPER TRAIL

If you have the slightest feeling that you might use a source—to paraphrase or quote—keep track of it. It is awful to finish a paper only to realize you have a quotation whose source you don't remember: Either you have to remove the source from your writing or you have to find it.

TIP: CITE VISUAL SOURCES

If you use visual material made by others—such as charts, graphs, posters, photographs, and so on—you need to document the source.

→ If you are working with MLA style, pages 124–25 will help you find visual source examples; for APA style, see page 191.

TIP: ORGANIZE YOUR LINKS

If you don't already know about them, take a look at websites like **www.diigo.com** or **www.citeulike.org** for tracking your online sources. Such websites can also help you see the sources other people have found useful on your topic.

HINTS & TIPS FOR COLLECTING CITATION INFORMATION

COLLECT IT NOW!

If there is any possibility that you might use a source, record its citation information immediately.

Nothing will vex you more than having to find a source at the last minute as you are putting the finishing touches on a paper.

DO COLLECT INFORMATION ABOUT ONLINE SOURCES

Even though you can bookmark webpages and go back to them later, two problems will confront you if you do not collect citation information immediately:

- You have to wade through all your other bookmarks to find the ones you want.
- The information on the page might have changed from when you first visited it.

If you are publishing your paper online, you might think that you do not need to provide a works-cited list because you can provide links directly to the webpages you cite. But many readers will still want to see the full list of all your citations in one place. In addition, because websites can change quickly (or disappear), a citation will reference when you saw the site so that readers won't be lost if a link takes them to a site quite different from the one you referenced.

KEEP ALL YOUR SOURCE INFORMATION IN ONE PLACE

Get in the habit of having a notebook or folder or single online document in which you keep track of all your sources.

You want to be able to put together your final, formal list of works cited all at once, and you want to be able to check your in-text citations all at once.

IF YOU KNOW THE STYLE EXPECTED FOR YOUR FINAL PAPER, PUT YOUR SOURCES INTO THAT FORMAT RIGHT AWAY

This will save you time when you are finishing your paper.

→ For MLA style, see pages 124–164.

→ For APA style, see pages 165–191.

→ For CSE style, see pages 192–196.

→ For CMS style, see pages 197–200.

KEEP IN MIND THAT YOU MIGHT NOT USE ALL THE SOURCES YOU COLLECT

Until you have the absolute, final version of a paper, you will not know exactly which sources you will need. Sometimes you can become attached to a source, or to all your sources, because of the time and energy you put into researching—but this doesn't mean you will need the source.

Remember that you cite only those sources you quote, paraphrase, summarize, or otherwise reference in your writing.

PART 4
ENGAGING WITH AND ANALYZING SOURCES

ENGAGING WITH SOURCES

QUALITIES OF WRITING THAT ENGAGES WITH SOURCES

HAS INTEGRITY AND ACCURACY

Engaged writing respects the hard work of a source's author. Such writing shows that a writer tried hard to understand the source on its own terms and to represent it truthfully in all references to the source.

→ See pages 65–71 to learn about analyzing sources for understanding.

→ Learn how to quote, summarize, and paraphrase accurately on pages 55–59.

USES SOURCES TO PROPEL A WRITER'S THINKING

Writing that engages with sources doesn't simply repeat what a source says. Although such writing quotes, summarizes, or paraphrases sources, it explains why it uses the sources and how sources move the writer's own thinking.

→ See sample analytic writing on page 62 and page 71.

DOESN'T JUMP TO AGREEMENT WITH A SOURCE

Using sources is not about piling up those that already agree with what a writer believes. Instead, sources help thicken and make subtle a writer's thinking, and help a writer see the complex relations that shape our lives together.

→ See sample analytic writing on page 62 and page 71.

APPROACHES SOURCES WITH QUESTIONS

In Part 2 we showed strategies for developing questions to bring to sources. Writers engaged critically with sources approach the sources with many questions in mind so that they read with the widest possibilities for learning.

→ Pages 73 and 74 help you develop further questions for sources.

USES SOURCES TO GENERATE MORE QUESTIONS

As writers analyze sources to build understanding of their arguments, they use that understanding to generate further questions: questions for the source itself, but also new questions for the issue being considered.

→ An annotated bibliography on pages 60–61 shows a writer summarizing sources and asking questions.

ENGAGES WITH SOURCES—NOT SENTENCES

Engaged writing does not draw only on single sentences from sources; instead, it shows that it understands the full argument of a source and draws on the ideas developed in the source.

→ See the final draft of Jamie Garza's paper in Part 7, on pages 126–135.

SUMMARIZING, QUOTING, AND PARAPHRASING

Whenever you summarize, quote, or paraphrase others' words, you show readers you are engaging with others' ideas: You show readers you are working to make sense of and build on available ideas and information. This is a hallmark of academic writing and of any deliberative writing (writing that is about considering with others the choices we might make as citizens and community members).

SUMMARIZING

- focuses readers on the main points of a source's argument.
- shows that you are considering extended arguments made by others.
- is (of these three approaches to working with others' ideas) the ability most needed for producing effective academic writing.

→ See pages 56–57 for more on summarizing.

PARAPHRASING

- allows you to modify language your readers might not understand (technical language, for example) into language they will.
- allows you to bring in the opinions of others if their ideas are not presented succinctly or in memorable ways.

→ See pages 56–57 for more on paraphrasing.

QUOTING

- emphasizes the exact words being used, which helps you emphasize ideas you want to highlight because they support your arguments or provide important counter-positions.
- carries the authority of the person being quoted into your writing.
- can bring vibrant and memorable language into your writing.

→ See pages 58–59 for more on quoting.

TIP: SUMMARY COMES FIRST, BECAUSE IF YOU CANNOT SUMMARIZE A SOURCE, YOU DO NOT YET UNDERSTAND IT.
If you cannot summarize the whole of a source's arguments, you do not yet understand the major ideas—or, importantly, how the ideas build from one to the next. If you cannot summarize, return to the source and make it your own. As you work, keep in mind that summarizing gets easier with practice—while your thinking and writing become richer.

SUMMARIZING AND PARAPHRASING OTHERS' WORDS

SUMMARIZING

A summary condenses the main points of someone else's words and ideas. When you summarize, you leave out illustrations, examples, and details not necessary for your arguments. Go for the main points:

In his article "Thrifty, Green, or Frugal: Reflections on Sustainable Consumption in a Changing Environmental Climate," David Evans considers differences between being thrifty and being frugal, to see how those two different approaches might help people consume less. He argues that thrift is still about consuming, just about consuming with more attention for those with whom one lives and helping them have better lives. Frugality is about not consuming and about caring for the future and for those who live in the broader world.

Summaries tend to:

- be shorter than the original.

- tell whose ideas are being summarized.

- indicate where the information was found.

- focus on the main point (or points) of the piece being summarized, drawing on information from throughout the piece.

PARAPHRASING

A paraphrase is a restatement of the original in your own words. You paraphrase when you do not want to quote, perhaps because you already have used many quotations or because the original words are not memorable or need modification so that your audience will understand them.

Here is **a quotation** from the journal article summarized to the left:

Firstly, frugality is a restraint on consumption that is not borne out of economic scarcity and so is not necessarily a restraint on expenditure. Secondly, it is a moral restraint that is grounded in ascetic critique of consumption, excess and waste. Finally, although this moral restraint does not have to be ecological in origin, it is ecological in consequence insofar as it works to reduce the environmental impacts of consumption.

Here is **a paraphrase** of the passage:

Evans distinguishes three characteristics of frugality: people can choose to be frugal even when there is plenty to buy; people choose to become frugal because they want to stop overconsumption and waste; and, finally, frugality results in less impact on the environment.

Notice that this paraphrase:

- retells in new words all the points of the passage's sentences.

- makes the passage more accessible to a nonspecialist audience.

- is more detailed than a summary: Summaries tend to be about whole arguments; paraphrases are usually of parts of arguments.

HOW TO SUMMARIZE TO AVOID PLAGIARISM

- Read the piece you want to summarize several times, jotting down the ideas and points that stick out for you—using your own words. (Use a thesaurus to look up synonyms for important terms.)

- Without looking at the piece, try to say out loud what you think the main point of the piece is. (This is easier to do if you can say it out loud to someone else.)

- Write down what you said, and check it against the piece to be sure you are accurate.

SUMMARIZING WELL

- Make your summary considerably shorter than the original.

- Weave summaries into your writing using the same sorts of introductory phrases and strategies you use with quotations. (→ See pages 58–59.)

- Use the same sorts of strategies for alerting readers to the authority of the authors of the piece you are summarizing as you use for quotations. (→ See pages 58–59.)

- Stay truthful to the ideas of the piece being summarized and focus on main points instead of details, facts, and examples.

HOW TO PARAPHRASE TO AVOID PLAGIARISM

- Several times, read the passage you want to paraphrase.

- On a piece of paper, break the passage up into its parts: *What are the main points of the passage?*

- Without looking at the passage or your notes, write down what you understand the passage to be communicating.

- Check your writing against the original to be sure you have the main ideas and have not inadvertently used the same words and structures in the original.

PARAPHRASING WELL

- Try to make your paraphrase shorter than the original.

- Weave paraphrases into your writing using the same sorts of introductory phrases and strategies you use with quotations. (→ See pages 58–59.)

- Use the same sorts of strategies for alerting readers to the authority of the authors of the piece you are paraphrasing as you use for quotations. (→ See pages 58–59.)

- Remember that the point of a paraphrase is to present the ideas of another as you think that writer wants others to understand them—so don't offer your interpretation or any comments until after you have finished a full and honest paraphrase.

ENGAGING WITH SOURCES
QUOTING OTHERS' WORDS

THE PATTERN

THE PARTS OF QUOTING WELL

Below is an example of quoting from a journal article. The example is color-coded to show the conventions that readers of formal texts have come to expect:

In defining his terms, sociologist David Evans asserts "thrift is the art of doing more (consumption) with less (money) and so thrifty practices are practices of savvy consumption, characterized by the thrill and skill of 'the bargain'" (551).

The color-coded sections to the right explain how to build conventional quotations.

USE QUOTATION MARKS

→ See pages 292–293 for using quotation marks.

USE THE EXACT WORDS

BUT IF YOU NEED TO REMOVE WORDS . . .

Use an ellipsis punctuation mark to show where you removed words:

In an article on tapeworms, science writer Carl Zimmer describes how some tapeworms called monogeneans that live inside fish "give birth to offspring without releasing them from their bodies. . . . A monogenean may contain twenty generations of descendents inside its body!"

→ See page 281 for more on using ellipses.

IF YOU NEED TO ADD EXPLANATION
Put the explanation in square brackets:

Leslie Collins notes that "over 1000 women leaders were killed in China in 1927 by [members of a political party opposed to the Communists]; many of the women were not Communists but simply active participants in the women's movement" (620).

→ See page 285 for more on using brackets.

USE A TITLE OR AFFILIATION
If your readers might not know why someone is worth quoting, introduce the person with a title, affiliation, or other relevant information to help readers understand the person's authority.

In her article in "Neurological Studies of the Eye," neurophysiologist Binti Musa has explained . . .

GIVE THE NAME OF THE PERSON YOU QUOTE

When you first cite an author, convention says to use the person's full name.

Sports historian James Riordan suggests that, after the revolutionary stirrings of 1905, factory owners' introduced soccer to their workers "to divert them from revolutionary actions" (27).

In later references, use just the last name:

Riordan believes that the factory owners' strategies were largely successful.

SIGNAL THAT YOU ARE QUOTING

Many verbs signal to readers that they are about to read quoted words:

acknowledges	agrees	analyzes	answers
argues	asks	asserts	believes
claims	comments	complains	concedes
concurs	condemns	confirms	contends
criticizes	denies	disputes	explains
holds	implies	insists	lists
notes	objects	observes	offers
opposes	points out	predicts	proposes
refutes	rejects	remarks	replies
reports	responds	reveals	says
shows	states	thinks	

KNOW YOUR CITATION STYLE

Each citation style specifies how to reference the page or paragraph of a citation's source. Readers can then find the exact place from which you drew your citation.

→ For MLA style, see pages MLA 124–165.

→ For APA style, see pages APA 166–191.

→ For CSE style, see pages CSE 192–196.

→ For CMS style, see pages CMS 197–200.

BLOCK QUOTATIONS

If a quotation will take up more than four lines in your paper, make it into a **block quotation**. Introduce the quotation as you would any other, but:

- Make the quotation its own paragraph.
- Indent the paragraph one inch from the text's left margin (or two inches from the paper's left edge), but don't additionally indent the first line.
- Put the parenthetical information at the end of the quotation, following the style you have been asked to use.
- Put the parenthetical information outside the punctuation mark that ends the quotation.

→ Page 127 shows a sample block quotation.

TIP: WHEN TO QUOTE

- Use the words of others when those words add what you cannot with your own words.
- Use words from sources your readers are likely to recognize because of their names, work, or affiliations. Readers' familiarity with a source means they will be more moved by it.
- Try to find words that will be funny, poignant, striking, or otherwise memorable for your readers, so that they will be more likely to pay attention.
- In your writing, when you consider the positions of people with whom you disagree, quote their words. This shows your audience that you are being fair by letting others speak for themselves.

ENGAGING WITH SOURCES
AN ANNOTATED BIBLIOGRAPHY

→ For help with writing summaries, see pages 56–57.

A *bibliography* is a list of the sources you use in a research project; an *annotated bibliography* lists sources using the format you would in a bibliography but also includes a summary of each source. An annotated bibliography also might include quotations or paraphrases that might be useful to your argument; it might also include your questions and comments about the source.

Annotated bibliographies help you summarize and reflect critically on your sources—and so are useful preparation for well-developed research projects.

ABOUT WRITING ANNOTATED BIBLIOGRAPHIES

- Each entry starts with a citation for the source being annotated. Cite the source in the style you are using for your paper.

  → See part 7 for citation syles.

- The annotation starts immediately after the citation, *not* on a new line.

- The annotations are in alphabetical order according to the source authors' last names.

- Annotations always give a summary of the source, using analysis for understanding; they also often define the source's key terms, as in the first example to the right. Annotations can go beyond summary to include response and evaluation (following the analysis steps shown on page 64). The first sample to the right offers summary; the second shows the writer also discussing questions and concerns the source raises for her.

A student's annotated bibliography

To the right, Jamie summarizes and comments on two of her sources.

→ To see how Jamie uses this work in her draft and final paper, go to pages 96–101 and 126–135.

ANNOTATED BIBLIOGRAPHY

Evans, David. "Thrifty, Green, or Frugal: Reflections on Sustainable Consumption in a Changing Environmental Climate." *Geoforum* 42 (2011): 550–57. *Science Direct*. Web. 6 Mar. 2014. Evans starts by talking about how environmental problems are tied to people consuming too much—and so people now wonder about consuming less. Evans looks at differences between being thrifty and being frugal, to see how those different approaches might shape how people consume less. Being thrifty is about "doing more (consumption) with less (money) and so thrifty practices are practices of savvy consumption, characterized by the thrill and skill of 'the bargain'" (551). Someone who is frugal "values work over leisure; saving over spending; restraint over indulgence; deferred over immediate gratification and the satisfaction of 'needs' over the satisfaction of wants and desires" (552). Evans argues that thrift continues to be about consuming; it is about caring for those with whom one lives and helping them have better lives. Frugality is about *not* consuming and about caring for the future and for those who live in the broader world.

Skidelsky, Robert, and Edward Skidelsky. *How Much Is Enough? Money and the Good Life*. New York: Other Press, 2012. Print. The Skidelskys start by describing how in 1928 a famous economist predicted that rising economic production meant that, in one hundred years, everyone would be able to work less and have more leisure time. The Skidelskys ask why this hasn't happened. Their book gives some history of economics as a discipline in order to show how societies and governments turned from supporting "the good life" and how we all came to value being consumers and owning more. The book gives some history of the idea of "happiness" to show that this is not the same as "the good life." The book discusses some problems of increased consumption and the environment. The book describes what the authors think makes a "good life": they argue that "a good life" meets all the basic needs of health, security, respect from and for others, personality (which means being able to express one's self freely), harmony with nature, friendship, and leisure. The book ends with discussing what governments ought to do to ensure good lives for citizens. I'm proud that I stayed with reading this book. It wasn't too hard to follow, and it raised many new thoughts for me. I learned that people used to be trained in using their free time—"leisure"—and that this was considered a sign of being free. "Leisure" in this way is new to me; I want to think about it more.

PUTTING SOURCES IN DIALOGUE WITH EACH OTHER

One sign of strong academic writing is that it puts sources in dialogue with each other. That is, rather than including sources one after the other, using each one to make or support one point, strong academic writing helps a writer learn by wondering what would happen if one source could talk to another.

When you put sources in dialogue with each other, you might find yourself with the following results:

- Finding how sources that seem very different are actually in agreement. In such cases, it is important to note exactly how the sources agree—as well as where they still disagree.

- Finding how sources that seem similar are actually in disagreement. In such cases, it is important to note exactly how the sources disagree—as well as where they still agree.

- Synthesizing across the sources to find a larger, more encompassing solution or perspective—as happens in the sample writing on the facing page.

- Determining that disagreeing sources all still hold plausible positions. In such cases, you do not need to try to do away with the differences. Instead, try to understand why each differing position seems plausible to you.

TIP: HOW TO START PUTTING SOURCES IN DIALOGUE WITH EACH OTHER

- Such writing comes more easily if you write after summarizing your main sources. You can do this summarizing as part of class work (as in the annotated bibliography on page 61) or informally, on your own. But having a solid hold on different sources' main ideas prepares you to put those sources in dialogue with each other.

- Even if you are asked to turn in such work formally, in class, start by just sitting down and writing. Don't think about shaping a crisp, formal piece of writing; instead, write down what would happen if the sources could talk to each other. After you have come up with an idea or two, then you can shape the writing to be formal.

A student puts sources in dialogue

To the right, Jamie Garza considers the sources she summarized (on page 61) and thinks her way to a new understanding of her topic.

→ See pages 96–101 for her draft and pages 126–135 for her final paper.

Minimalism Is About Choosing Who We Want to Be

As I've been learning about minimalist lifestyles and why one might choose to live that way, I've come across many people talking about "wants" versus "needs." Being minimalist is about having less stuff—and being careful to know what one needs instead of what one just wants is how one decides what stuff is worth keeping and what stuff isn't.

But I haven't thought about the differences between being thrifty and bring frugal, as David Evans describes in his article. Some people want to be minimalist so they can save for bigger or better things for themselves, and that is thrift. Some people want to be minimalist in order to use less stuff in general, in order to save the planet; that is being frugal. Evans says that being thrifty is about caring for one's self and for those with whom one lives; being frugal is about caring for the wider world, for the future and for hoping that people in other places can have enough.

And I certainly haven't thought about how being minimal might help one live "the good life," as the Skidelskys describe. "The good life," as they describe it, seems to be about caring both for one's self and about others and the wider world—and so the good life seems to merge being thrifty with being frugal.

More importantly, though, I think I'm starting to see from these two readings that being minimal is about a choice, a large choice. There's the large choice of trying to help the planet and others, that both Evans and the Skidelskys discuss, but there's also the perhaps more important large choice of who we want to be. Do I want to be known as a consumer, someone who maybe is owned by her stuff, who cares mostly about stuff . . . or do I want to choose, consciously, to live "the good life"? Do I want to choose to live with the freedom of choosing this, to have the freedom of shaping myself and the world around me? Do I want time to think about who I am and can be? Do I want time to consider how I live with others? By thinking about the Evans article and the Skidelsky book, I realize that I want to understand better how there are many reasons to be minimal—but only certain of the reasons involve really choosing to care not only for myself and who I think I can be but to care also for those directly around me *and* the larger world we all share and so to seek a good life.

WHAT IS ANALYSIS?

Analysis is about breaking something into its pieces to learn how the pieces fit together.

For example, social scientists analyze crises that result from human action (such as wars and economic depressions) and crises that result from a mixture of human and natural causes (deaths from heat waves or hurricanes). They try to understand the political, social, economic, and technological structures of towns, cities, countries, and regions; then they can ask how actions and events affect those different structures. They hope in this way to learn what caused a crisis and how to avoid a future crisis.

Similarly, communication specialists analyze the texts we give each other. Some specialize in analyzing political speeches, some in television advertising, some in film, some in literature, some in digital communication. These specialists bring different analytic tools to their work. In this book, we use the analytic tools of rhetoric.

In the upcoming pages, we follow the scheme shown below, to help you move from *analyzing to understand* to *analyzing to ask questions*.

ANALYSIS

By breaking a text down into its parts and identifying its strategies, we can:

understand.

If we can describe the parts of a text and how they fit together into a whole, then we can say we understand the text and what its composer's purpose might have been in producing it.

ask questions.

Once we understand a text, we can ask:

Does the text achieve the composer's purpose?

- Do the strategies used in the text fit with its purpose?
- Is the intended audience likely to be persuaded by the strategies used?

What do I think about that purpose and the strategies used to achieve it?

- Can I support the purpose?
- Are the strategies used valid?
- Do I think the strategies are ethical?
- Do I think the text's composer respects the text's audience?

ANALYZING TO UNDERSTAND

To analyze a text to understand what a composer might be intending with it, we need to carry out two tasks:

1 IDENTIFY THE PERSUASIVE STRATEGIES CHOSEN BY THE TEXT'S COMPOSER.

By *strategy* we mean anything you can identify in a text that is a choice made by the text's composer: *What choices did the composer make so that the text would be persuasive for a particular audience in a particular context?* The following list suggests the range of choices a text's composer can make, in attending to both the small and the large details of a text:

- **The kinds of arguments used.**
  - → See the following pages for various kinds of arguments writers can make.

- **The kinds of evidence used.**
  - → See pages 76–77 for the kinds of evidence available to writers.

- **The order of a text's paragraphs.**

- **All matters of style: word choice, sentence length, and so on.**
  - → See Part 6 of this book to learn more about aspects of style in writing.

- **Other features, such as colors or illustrations and photographs.**

2 CONSIDER HOW THOSE STRATEGIES HELP US IDENTIFY A TEXT'S AUDIENCE, PURPOSE, AND CONTEXT.

After you identify a wide range of strategies used in a text, ask *Why might this text's composer have chosen each of these strategies?*

- **Ask about audience:** *What values or beliefs do these strategies suggest the composer believes the audience to hold?*

- **Ask about purpose:** *How would these strategies encourage such an audience to think, feel, or behave?*

- **Ask about context:** *What do these strategies tell us about the situations in which the composer imagined the audience would encounter this text?*

As you address these questions, keep in mind what we discuss in more detail in Part 5: a writer's audience is both real *and* imagined: the audience consists both of the actual people who read the text and of the kinds of people (and their values and beliefs) imagined by the writer while writing.

ANALYZING TO UNDERSTAND

IDENTIFYING RHETORICAL STRATEGIES

The analytic tools of rhetoric (→ see Part 1) help us identify the main strategies a writer chooses in shaping a text.

THE ORIGINS OF THESE TERMS

Ethos, *pathos*, and **logos** come from Ancient Greece. In the fourth century B.C.E., Aristotle classified these as the three *artistic* proofs composers could create; he called them artistic because, unlike facts or others' words (which cannot be changed), composers actively shape *ethos*, *pathos*, and *logos* in a text.

Ethos originally meant one's community; it also thus implied the customs or habits one acquired from that community. From that original meaning it is a short jump to *ethos* meaning an individual's character and expertise.

Pathos was used to discuss a person's experiences or feelings—and so, for Aristotle, *pathos* named any strategy for shaping an audience's emotions.

Logos may make you think of logic, and that is appropriate: Both words developed from the same Ancient Greek word. *Logos*, as a name for a strategy that looks at the arrangement of a text, includes logic. Logic is about how ideas are structured— arranged—to have a very specific kind of effect. So when you hear the word *logos*, it is fine to think about all kinds of arrangements that are used to structure texts, including the particular set of arrangements we call logic.

AUDIENCES MAKE ASSUMPTIONS ABOUT THE COMPOSERS OF TEXTS

Whenever you use a text, you develop a sense of the person who made it.

Listening to the radio, you probably develop—without thinking—a sense of any speaker's gender and age, and probably also a sense about whether the person is serious, funny, or well-informed. You could be wrong in all your assumptions—but that doesn't stop you from making assumptions.

We make similar assumptions when we read and even when we look at photographs, posters, or video games: We develop, consciously or not, a sense of who made the text and whether the person is trustworthy, authoritative, knowledgeable, or intelligent.

Throughout all of this, we need to keep in mind, however, that we never know a real person through the assumptions we make. Instead, text producers choose how they want to appear in their texts: Writers choose tone of voice, the evidence they use, and how they describe others. Because the evidence is limited—and sometimes carefully crafted—the sense we develop of composers is always therefore limited and partial.

A composer can use any strategy to shape how audiences understand who the composer is. In traditional rhetorical terminology, the sense that audiences develop about a text's composer is called

ETHOS.

PEOPLE COMPOSE TEXTS TO MOVE OTHERS

Every text is composed for a purpose—and for that purpose to be achieved, the audience has to shift. The shift can be as simple as the audience's attention being redirected from one object to another—but most often it is larger: the audience might shift from passivity to engagement, from not knowing or caring about a topic to knowing and caring, from feeling hopeless to wanting to act. In all of this, there is a shift in the audience's emotions.

What emotions does an audience hold on a topic before they read, see, or hear a text—and what emotions does the composer hope the audience will hold afterward?

And—given the emotions a text's composer hopes an audience will feel after engaging with the text—what compositional strategies should the composer choose?

In rhetoric, a composer's use of strategies to shift an audience's emotions is called

PATHOS.

EVERY TEXT UNFOLDS IN TIME

Even in posters and book covers, we see some elements first and some second because some elements are big or at the top. We have to look longer to see the arrangements of novels, essays, films, and video games. We may read a book's conclusion first, but in the table of contents we see that the composer put the chapters into a particular order. On a website we can look at individual pages in any order, but we see that the designers have designated one page as the home page—and we still have to look at each page starting at the top.

To move audiences, composers make choices about the order in which (they hope) audiences experience their work.

Choices about order can concern the

- **Large scale**. What introduces someone to the text and what concludes it, or what does someone see first, then second, and so on?

- **Middle scale**. How are intermediate parts of a text given shape, such as sections or paragraphs in writing, the arrangements of one photograph in an advertisement that contains ten photographs, and so on?

- **Small scale**. In writing, how might a sentence's word order shape how readers read? In a movie, how might background music or ambient sounds shape a viewer's experience?

In rhetoric, a text's arrangements (including its logical arguments) are referred to as the strategy of **LOGOS.**

ANALYZING THESIS STATEMENTS

Figuring out the thesis statement shaping this opinion piece from the "The Minimalist Student" blog (by Jessica Dang) can help you decide whether you want to accept its arguments, as we describe on the facing page.

Why Minimalism Brings Happiness

WHEN I WAS PACKING for university, I found it extremely difficult to let go of some of the things I owned. I knew I couldn't take everything with me, but I kept asking myself "How could I possibly throw this away? What if I need it one day? What about all of the memories?"

Now that I've moved, and left that stuff behind, I don't even miss it. Whether or not I got rid of it, it barely makes a bit of difference to me now.

I've learned that over time people forget, or their need for a particular object eventually diminishes. Either they store it away or they get rid of it.

You might think nostalgically about the toys you cared about when you were a child, but what is making you smile now is not the thing itself but the memory of it. I've heard it a hundred times, "You don't need things to make you happy." It takes something life changing like moving across the country to realize how true this is.

Speaking of which, for a lot of people, minimalism is about being able to move. It's about being able to go almost anywhere at any time because you don't have many possessions to carry. When you keep things you don't need they become a burden that ties you to a place. Moving to university was a good time to let go of a lot of stuff. And when I visit home for the holidays, I'll probably get rid of even more, to lighten the burden.

Of course, there are exceptions. There are some things that are irreplaceable, very rare, or expensive or that we simply love and cherish for some reason or another—we are human after all. But after we keep those, how much is left that we don't really need?

Hence, minimalism. And why does minimalism bring happiness? This was a bit of a roundabout way of saying that it's because what really makes me happy is freedom. And the key to freedom is minimalism because minimalism reduces our attachment to things.

Attachment to too many objects creates clutter and can severely hinder our freedom to do whatever we want, whereas minimalism helps us start new projects, move, travel, learn new things, meditate, work, expand, be debt free, be healthy—really living life to our full potential.

I left the nest to fly onwards and upwards. I can't do it with old things weighing me down. And that is why I have adopted minimalism with open arms.

TIP: FINDING THESIS STATEMENTS IN ANOTHER'S TEXT

Rarely will you find a thesis statement written openly in a text. Usually, you need to figure it out from the main points you see a writer making.

This approach to thesis statements comes from Stephen Toulmin, a mid-twentieth-century philosopher. Through his studies into the structure of argument, Toulmin came to believe that all arguments are composed of **evidence**, a **claim**, and a **warrant**.

When you read another's argument, you can pull out and analyze a thesis statement to decide whether you want to be persuaded. Here is the thesis statement for the blog post:

> **Having fewer possessions gives us the freedom to do whatever we want;** *therefore* **having fewer possessions brings happiness.**

A THESIS STATEMENT IS COMPOSED OF THREE PARTS:

1 Having fewer possessions gives us the freedom to do whatever we want.   THEREFORE   2 Having fewer possessions brings happiness.

3 Being free to do what we want is happiness.

EVIDENCE,
which states one reason the claim should come to pass. Notice how the reason has two parts: (1) *Having fewer possessions* and (2) *the freedom to do whatever we want*. In a thesis statement, general evidence is given, but the writing built around a thesis statement—as in the blog post to the left—offers more specific evidence. The blog post is short and so can't offer much evidence, but it does offer as evidence the examples of how *owning fewer possessions enables one to move and travel more easily, have more time to meditate, take on new projects, or attend to health, and feel more free.*

a CLAIM,
which is a statement about a condition, policy, or event that a writer believes should come to pass. Notice how the claim is made up of two parts: (1) *having fewer possessions* and (2) *happiness.*

a WARRANT,
which is an idea or value that links the evidence to the claim. A writer believes the audience will accept the warrant without argument—and so, while the warrant is not stated explicitly, the strength of the thesis statement depends on whether the audience accepts the warrant. Notice how the evidence and claim each repeat a similar phrase (*Having fewer possessions*); the warrant links the evidence and claim logically—by linking the unrepeated parts: *the freedom to do whatever we want* and *happiness.*

TIP: WHY SHOULD READERS FIGURE OUT THESIS STATEMENTS?
By figuring out the thesis statement shaping the blog argument to the left, we see that the writer wants us to accept, without question, that *happiness is the freedom to do whatever we want.* If you do not accept that warrant, then you should not accept the argument.

ANALYZING TO UNDERSTAND
A SAMPLE RHETORICAL ANALYSIS

As we wrote earlier, analysis's first step aims at understanding. Can you describe a text's purpose(s) and for what audience it was intended? Can you find evidence in the text that supports your understanding, evidence such as quotations or how you see ethos, pathos, and logos being used?

Your understanding may differ from another's analysis of the same text, but as long as you can point to evidence in the text to support your analysis, then you have built your own understanding.

On the opposite page is a written rhetorical analysis of the poster below.

The introduction
This essay's introduction tells readers something about what the essay argues, enough to give readers direction and (the writer hopes) curiosity.

Building to analysis
Notice that this writer describes how she thinks the audience will see the poster's elements. Only after describing that—her evidence—does the writer describe how those elements might shape the audience's experience.

Identifying a main strategy
In writing a short analysis like this, identifying the main rhetorical strategy of the text can help a writer stay focused on the evidence relevant to that strategy.

Being critical?
This analysis never judges the poster: It does not say whether the poster is effective or not. The analysis instead focuses on how the poster builds its effects. This is critical reading for understanding;
→ see page 73.

She wants to be a dancer, not a child soldier.

bring back
the child
stop child recruitment

Recruiting children is against Sri Lankan and International laws. The Government of Sri Lanka has a zero tolerance policy on the issue.

unicef

At first glance, this poster shows a girl dancing. At first glance, the audience sees her in brightly colored clothing and jewelry, in what appears to be a traditional dance pose. When they first see this poster at a distance, the audience is positioned as spectators: They see a cultural event both beautiful and pleasurable. However, the poster's logos—how its elements are arranged for the audience—changes this first-glance understanding.

Once they step closer (perhaps because they notice the girl's face is not as brightly colored), viewers see the girl performing a very different task. They see the girl is a soldier. Dressed in a drab uniform, she salutes someone looking directly at her. The photograph of the girl's face positions viewers as though they were the person being saluted. Instead of watching a dance, viewers are now in a position of military power over the girl.

As its main strategy, this poster arranges the two photographs to put the audience in two different relations with the girl. The poster asks viewers which relation they want.

The poster was produced by the United Nations Children's Fund (UNICEF) and the government of the Asian country Sri Lanka. The poster's words (most of which can only be read up close) respond to viewers making either choice.

The most visible words address viewers choosing to see the girl as a dancer. The first words a viewer sees are "She wants to be a dancer, not a child soldier." These words tell the audience what the girl wants; they tell the audience to listen to the girl and her hopes and not to impose awful grown-up tasks on her. Below those words sits a logo, drawn childishly, of a child who has crossed out a gun with a red crayon. The childish style encourages the audience to think of the innocence of children and so of the girl-dancer's innocence. Next to the logo are the words "Bring back the child" and "Stop child recruitment." The first command echoes the childish drawing, asking the audience to think of the child lost in the child soldier. The second command demands that the audience help prevent children from being made to fight.

The viewer who would want to be saluted by the girl is addressed in the small type at the poster's bottom. There the audience is told that "Recruiting children is against Sri Lankan and International Law. The Government of Sri Lanka has a zero tolerance policy on the issue." These words use a different kind of emotional appeal than all the other elements. These words at the bottom inform the audience that whoever participates in child recruitment should fear the law.

The poster's rhetorical work is complex even though the poster has few elements. The two photographs make the audience feel they must choose between two different relations with the girl—but clearly the poster wants its audience to choose to help the girl and other children because the largest and most colorful elements speak on behalf of children. The smallest, final elements threaten those who choose to be (or are) the person being saluted.

ANALYZING TO ASK QUESTIONS

BEING CRITICAL

Once you have analyzed a text to try to understand the purposes its writer might have held and to get a sense of how all its parts fit together to make a whole, you can ask how well the text achieves those purposes and whether you think its arguments and evidence are valid.

This is critical reading and thinking. Out of critical reading and thinking we develop critique, and—out of critique—criticism.

Critical reading and thinking, and critique and criticism, are valued skills not only in college but also in living carefully with others. Not everyone means the same thing by *critical*, *criticism*, and *critique*, however. For some, these three words amount to the same thing: to criticize or find fault with something. In this book, on the other hand, we use the following definitions:

CRITICAL
To be critical is to exercise careful and informed judgment or evaluation.

CRITIQUE
To critique a text is to evaluate it by considering its strengths and limitations, its conformity to standards, or its effectiveness across a given audience, purpose, and context. Critique can involve making a judgment about a text, but it can also be a series of observations about how a text works.

CRITICISM
Criticism results from critique and is a coherent statement of evaluation or interpretation of a text. There are different methods for critique and criticism; the method we offer here is rhetorical.

Although we have been distinguishing "reading to understand" from "reading to ask critical questions," the above definitions suggest that reading to understand involves making careful interpretations of and judgements about a text and its purpose, context, and audience—and so reading to understand is also about being critical.

As you analyze, respect writers' efforts to shape a text as a whole: Consider a text's overall structure before moving on to critique its parts.

ANALYZING TO ASK QUESTIONS

QUESTIONS FOR CRITICAL READING

QUESTIONS ABOUT AUDIENCE

- Whom is the composer including in the audience? Whom is the composer excluding from the audience—and why?

- What does the composer assume the audience knows, values, or believes?

QUESTIONS ABOUT PURPOSE

- Why does this purpose matter at this time and in this place?

- Is the purpose clearly stated or easy to determine? If not, why might the composer have decided not to make the purpose obvious?

QUESTIONS ABOUT CONTEXT

- Where does the audience encounter the text? How might this shape their responses?

- When is an audience likely to encounter the text, and how might this shape their responses?

QUESTIONS ABOUT STRATEGIES

ETHOS

- Has the composer appropriate background or experience for pursuing this purpose?

- Does the composer seem open to multiple perspectives? Is the composer treating those perspectives fairly?

- What cultural backgrounds and expectations shape the composer's positions?

- Is the composer using a tone of voice appropriate to the purpose?

- Is the composer acting as a teacher, a lecturer, a parent, a peer, a friend? Is this role appropriate for the purpose?

- Does the composer respect the audience as intelligent and thoughtful people?

PATHOS

- What emotions is the intended audience likely to have about the issue? How does the text acknowledge those emotions and then try to shift them?

- Do the emotional appeals seem appropriate to the purpose(s)? Do they seem reasonable to you—or overblown?

LOGOS

- What claims, reasons, and warrants are explicit or implied? (→ See page 69.)

- Are sources cited so that the audience can check them? If so, are the sources relevant and credible? (→ See pages 34–39.)

- Why might a composer start with particular examples or evidence? To what do these draw the audience's attention—or distract them from?

- How does the composition end? How might the end affect how the audience looks back over the composition?

ANALYZING TO ASK QUESTIONS
QUESTIONS FOR CRITICAL WRITING

WRITING CRITICALLY ABOUT THE TEXTS OF OTHERS

The questions below can help you approach writing assignments for which you need to make evaluations or judgments about texts.

- **Who might care about the text's arguments?** Asking this helps you discover the differing audiences for a text. By listing as many different kinds of people as you can who might care about the text's arguments, you can gain a more subtle and complex sense of what is at stake with the argument.

- **How can you think most broadly about the purposes, contexts, or audiences that shape the text you are analyzing?** You can, for example, ask just about local events shaping the context of a text, but what might have been happening nationally or internationally to shape that composer's choices?

- **How are purpose, context, audience, and strategies related in the text(s) you are analyzing?** It is easiest to write a paper that analyzes how (for example) only the context of a text shapes the text; you will learn more by considering how (for example) the sense of audience you see the author holding relates to the particular strategies chosen by the author.

THINKING CRITICALLY ABOUT YOUR OWN WRITING

The following questions can help you before you write, to clarify your own purposes. You can also ask such questions after you write, as you reflect on what you have written, to help you understand your thinking more carefully and approach later assignments more knowledgably.

- **What do you want this writing to do?** *What do you hope readers will do or think or feel after they read?* Or, when you analyze finished writing: *What in your writing most helped you achieve your purposes?*

- **Are you writing to consider different positions or interpretations, or are you writing to defend a position?** Writing to consider different positions generally engages you with thinking carefully about the positions; writing to defend a position often sets you up to consider only evidence in favor of that position or to consider only the weakest opposing evidence.

- **Are you writing to address the questions and concerns of others, or are you focusing only on what matters to you?**

- **What sort of relations with others does your writing shape?** Does your writing treat readers as smart and thoughtful, or . . .? Does your writing position you as a teacher talking to students, a parent talking to a child, a colleague talking to equals, or . . .?

- **How could you shape your writing differently?** What other possible argument could you make? What other arrangements, tones of voice, or strategies could you use? What conditions—what was happening at home, at your job, or in the news—are affecting how you write?

ANALYZING TO ASK QUESTIONS
DEFINITIONS AND DISTINCTIONS

DEFINITIONS

Happiness is being free to do what we want.

Happiness is the mental or emotional state of well-being characterized by positive emotions.

Happiness is the absence of pain and worry.

Happiness is about taking from others; a meaningful life is about giving to others.

Happiness is a sunny Saturday afternoon after work when I am with my friends.

On pages 68–69, we write about a blog entry by Jessica Dang; we show how the entry's argument depends on Dang's definition of *happiness*, which is the first definition listed above. Could Dang have made her argument about happiness and minimalism if she had defined happiness using one of the other definitions above?

Any time we write, we use words that different people might understand differently—even if they are looking at the same dictionary.

Any time we write, then, defining our terms matters. *If we want to make a particular argument, what definitions help readers understand our purposes?*

Any time we read, too, we need to consider how writers define their terms. *Do we agree with their definitions? What do we accept when we accept their definitions?*

DISTINCTIONS

Is *being thrifty* different from *being frugal?*

Look at the first entry in the annotated bibliography on page 61: The entry summarizes an article focused on the distinction between being thrifty and being frugal. That distinction might seem subtle, but it helps the article's writer understand how each of those ways of being connects us differently to our families, our friends, and to others in the broader world.

By learning about that distinction, Jamie Garza (whose paper for a class assignment we've been watching develop since Part 1) can think more deeply about the choices one makes in taking on a minimalist lifestyle. By paying attention to this distinction, she can make more careful choices in her own life.

Distinctions enable us to compare objects, ideas, or processes. By allowing comparisons, distinctions allow us to understand what is similar and different about the objects, ideas, or processes. When we make distinctions, then, we come to understand which objects, ideas, and processes are better for which situations; we come to understand better our options in moving through the world and the possible consequences of our actions.

Distinctions start with and depend on definitions, but they take us beyond definitions into thinking more deeply about connections and relationships.

Good writing, like good thinking, depends on careful distinctions.

DEFINITIONS, DISTINCTIONS, AND CRITICAL THINKING

If thinking critically involves the processes of understanding, analyzing, synthesizing, and evaluating, then thinking critically involves being able to define and to make distinctions, since defining and making distinctions are necessary to all those other processes.

WHAT COUNTS AS EVIDENCE

Evidence can persuade audiences that a position on a topic is worth considering.

ANALOGIES

When you use an analogy, you compare two objects, events, or processes so that the more familiar can explain the less familiar. For example, a long description of how the brain is like a computer would be an analogy in which the composer relies upon the audience's knowledge of computers to explain how the brain works.

But analogies also carry assumptions from the more familiar object to the less familiar. For example, the analogy of the Internet to a highway system—the *Information Superhighway*—carries the assumption that the Internet should be a public resource as highways are and so should be regulated, supported, and repaired with public funds as highways are.

Consider this when reading and using analogies:

- Analogies prove nothing. They do not guarantee that situations will play out as the analogy suggests. Instead, composers use analogies to shape an audience's attitudes: A compelling analogy can persuade audiences to consider an object or process in a positive light, which is a large part of any successful argument. A compelling analogy is therefore both a pathos appeal and a form of logos.

PERSONAL EXPERIENCE

Personal experience is limited evidence precisely because it is personal. Without considerable research, you cannot know how many other people share any experience; you cannot know if others draw the same knowledge from their experiences as you do. The same holds true for using others' experiences as evidence. A friend who went to Burundi on a missionary trip might know something about how donations are spent there, but those observations have little place in your writing unless your friend is also an expert on the economics of donations or the observations are backed up by other evidence.

Personal experience can become facts or statistics when it is joined with and examined alongside the experiences of others through field research.

When you see others using personal experience as examples in their writing, whether the experiences are their own or belong to others, ask these questions:

- Is the experience used as logical evidence in support of the composer's ability to discuss this topic (ethos) or as an emotional appeal (pathos)?

- If the experience is used as logical evidence, does the writer acknowledge that the experience is necessarily limited? Is other evidence also given as support?

In composing your own texts, keep in mind:

- When you use the experiences, observations, anecdotes, or opinions of others, use them only to illustrate examples and to humanize other evidence of the kinds we describe on these pages.

EXAMPLES

Examples can make arguments specific and concrete. Detailed examples can help audiences visualize what might otherwise be only abstract. Whether you are analyzing others' examples or considering how to use them in your own work, consider:

- Do the examples make clear the general or abstract point they are meant to explain—or do they distract from the point?

- How do the examples support the general or abstract points being made? Are the examples too specific, causing the general points to get lost?

In addition, for **visual examples**, consider:

- Are examples used to support and explain, or do they distract from the purpose?

- Are the examples labeled, to give proper attribution and to help readers understand their relationship to the words?

EXPERT TESTIMONY

The words of experts—their testimony—can be authoritative on the topics about which the expert is knowledgeable.

To analyze expert testimony:

- Do an online search on the person (or organization) to see if the person has the credentials—the education and experience—for offering the evidence.

- Ask others what they know about the person or organization.

As you compose your own texts:

- Ask people from your audience if they know and trust the experts you are citing.

- If your audience might not be familiar with an expert you cite, explain the person's authority.

FACTS

A fact is a statement about an event or condition that exists or has happened. Readers can check statements used as facts in writing to see if they are true or false. If someone claims it is a fact that cold climate turtles hibernate, we ought to be able to go see such hibernating turtles for ourselves.

Facts can be presented in words and through numbers, accounts of firsthand experience, illustrations, charts, and graphs.

To evaluate facts, ask the following:

- Are sources given for the facts and statistics? If so, are they authoritative? If not, do you trust the author enough to accept the facts?

- Do the facts and statistics support the conclusions that are based on them?

- Can you find other facts that contradict those you are questioning?

When you are using facts and statistics in your own compositions, consider:

- Will your audience accept the authority of the sources from which you've drawn the facts or statistics?

- Have you made clear how the facts support the points you are making?

- If you are working with a source that offers a wide range of facts or statistics—census data, for example—are you using the facts responsibly, using them fully, and not choosing only those that support your points?

ANALYZING TO ASK QUESTIONS

CRITICAL REASONING

FORMAL & INFORMAL ARGUMENT

Formal argument is called *formal* because it depends on the arrangement or form of ideas; it usually has explicit statements of premise and conclusion. Informal argument can simply be about taking others from evidence toward conclusion without any explicit statement of premises; it can also be about simply showing others a new position they hadn't considered before.

DEDUCTION

A thesis statement depends on deduction: From general premises, one deduces a specific conclusion. The form of deduction is often called a *syllogism*, which looks like this:

A leads to <u>B</u>.

<u>B</u> leads to <u>C</u>.

Therefore, <u>A</u> leads to <u>C</u>.

For example:

Modern language classes expose <u>students to other cultures</u>.

<u>Classes that expose students to other cultures</u> prepare <u>students to live in a global economy.</u>

Therefore, <u>modern language classes prepare students to live in a global economy</u>.

Try to rephrase this syllogism into a thesis statement (as on page 77) about the value of modern language classes—and notice that, if you wished to persuade readers of the conclusion, you would need to persuade them only of the first and second statements, because the conclusion follows logically from the first two statements.

INDUCTION

Induction moves from the specific to the general, from specific observations to a general statement about a shared condition:

There is a crow, and it's black.

There's another black crow.

There's another black crow.

Therefore, all crows must be black.

That sample may seem silly to you, but writers use induction all the time: Imagine a writer describing three specific examples of how someone's thinking had been shaped by their experience and then concluding that all thinking is based on individual experience.

USING FORMAL AND INFORMAL ARGUMENTS

Formal and informal arguments provide the skeleton for all persuasive writing—and so you should look for both such forms in the writing of others. Attend to using such arguments in your own writing, too, as we have discussed with thesis statements and using examples. Each form of argument helps you move readers to the conclusions you hope they will consider, but each has its challenges. Deduction requires readers to accept the general premises, and so requires writers to focus on the premises (and analytic readers to look closely at the premises). Induction requires readers to leap from specific examples to a conclusion, but how do you persuade readers you have provided enough examples (or how do you as a reader decide that enough examples have been given)?

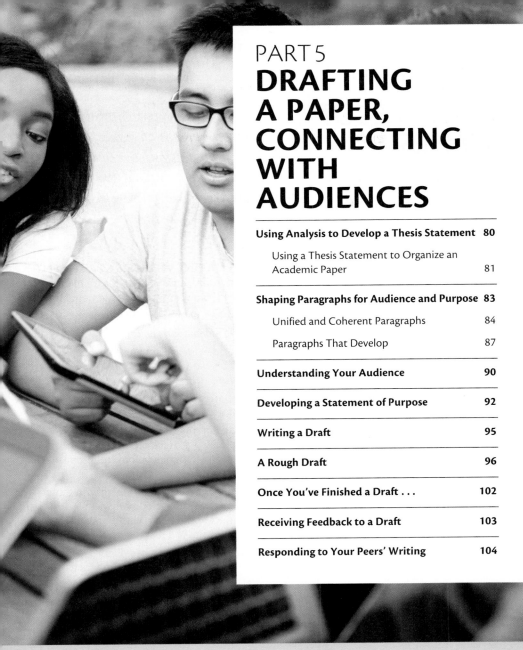

PART 5

DRAFTING A PAPER, CONNECTING WITH AUDIENCES

USING ANALYSIS TO DEVELOP A THESIS STATEMENT

Jamie Garza has done initial online and library research into minimalist lifestyles, as the notes on page 51 describe. Because Jamie asked the research questions she did (page 17), she was able to read her sources analytically, looking for specific information, critically questioning what she found, and judging the credibility of her sources.

Jamie learned that the term *minimalism* was first used to describe an art movement of the 1960s and 1970s, but that it is now often used to describe a lifestyle people choose when they want to own fewer things.

Thinking analytically about this situation, Jamie wondered why people would want a minimalist lifestyle—and so she read her sources looking for the reasons people choose minimalism. She found that many people think that owning fewer possessions helps them be happier and more free; in a book she read, those qualities were tied together (with other qualities) to a notion of "a good life."

Reading critically, she noticed that, while her sources listed many different reasons for thinking of "a good life" in these ways, one common underlying reason was a desire for taking better care of what one does own, the planet, and one's self.

A THESIS STATEMENT

Based on her research, Jamie wrote this thesis statement following the form shown on page 69:

> Choosing a minimalist lifestyle focuses people on respecting their possessions and so on the environment and how they use their time; therefore, a minimalist lifestyle helps people live a good life.

EVALUATING A THESIS STATEMENT

Effective and engaging papers are most likely to come from thesis statements that:

1 Have a concrete and focused claim.

2 Have a debatable claim.

3 Rely on evidence supported by credible and relevant sources.

Using the three points above to think about Jamie's thesis statement, here's an evaluation:

1 The claim that *a minimalist lifestyle helps people live a good life* concretely focuses readers' attentions on how minimalism and a good life are connected.

2 From her reading and talking with others, Jamie knows that not many people connect minimalism with a good life, and so her claim is debatable.

3 In addition to drawing evidence from popular sources like blogs and magazine articles, Jamie will use credible academic sources—written by economists and sociologists—to make her argument.

USING A THESIS STATEMENT TO ORGANIZE AN ACADEMIC PAPER

If a reader cannot figure out why one paragraph follows another in a text, the reader will be confused—and the text loses its force. But **the reader** won't be able to figure out why one paragraph follows another if **the writer** hasn't figured it out.

Writers must be able to say why each paragraph is where it is. To do this, they need a conceptual framework—and having a thesis statement for a piece of writing helps them develop a conceptual framework. A thesis statement can show a writer the major steps to take in writing.

START
WHAT'S ACCEPTED
What readers and you agree is the case

WARRANT

INTRODUCTION

EVIDENCE

BODY

FINISH
WHAT'S NEW
What you would like readers to consider

CLAIM

CONCLUSION

Rhetoricians in ancient Greece noted that speakers were more likely to persuade when they began on a point of agreement with their audience. When a speaker starts that way, the audience feels more connected with the speaker and so is more likely to listen generously. Because persuasive (or argumentative) research writing is about moving audiences to consider a different position than they may otherwise hold, those observations about persuasion led to the pattern diagrammed above for organizing persuasive compositions:

1 INTRODUCTION: Use your warrant
Start by discussing something around which you and your audience hold the same values or opinions.

2 BODY: Give your best evidence
Offer evidence for a new perspective on what you hold in common with the audience.

3 CONCLUSION: Make your claim explicit
Make your claim: Tie together for your audience how what they already accepted (the warrant), when seen through the lens of your evidence, points to the conclusion, your claim. (Note that your conclusion is the concluding part of your paper; this could be the last paragraph, but in a five-page paper is more likely the last two or three paragraphs; in a seven-page paper, this could be almost the whole last page.)

See the next page for an example of a student using a thesis statement to organize a paper.

AN EXAMPLE OF A THESIS STATEMENT ORGANIZING AN ACADEMIC PAPER

THE THESIS STATEMENT

Here is Jamie's thesis statement. (→ See page 69 on thesis statements.)

> Choosing a minimalist lifestyle focuses people on respecting their possessions and so on the environment and how they use their time; therefore, a minimalist lifestyle helps people live a good life.

THE WARRANT

Based on her thesis statement, Jamie's warrant—what she believes her audience already believes—goes something like this:

> When we focus on respecting our possessions and so the environment and on how we use our time, we live a good life.

Note that this warrant implies that Jamie believes her readers will readily accept that a good life depends on respecting our possessions and so the environment and on how we use our time.

A STRUCTURE FOR A PAPER

Following what we've written on page 81, Jamie draws up the following conceptual framework, the large-scale organization for her paper:

> 1 I'll start by discussing what we think a good life should be.
>
> 2 I'll spend the largest part of my writing presenting evidence showing how people who choose a minimalist lifestyle focus on respecting their possessions and so on the environment and their time.
>
> 3 I can conclude by stating that, given my evidence, more people ought to consider a minimalist lifestyle.

→ See pages 92–94 and 96–101 to learn how Jamie blended this conceptual framework with a statement of purpose to compose a first draft.

SHAPING PARAGRAPHS FOR AUDIENCE AND PURPOSE

WHY THINK ABOUT PARAGRAPHS NOW?

If you possess a thesis statement, you also possess a sense of the overall shape your writing needs to take, as we described on the previous pages: You ought to be able to describe what needs to happen in the introduction, the body, and the conclusion of your paper. Once you have that, you can think about what needs to happen in the smaller units of your writing, your paragraphs.

PARAGRAPHS

Writing is not simply about conveying ideas to someone else. It also involves conveying the structure and relations of the ideas that have led writers to hold the beliefs, opinions, and values they do.

Paragraphs break reading—conceptually and visually—into units a reader can easily see. Because readers can see them, paragraphs help readers remember and so think about the structure and relations of the ideas in a text.

Readers' expectations about paragraphs have developed over several centuries. What we present on the following pages are current expectations about paragraphs in formal writing.

PURPOSES OF PARAGRAPHS

There are three main categories of paragraphs:

1 **Introductory paragraphs**, which orient readers to the general concerns of a paper.

2 **Body paragraphs**, where the main arguments of the writing are developed.

3 **Concluding paragraphs**, which summarize the paper's argument and add nothing new to the argument.

Here in Part 5, we discuss body paragraphs. In Part 6 we discuss revision, with a focus on introductory and concluding paragraphs on pages 109–110, because it is after completing a first draft that writers can tweak those paragraphs into their most effective shape.

QUALITIES THAT READERS EXPECT IN PARAGRAPHS

UNITY

In the twenty-first century, readers expect a paragraph to contain sentences focused around one idea or point.

COHERENCE

Readers expect the ideas in any sentence in a paragraph to grow out of the sentence preceding it.

DEVELOPMENT

Readers expect paragraphs not to repeat the same idea over and over. Instead, they expect each new paragraph to add something new to their understanding of the idea being discussed.

SHAPING PARAGRAPHS FOR AUDIENCE AND PURPOSE

UNIFIED AND COHERENT PARAGRAPHS

Whether you write for an academic journal or a music blog, your readers expect paragraphs to be unified and coherent.

To be unified, each sentence of a paragraph is on the same topic.

To be coherent, each sentence of a paragraph will seem to a reader to follow directly from the sentence that preceded it.

WRITERS USE STRATEGIES LIKE THESE TO ACHIEVE COHERENCE:

- repeating important words and phrases
- repeating important concepts by using synonyms for the concepts
- using pronouns to show that successive sentences refer to the same topic
- using parallel structures (→ see page 115)
- using words that show relations and connections among sentences (→ see pages 85–86)
- having a consistent point of view
- using the same tense throughout

When a paragraph is coherent, a reader should be able to draw connections between various parts of the paragraph, as the examples to the right show.

ground were the result of deep and personal individual reactions to a new environment.

The knottiest mystery of survival is how one unequipped, ill-prepared seventeen-year-old girl gets out alive and a dozen adults in similar circumstances, better equipped, do not. But the deeper I've gone into the study of survival, the more sense such outcomes make. Making fire, building shelter, finding food, signaling, navigation—none of that mattered to Juliane's survival. Although we cannot know what the others who survived the fall were thinking and deciding, it's possible that they knew they were supposed to stay put and await rescue. They were rule followers, and it killed them.

In the World Trade Center disaster, many people who were used to following the rules died because of it. They were

UNITY

In the full paragraph above, the first sentence describes a *mystery*—and then every sentence that follows works to explain that mystery.

COHERENCE

In this paragraph, the writer has chosen a straightforward, emphatic tone throughout. The writer repeats *survival* often because that is the paragraph's unifying idea. The writer refers to a young woman in two different ways. After a first reference to those who did not survive the airplane crash that the young woman did, the writer uses pronouns to refer to them.

LINKING WORDS THAT BUILD COHERENCE IN PARAGRAPHS

By using words from the lists below in a paragraph's sentences, you help your readers understand why the sentences belong together. When you use the words below, you can repeat them to build parallel structures (see page 115) that also show how the sentences belong together. If you do use such repetition, read your paragraph aloud to check that you have not built a boring, singsong rhythm (unless a boring, singsong rhythm supports your purpose).

To show that information in one sentence adds to information in a preceding sentence: *additionally, also, and, besides, equally important, furthermore, in addition, moreover, too*

To emphasize the information in a sentence: *indeed, in fact, of course*

To help readers understand that you are building a sequence of events or a description of a process: *again, also, and, and then, besides, finally, first. . . second. . . third, furthermore, last, moreover, next, still, too*

To build sentences to describe events that take place over time: *after a few days, after a while, afterward, as long as, as soon as, at last, at that time, at the same time, before, during, earlier, eventually, finally, immediately, in the future, in the meantime, in the past, lately, later, meanwhile, next, now, simultaneously, since, soon, then, thereafter, today, until, when*

To help readers compare information in one sentence with that in another: *also, in the same manner, in the same way, likewise, once more, similarly*

To help readers see any important differences between your sentences: *although, but, despite, even though, however, in contrast, in spite of, instead, nevertheless, nonetheless, on the contrary, on the one hand. . . on the other hand, otherwise, regardless, still, though, yet*

To indicate to readers that a sentence contains an example: *for example, for instance, indeed, in fact, of course, specifically, such as, to illustrate*

To help readers see cause and effect: *accordingly, as a result, because, consequently, for this purpose, hence, so, then, therefore, thus, to this end*

To make clear to readers the spatial relations among objects you are describing: *above, adjacent to, behind, below, beyond, closer to, elsewhere, far, farther on, here, in the background, near, nearby, opposite to, there, to the left, to the right*

To concede that your arguments are open to question: *although it is true that, granted that, I admit that, it may appear that, naturally, of course*

To show that sentences are summarizing or concluding: *as a result, as I have argued, as mentioned earlier, consequently, in any event, in conclusion, in other words, in short, on the whole, therefore, thus, to summarize*

USING THE LINKING WORDS AND PHRASES, REPETITION, AND PARALLELISM TO BUILD COHERENCE

The paragraph below shows how each sentence connects to the next through repetition of words and phrases, as we described on page 84. This paragraph also shows how coherence is built through linking words and parallelism.

You can see that only a few linking words are used; too many linking words can fragment a paragraph. Generally, writers use only a few but combine them with the other strategies we listed on page 84 to link sentences.

"war"

War is used in four out of this paragraph's seven sentences, helping keep the paragraph unified around its topic of how the Civil War changed the U.S. without destroying it.

parallelism

This sentence has three clauses, each of which has the same structure: *was not, were not,* and *was no;* the clauses are linked with semicolons. This structure shows that the three ideas have equal weight.

"in fact"

In fact precedes an explanation here and emphasizes the explanation. In this way, *in fact* indicates that the words following it amplify the words that precede it.

> It is a remarkable fact about the United States that it fought a civil war without undergoing a change in its form of government. The Constitution was not abandoned during the American Civil War; elections were not suspended; there was no coup d'état. The war was fought to preserve the system of government that had been established at the nation's founding—to prove, in fact, that the system was worth preserving, that the idea of democracy had not failed. This is the meaning of the Gettysburg Address and of the great fighting cry of the north: "Union." And the system was preserved; the union did survive. But in almost every other respect, the United States became a different country. The war alone did not make America modern, but the war marks the birth of a modern America.

"This"

This refers to "that the system was worth preserving, that the idea of democracy had not failed." The pronoun carries those concepts into the next sentence, linking them.

"And"

And indicates to readers that the sentence it begins adds information to the sentence before it.

"But"

But signals to readers that there will be a change from what the preceding sentences were arguing.

SHAPING PARAGRAPHS FOR AUDIENCE AND PURPOSE
PARAGRAPHS THAT DEVELOP

WHAT DOES "DEVELOPMENT" MEAN FOR PARAGRAPHS?

No matter its specific purpose, all writing intends to move readers: It can move them from knowing nothing about a proposal in an upcoming election to understanding why some people are against the proposal. If writing is to move readers, it has to begin with ideas familiar to them and then, from paragraph to paragraph and within paragraphs, develop those ideas toward the writer's purposes.

Effective paragraphs thus start with a sentence that develops out of the preceding paragraph—and then each sentence that follows develops or adds to the idea of the first sentence. You can shape this development from the familiar to the unfamiliar in many ways.

Simpler kinds of paragraphs (description, definition, and narrative) usually appear near a composition's beginning because they help writers lay out the ideas and terms at stake. Later, when a writer hopes to persuade readers toward particular connections among ideas, more complex kinds of paragraphs (classification and division, comparison and contrast, cause and effect, syllogistic, and analogical) function more effectively.

→ Because introductory and concluding paragraphs have very specific stylistic functions, we discuss them in Part 6 on style; see pages 109–110.

PARAGRAPHS THAT DEFINE

If you are unsure whether readers will understand a term, define it. If you use a term special to a discipline, define it for a general audience. If a term is central to your argument, defining it allows you and your readers to be in agreement about the term. (Because writers and readers need to develop shared understandings of terms if discussion is to be possible, definitions of new or contested terms usually come early in writing.)

Sometimes a one-sentence definition is all you need—but if a term or concept is complex or central to your purpose, then use a whole paragraph to build a definition.

The paragraph below shows how one writer defines a term he thinks his readers won't know: *grass farmer*.

Grass farmers grow animals—for meat, eggs, milk, and wool—but regard them as part of a food chain in which grass is the keystone species, the nexus between the solar energy that powers every food chain and the animals we eat. "To be even more accurate," Joel has said, "we should call ourselves sun farmers. The grass is just the way we capture the solar energy." One of the principles of modern grass farming is that to the greatest extent possible farmers should rely on the contemporary energy of the sun, as captured every day by photosynthesis, instead of the fossilized sun energy contained in petroleum.

PARAGRAPHS THAT DESCRIBE

Paragraphs that describe people, places, or things serve two functions. First, they appeal to our senses and so make what is being described more immediate, engaging our attentions. Second, such paragraphs help writers set the scene: They provide the background within which discussions, controversies, and experiments occur. Because they engage readers and set the scene, writers often use descriptive paragraphs at a writing's beginning—but whenever writers need to make a scene clear or describe a situation that affects their arguments, such paragraphs are useful.

The paragraph below appeals to readers' expectations and emotional senses by using concrete adjectives and nouns (*crushworthy*, *flamboyant*, *shy*) and by using words spoken by the person being described.

As a rock star, he's a strange case: A crushworthy frontman and a bit of a peacock, he's given to showy, flamboyant stage performances. But in person, he's shy and sweet, a married, practicing Mormon (who enjoys the occasional beer or cigarette). When he talks about Vegas, he constantly ends up talking about his roots. "Vegas is my hometown, and it's turned into a place that's really sentimental to me," he says. "I think a lot of people can identify with that."

PARAGRAPHS THAT GIVE EXAMPLES

Compare this sentence, *No wonder people don't watch television news—there are so many commercials!*, to this:

No wonder people don't watch television news anymore—there are so many commercials! Last night, I counted 12 commercials during one 30-minute local newscast and 15 during a 30-minute national newscast.

Examples give readers vivid, concrete evidence and so give them reasons to consider the situation you are discussing.

PARAGRAPHS THAT USE ANALOGY

An analogy uses a concept an audience already understands to explain a concept they don't. Use paragraphs based on analogies to explain complex concepts or processes. When you use an analogy, whatever associations your audience has with the more well-known concept will shape their attitudes toward the more complex concept.

The paragraph below draws on readers' understandings of computers to help them understand how and why humans can be physically but not socially adept.

Understanding of the physical world and understanding of the social world can be seen as akin to two distinct computers in a baby's brain, running separate programs and performing separate tasks. The understanding develops at different rates: The social one emerges somewhat later than the physical one. They evolved at different points in our prehistory; our physical understanding is shared by many species, whereas our social understanding is a relatively recent adaptation, and in some regards may be uniquely human.

PARAGRAPHS THAT NARRATE

Paragraphs that narrate tell stories. Stories personalize issues. When we hear the fortunes—or misfortunes—of others, we imagine ourselves in those situations. We know what feelings must be involved and might feel them ourselves. Stories can thus build emotional connections—positive or negative—between readers and topics.

Because stories are always about the experiences of one person or a few people, rarely can they stand alone as evidence: Readers will question a writer's attempts to generalize from limited experience to a broad claim. But stories can be useful in introductory or concluding paragraphs to engage readers emotionally with a topic or to make the topic memorable.

The paragraph below is the introduction to writing about the safety of car seats; this story makes the topic real—and scary—so that the writer can then develop more general points about car seats.

A couple of weeks ago, I was sleeping in the front passenger seat of our car when it slammed into the vehicle in front of us. We were on the highway coming home from a family trip. The other three people in our car weren't hurt. But I'd reclined my seat, and my seat belt, which was riding high, left a long welt around my rib cage and along my stomach. As it turned out, I had internal bleeding from a lacerated spleen and three cracked ribs. I spent two days in intensive care.

PARAGRAPHS THAT DIVIDE

Academic writing often hinges on divisions because making divisions—distinguishing what something is from what it is not—is a basis for analysis. Paragraphs that divide are often followed by paragraphs that further define or that compare and contrast what was divided, in order to develop the arguments of the original division.

The following paragraph divides—makes distinctions between—knowledge (and manners of knowing) and art. Try to imagine the writing that would follow the paragraph and how this writer would more carefully define both *knowledge* and *art* and would elaborate why it matters to make these distinctions.

The historian Lucien Febvre has argued that "art is a kind of knowledge." I will argue, instead, that art is neither a kind of knowledge nor a manner of knowing. On the contrary, art is about making.

PARAGRAPHS THAT BLEND ORGANIZATIONS

Depending on your arguments, paragraphs can get complex: Writers need paragraphs to perform multiple functions. Keep in mind, however, that when paragraphs blend organizations, they still need to be unified and coherent.

UNDERSTANDING YOUR AUDIENCE

THE CONCERN

In Parts 1–4 we have followed Jamie's development of ideas for writing about minimalism, freedom, and happiness. As you saw, Jamie put together a thesis statement:

Choosing a minimalist lifestyle focuses people on respecting their possessions and so on the environment and how they use their time; therefore, a minimalist lifestyle helps people live a good life.

**But who needs to know this?
For whom does this argument matter and why?**

Through her research, Jamie has accumulated some supporting evidence for her thesis, but what of that evidence will be most persuasive? Into what order should she put her evidence? What examples will be most compelling to her readers? What tone of voice should she use in her writing?

Jamie can answer these questions only if she has some sense of who will read her writing and why.

Jamie can say, *I am writing to people who think that owning stuff is necessary to happiness and freedom*—but that level of understanding of audience is vague; it does not help her make the choices posed by the questions above.

How can Jamie—or any writer at this stage of the composing process—develop a more discerning and useful sense of her readers so that she can make specific choices about her writing?

ADDRESSING THE CONCERN

Experienced writers will tell you that they cannot compose effective writing if they do not understand their audiences.

Concrete and persuasive writing grows out of thinking about what readers believe and why. For example, if Jamie is writing to people who believe that owning more things helps them be happy, she needs to ask, *Why might someone think owning stuff helps us be happy? Are people really happier when they own more?*

There is also another important question Jamie has to ask, a question that any writer has to ask when addressing an audience that might not know about the topic: *Why should my readers care about any of this?*

All these questions suggest further research as well as decisions a writer like Jamie has to make about readers. Jamie has to research her readers—and their beliefs and opinions—because if she is going to be persuasive about a minimalist lifestyle, she will have to address what matters to her readers about owning things.

Jamie needs to develop a thicker characterization of her audience, so she needs to think about her audience as concretely as possible. If she can think of them as real, living, breathing people with emotions and attitudes toward events, then she can write to them almost as though she were talking with them, taking into consideration their opinions, thoughts, and feelings.

READERS AS PEOPLE WITH KNOWLEDGE, BELIEFS, AND OPINIONS

What people know or believe about a topic, and how strongly they hold that knowledge and those beliefs, will shape their opinions and so the attitudes they bring to reading any paper.

If you are to be persuasive, you need not only to know your readers' ranges of knowledge, beliefs, and opinions but also why they hold them. Only then can you address your readers respectfully to ask them to consider other possible beliefs and opinions.

You need, therefore, to talk to potential readers, asking about:

- what they know about your topic.
- their emotional responses to the topic.
- how they have learned what they know of the topic.
- values, beliefs, or commitments related to the topic.
- questions they might have about the topic.
- their self-identity as it connects them to the topic. How do they see themselves connected to the topic because of their specific relations to others? That is, does it matter that a reader is a mother, a daughter, unemployed, a Republican or a leftist, rich or not, a boss or a worker, a student or a teacher, or. . . ?
- recent events—local, national, or international—that might shape their responses to the topic.

If you cannot talk directly with readers, ask yourself the same questions, imagining how people with different backgrounds would respond.

FOR EXAMPLE. . .

Jamie talks to her readers—others in class—and writes in response:

> When we all talked in class yesterday about our topics and thesis statements, hardly anyone in class has heard about a minimalist lifestyle. And when I describe it to them, they all think it sounds nuts. They talk about hanging out at the mall and how much fun it is to shop. They all want to have big houses some day and lots of toys. Why would anyone want to give away what they own and own so much less?
>
> When I ask them what "happiness" is, they usually say something like "getting time with friends," "not having to work," "being free from all this stress," or "time to kick back."
>
> When I ask them what "freedom" is, they say something like "being able to do whatever I want whenever I want."
>
> So when I ask them whether they think having to work less and having more time with friends might happen if they needed less stuff, they get a little interested. I can see that, like me, hardly anyone has thought about how these ideas might be connected. So I think they'll be interested. . .

TIP: USING CARE WITH AUDIENCE CHARACTERISTICS

To define someone just by age, gender, ethnicity, level of education, or class—or even to define with all those characteristics—is to miss the complex mix of experiences and culture that shapes each of us. You can never know for sure how a person's particular life will affect his or her responses.

DEVELOPING A STATEMENT OF PURPOSE

MOVING FROM A THESIS STATEMENT TO A STATEMENT OF PURPOSE

A thesis statement is a short statement summarizing the logic of your argument.

→ See pages 69 and 81–82.

Because humans respect logic but are also, well, human, writers must consider the emotions shaped for readers within any piece of writing. Writers must also consider how readers construct a sense of the writer—the writer's authority, believability, and general character—based on the writer's words. (→ See pages 66–67 for more on these strategies of *pathos* and *ethos*.) A statement of purpose helps you do this.

A statement of purpose weaves together a thesis statement's logic with what writers learn about their audience's knowledge and beliefs and with what writers understand about the context of their writing.

A statement of purpose is not itself a formal piece of writing. Instead, it is thinking-on-paper—a way to help you consider what you really hope your readers will think, feel, or do as they read your writing and when they are done reading it.

WRITING A STATEMENT OF PURPOSE

To prepare, you need to:

- Have a thesis statement that you've developed following the guidelines on pages 69 and 81–82.
- Have thought about your audience in the ways we've described on pages 90–91.
- Set aside some time (30 minutes to one hour) when you can be relaxed and write without being distracted.

To write a statement of purpose, write in response to the following questions:

- Who, to the best of your ability to describe them, are your readers? What do they know—or not know—about your topic?
- When they finish reading your writing, what do you hope they will think, feel, or do?
- Is your audience likely to accept your warrant with little discussion? What sort of immediate responses are they likely to have to your evidence and claim in your thesis statement?
- What sort of shifts—in emotion, in opinion—is your audience going to have to make, if you are to persuade them to reconsider their likely initial response to your topic, so that they have the response you hope they will when finished reading?
- How is the context in which you write (and in which your readers will read) likely to affect how your audience responds?

A statement of purpose is informal writing but helps you move from writing-to-learn to writing-to-communicate. A statement of purpose saves you time by helping you make important decisions about your writing before you start it, before you get yourself too tied down to a first draft.

FOR EXAMPLE...

This thesis statement is for a research paper:

> Nuclear power plants have become safer and more reliable; therefore, we can build new nuclear power plants in the United States to help take care of our energy needs and reduce reliance on foreign oil.

One possible statement of purpose from that thesis statement is this:

> My audience is a general audience, of different ages and backgrounds. They've heard or read about Chernobyl, Three Mile Island, Fukushima, and the government's tests in Utah in the 1950s. So they'll probably start reading with some real fears that nuclear energy, not carefully handled, can result in horrible children's cancers, as in Chernobyl. They also probably have some fears based in the science fiction movies they've seen.
>
> Because of those fears, I doubt I can change their minds completely—but I'm hoping to persuade them just *to look again* at nuclear power. I believe recent developments might help.
>
> My readers also share concerns that might encourage them to be more open. They are concerned about how current energy sources—oil, coal, fracking—affect the environment. They are concerned about the costs of power production and use. So if I can show how nuclear power might just be cleaner and less expensive, they are likely to look at it again.
>
> Should I start by addressing their fears, or should I start by talking about a form of energy that's cleaner and less expensive?

TIP: **JUST WHAT CAN YOU ACHIEVE WITH WRITING?**

Have you ever had your mind changed *completely* on a topic (especially a controversial topic such as gay marriage or genetic engineering) by reading one article written by someone you don't know? Chances are your answer is **No**.

Most often, when we change our minds completely on such topics—or on almost any topic—it's because we've had extended conversations with those we know and trust.

The writing of strangers—even of respected, experienced writers—might give us a little nudge to reconsider a position, but it will rarely change our minds completely.

When you write a statement of purpose, therefore, keep your purpose within reach. Don't expect to *convince my readers that gun control is bad* or *make my readers finally understand how harmful our dependence on oil is*. Instead, using verbs such as the following in your statement of purpose helps you design achievable purposes:

inform	suggest
recommend	consider
acknowledge	propose
ask	reflect
attempt	understand

→ On the next page we show Jamie's statement of purpose, so you can see how her writing continues to develop toward her draft on pages 96–101.

FOR EXAMPLE...

Here is Jamie's thesis statement:

> Choosing a minimalist lifestyle focuses people on respecting their possessions and so on the environment and how they use their time; therefore, a minimalist lifestyle helps people live a good life.

Here is Jamie's statement of purpose:

> By talking with people in class, who are my audience, I learned that many don't know what a minimalist lifestyle is and don't think such a lifestyle will help them be happy or free (or live "a good life," the bigger term I want to explain).
>
> What I learned from talking with them is that, like me, they haven't really thought about this stuff. Like me, they just grew up thinking that shopping and owning lots of stuff is fun and that it all helps you be happy. I had to run into the guy in our building who was getting rid of all his stuff, and do my research, to start thinking about how maybe owning a lot of stuff (and having to do all the work to get it and then take care of it) isn't really good for me—or for anyone, or for the planet, even.
>
> When they finish reading my paper, I don't think anyone is going to turn around and become a minimalist! It's such a huge change in what we think and do that it's like asking someone to stop breathing! But maybe I can help them start to think about things a little bit more, just like I have. When they finish reading my paper, I think I'd like it if my readers start to question whether owning a whole lot of stuff really does help them be happy or more free. I'd like them to start really thinking about what "happiness," "freedom," and "a good life" mean. I'd like them to feel what I felt, that little excited buzz when I first understood that maybe I could work less and have more time for friends and doing the stuff I want if I didn't spend all my money on crap. (Sorry for that word, but that's how it all sounds to me now!)
>
> When I reread what I just wrote, I think that what it means is that my paper can't lecture my readers. I need to write in a way that asks them to think (without telling them to think!). I need to ask questions and to make suggestions. I need to use examples that are interesting (like maybe about how weird it was to see that guy's stuff piled up in the hallway, with him giving away new stuff every day). I need to figure out how to shape what I write so that it doesn't have a know-it-all Miss Priss tone of voice. (I know I do that sometimes.) I can't imply that what they own is crap!
>
> But from talking with people I did learn that they care about being happy. They do care about being free. They do want to think for themselves. So I am appealing to something they want. So maybe if I start with what I think they want—that "good life"—just as I described in my rough outline from my thesis statement, that is exactly the right place to start.

WRITING A DRAFT

ARE YOU READY TO WRITE A FULL ROUGH DRAFT?

❑ Do you have a thesis statement and have you gathered good evidence in support of the reasons for your thesis's claim?

❑ Do you have a statement of purpose that helps you understand how to shape your thesis for your particular readers?

PREPARING TO WRITE A DRAFT

- Review your notes about your sources.
- Keep your sources (or copies of your sources) nearby so you can check that you are summarizing, paraphrasing, or quoting according to academic conventions.

  → See pages 55–59 on how to summarize, paraphrase, and quote in academic papers.

- Set up your writing area so that you have few distractions.
- Arrange your time so that you have at least one hour, but preferably two or three hours, to write at any one sitting.
- Do not expect to complete a five- to seven-page draft in one sitting. Plan for at least two or three different times to write.
- Expect satisfaction for finding new ideas and hard work. By setting aside time to think and write, you prepare yourself to think and write well.

WHILE WRITING

- Don't stop the flow by fixating on grammar or spelling; focus instead on writing. Because this is a draft, you have time later to revise and edit. Even if English is not your home language, you should wait until you have writing that seems solid before you shift to editing and proofreading.
- If you get stuck in your writing, you have at least three options:

  1 Get up and walk away; come back to the writing later, after you've had a chance to rest, go for a walk, chat with some friends, or otherwise refresh your mind.

  2 Reread your writing from the beginning to see if this sparks your thinking.

  3 Review your thesis statement and statement of purpose to see if you have covered all that you know you need to cover; if you've missed anything, start writing about it.

BE OPEN TO CHANGE AS YOU WRITE

Although you have a thesis statement and a statement of purpose, sometimes drafting a paper leads you in other directions. As you develop your ideas, they might take you toward a different argument than you thought you had. Experienced writers know this happens. They know they might need to reshape a thesis statement after a first (or even second) draft; they also might need more research to support the new ideas.

Every act of writing helps us learn more precisely what it is we are thinking.

A ROUGH DRAFT

Jamie has produced a very rough draft for an assignment that asks for a four- to six-page paper. She is using this draft just to get her ideas onto paper, to see how they look, and to get a sense of how they will work for her readers.

We've indicated some of her initial choices, as well as places where she is not yet sure of her choices; and we've indicated where in this book she can look for further assistance.

→ Jamie's polished revision of this draft is on pages 126–135.

Title

After you read the draft, return here: Do you think Jamie's title accurately prepares a reader for what is to come? Could it be more focused?

Opening anecdote

Do you think this personal story pulls readers into her topic and argument in the way Jamie described in her statement of purpose? (→ See Jamie's statement of purpose on page 94.)

Do you think this story is the right length for a paper like this?

Tone of voice

Does Jamie's chosen tone of voice in this paper sound appropriate for an academic audience?

Introduction

Does this introductory paragraph help readers understand clearly and easily what is to follow?

→ Page 110 gives suggestions for introductions that meet academic expectations.

Do you think this paragraph engages readers sufficiently with Jamie's warrant? Do you think this paragraph comes early enough in the writing? Why—or why not?

Introducing quotations

Does Jamie give enough information about Leo Babauta or Jessica Dang for a reader to understand why their words matter here?

→ See page 59 for academic conventions on introducing quotations.

→ See Jamie's final draft on pages 126–135 to see how she revises these references.

Jamie Garza
DRAFT

CHOOSING A LITTLE

This guy used to live in the apartment next to ours. He started putting things out in the hallway. He put up a sign saying, "Free!" At first, he put out stuff that looked like he was moving: old clothes, old textbooks, an old kitchen pot. But he kept putting stuff out. He put out clothes that looked like they'd never been worn. He put out a new toaster and even a good waffle iron. My roommates and I started worrying about him. We knew him just from seeing him in the hallway. He seemed like a nice guy—but it started to look as though he was losing it, giving everything away. We thought he'd be naked soon and unable to cook.

So one day when we saw him we asked him if he was okay. He said, "Sure," and asked us why we were asking him! We told him we were worried that he was losing it and giving everything away. He laughed and said that he was just working on a minimalist lifestyle.

None of us had ever heard of that, so we asked him to tell us.

He explained that minimalism is about trying to live with as little as possible, so that you can save money and live more freely and so be happier. He suggested we do a Google search to learn more.

So I did. This paper shows my research into why people get into minimalism. Most people, it seems, go into minimalism because they believe it will help them be happier and more free. Perhaps to achieve "a good life." Isn't that what we all want?

Leo Babauta defines "minimalism" this way:

It's a way to escape the excesses of the world around us—the excesses of consumerism, material possessions, clutter, having too much to do, too much debt, too many distractions, too much noise. But too little meaning. Minimalism is a way of eschewing the non-essential in order to focus on what's truly important, what gives our lives meaning, what gives us joy and value.

Jessica Dang says that minimalism is "about being able to go almost anywhere at any time because you don't have many possessions to carry." Dang says that having fewer possessions brings happiness because it brings freedom. For Dang, freedom

1

Transitions

Do you think readers will understand why Jamie moves from the paragraph above to this one?

→ See page 111 to learn about transitions that help readers follow your arguments.

Quotations lacking introduction or attribution

Rarely in academic writing do writers use quotations without introducing them, most often by describing the authority of the quotation's source.

→ See pages 58–59 for suggestions for how to weave quotations into your writing.

Never in academic writing do writers use quotations without an attribution.

→ See pages 58–59 for how to give the expected attributions for quotations.

Helping readers

Has Jamie given her readers enough information to know who "the Minimalist blogger" is?

→ Jamie's final draft on pages 126–135 shows how she revises her paper so her readers can follow references like this.

Style, sentences, and academic writing

Jamie's paper has many simple sentences, and this paragraph is composed only of simple sentences. Academic writing usually mixes simple sentences with compound, complex, and compound-complex sentences.

→ Pages 247–259 define and describe these different sentence patterns.

How does this paragraph sound to you as you read it? Does the repetition of simple sentences create emphasis, or is it distracting?

→ See pages 113–119 on style and sentences.

Staying focused

Does this comment help Jamie develop her argument? If a comment doesn't move an argument forward or help readers learn something necessary to the argument, academic convention says to remove it.

means being able "to do whatever we want." Minimalism helps people "start new projects, move, travel, learn new things, meditate, work, expand, be debt free, be healthy—really living life to our full potential." Those two definitions show that there are many different reasons people go minimal. But maybe there is one big reason, having "a good life."

"Thrift" can be "doing more (consumption) with less (money) and so thrifty practices are practices of savvy consumption, characterized by the thrill and skill of 'the bargain'." Being thrifty is about spending carefully. You might decide you want to spend less on clothes so you can go on a big trip. But you are still spending less so you can focus on buying other stuff.

Instead, someone who is frugal "values work over leisure; saving over spending; restraint over indulgence; deferred over immediate gratification and the satisfaction of 'needs' over the satisfaction of wants and desires." Thrift is still about consuming. Being frugal is about not consuming and about caring for the future and for those who live in the broader world.

If you want to be minimalist in the way the Minimalist blogger describes, then you want to be frugal. You want to be frugal because you are trying to get to that last bit in the Minimalist's definition: you want to stop losing yourself in new stuff that you buy and instead find meaning, joy, and value.

This doesn't mean that you stop buying stuff. It means you buy more carefully. You buy less. You buy what will last. You take care of it. You want to care for the planet. You don't want to just throw lots of stuff away.

And I think if you do that for stuff you do it for yourself and people around you.

Did you know that in ancient times people used to be taught how to use their leisure time? A book I read titled *How Much Is Enough? Money and the Good Life*, by two economists (I think they are father and son) describes how people used to learn how to think about their time and how to use it. Their book gives some history of economics as a discipline to show how societies and governments turned from supporting "the good life" and how we all came to value being consumers and owning more. The book gives some history of the idea of "happiness" to show that this is not the same as "the good life." The book discusses some problems of

Summarizing to help readers

Jamie offers a fine summary of the Skidelskys' arguments about "the good life"—but notice how she does not offer her own understanding of their arguments or connect those arguments to her own. By not making those connections, she runs the risk that readers will not follow *her* argument.

→ See pages 56–57 about summarizing.

Does your conclusion make the points you want?

As we described on pages 81–82, an academic paper can conclude by making the paper's claim explicit. Does Jamie do that here?

→ Page 109 suggests strategies for concluding a paper.

If you were to summarize Jamie's argument here, what would you say? Does your summary match what Jamie described in her thesis statement?

→ See Jamie's thesis statement on page 82.

Making a works-cited list

For a rough draft, it is usually fine to start a works-cited list on the same page as the rest of the paper (but check with your teacher). For a final draft, however, the works-cited list should start on its own page in MLA format.

→ See pages 134–135 for help in constructing a works-cited list in MLA format.

→ See page 170 for help in constructing a reference list in APA format.

Enough?

Three considerations help you determine whether your list contains the citations it should:

- Have you cited every source you referenced in your paper? If you look back through Jamie's draft, you will see that she has put into her Works Cited list every source she referenced.

- Have you cited a range of sources? Jamie has referenced both academic and nonacademic sources in this paper, showing that she has—appropriately—not settled with just one kind of source.

- Have you cited enough sources? Jamie has cited only four sources so far. Most teachers will want at least a few more for a paper of this size.

increased consumption and the environment. The book describes what the authors think will make a "good life": they argue that "a good life" has the basic needs of health, security, respect from and for others, personality (which means being able to express one's self freely), harmony with nature, friendship, and leisure. The two authors argue that having these needs met, and so having time for leisure, is what really makes people free.

By researching minimalism I am learning that being minimal is about a choice, a large choice. There's the large choice of trying to help the planet and others, that both Evans and the Skidelskys discuss, but there's also the perhaps more important large choice of who we want to be. Do I want to be known as a consumer, someone who maybe is owned by her stuff, who cares mostly about stuff. . . or do I want to choose, consciously, to live "the good life"? Do I want to choose to live with the freedom of choosing this, to have the freedom of shaping myself and the world around me? Do I want time to think about who I am and can be? Do I want time to consider how I live with others? If I choose to care for myself, for those directly around me, and for the larger world we all share and so to seek a good life, then I think I need to learn how to be minimal.

Works Cited

Babauta, Leo. "Minimalist FAQs." *mnlist.com*, mnmlist.com/minimalist-faqs. Accessed 17 Mar. 2016.

Dang, Jessica. "Why Minimalism Brings Happiness." *Minimal Student,* 15 Jan. 2010, www.minimalstudent.com/why-minimalism-brings-happiness.

Evans, David. "Thrifty, Green, or Frugal: Reflections on Sustainable Consumption in a Changing Environmental Climate." *Geoforum,* vol. 42, 2011, pp. 550–57. *ScienceDirect*, doi:10.1016/j.geoforum.2011.03.008.

Skidelsky, Robert, and Edward Skidelsky. *How Much Is Enough? Money and the Good Life.* Other Press, 2012.

3

ONCE YOU'VE FINISHED A DRAFT. . .

HELP OTHERS GIVE YOU FEEDBACK

After you finish a draft, you might want to know whether readers see your main argument, think you have provided sufficient evidence, or are moved by your examples.

If you do not tell readers that you need that specific feedback, they might focus on other aspects of your writing or they might only give you polite, positive responses. By telling readers where you want their help—and that you want them to be honest in their responses—you will learn what you need to learn.

Let readers know, too, that you want them to tell you what they think the paper's strengths and weaknesses are, so you can learn how others read.

HOW TO ASK FOR FEEDBACK

When you are giving a draft to others to read, attach a short note, asking for what you need:

Hi—

I've been working hard on this draft to make my thesis clear to readers and to develop it step by step. Can you tell me what you think my thesis statement is? Can you also tell me whether my paragraph transitions make sense?

Thanks!

AFTER YOU'VE RECEIVED FEEDBACK

Once you've received feedback, do not hesitate to ask the person who wrote it any questions you have about the feedback.

HELP YOURSELF CHECK YOUR DRAFT: MAKING AN OUTLINE

Once you are confident in your arguments and know that your conclusion is what you want, check back over all your other paragraphs: *Does each follow what precedes it and lead to what comes next?*

Experienced writers often make outlines for their papers *after* they have a first (or later) draft:

- Summarize each paragraph in one sentence. (If you cannot summarize a paragraph in a single sentence, then you probably need to break the paragraph into two or more new paragraphs.)
- List the paragraph summaries in order.
- Check that the outline steps logically from the introduction to the conclusion. If not, you may need to add, take out, or clarify paragraphs to have different summaries.

HOW OTHERS CAN HELP YOU CHECK ORGANIZATION

When you have a draft, cut it apart so that each paragraph is on its own piece of paper. Shuffle the pieces and give them to someone else; ask that person to tape the paragraphs back into a whole, leaving out any paragraphs that don't make sense or marking any places where it is impossible to tell what should come next.

Sometimes the other person will hand you back something with a clearer order, and you will learn where you need to make clarifications, additions, or subtractions.

RECEIVING FEEDBACK TO A DRAFT

→ See Jamie's paper, revised to account for this and other feedback, on pages 126–135.

Below, Jamie's teacher responds to Jamie's paper. *Receiving such feedback can be hard if you've put a lot of effort into writing.* You might not want to hear that you have more work to do. But it's important to receive feedback well because feedback helps you strengthen your writing. *Read feedback as soon as you get it but then put it aside for a day or two.* Read it again with a little distance, and you'll be in a better position to understand and use it.

Jamie—

This is a fine start. Your topic (as you know from class discussion) fascinates your readers, and you raise issues to intrigue them throughout the paper. You found two solid and useful academic sources (but at least one more source would help show that you've done the research you should). Most importantly, however, I do get a little lost in the argument the paper is trying to make: At the end, are you asking your readers who they want to be or whether they want "a good life"? And I have to admit that, by the end, I lose the connection between minimalism and the "good life."

> *Is she saying I absolutely have to have another source? I need to ask.*

> *This helps me to know that readers aren't seeing these connections.*

To me, then, it looks as though you still need to clarify for yourself what you want to argue. Go back to your thesis statement and statement of purpose to see if your paper really does develop the argument you want. You might need to revise the paper to refocus it, or you might need to rethink your thesis statement and statement of purpose. You have to decide—but I want you to know that you need to decide because you're raising some complex issues, and you need to find a crisp way through them to determine what matters to you and to the people you want better to understand what's going on.

> *OK, so WHAT am I arguing? I guess if she's not seeing it, then I'd better figure out if I really know. I thought my thesis statement was pretty good— so maybe I need to check it against my paper.*

Also, the opening anecdote uses up a lot of space in getting to your main concern (and it is written in too informal a style for an academic paper). Can you shorten and focus it so that you get more directly to the question that concerns you in the writing?

Please, too, review how to format quotations; you are close!

I look forward to seeing your revisions of this. You should take confidence from the strengths of this draft so that, as you revise, you focus on the matters I've suggested above. Please come talk if you have any questions.

> Jamie writes notes in the margins to help her think about this feedback.

Thanks! Professor Maathai

RESPONDING TO YOUR PEERS' WRITING

When you are asked to respond to someone else's writing, consider these questions:

- **What kind of feedback does the writer need?** Perhaps the writer only needs help checking grammar and spelling—but perhaps the writer needs feedback on the order of ideas, in which case correcting spelling is useless because the words you correct might go away in the revision. If a writer asks for help and does not specify what kind, ask.

- **Have you prioritized your feedback?** You know how unhelpful it is to get a long, unordered list of feedback. When you prepare feedback for another person, pick the two to five most important observations you have—the observations you think will most help the writer revise—and present only those.

Dear Jamie,

I like how the paper starts with a story. I could relate! That was a cool way to introduce "minimalism."

As I read, I learned about differences between being thrifty and being frugal. But I am not sure yet how that connects with living a good life. Shouldn't looking after people right around you and looking after the bigger world both be part of having a good life? And does a good life connect to minimalism because when you need less stuff you are more likely to have your basic needs met? Or does minimalism connect to the good life in some other way? You asked me to tell you what I thought your main argument was, and I guess what I'm trying to tell you is that I can't tell. I'm sorry!

So I'm not sure these comments are helpful. Let me know.

Thanks! Hana

Respond to the writing, not the writer.

Respond with "This introduction didn't help me understand what the paper was about," not "You can't do introductions well." The first helps a writer understand what revisions are needed; the second just makes the writer feel bad and gets in the way of helping the writer improve.

Give reasons for your comments.

Instead of saying "I get lost in this paragraph," you can say, "This paragraph starts out about the effects of video game violence on children but then ends by talking about television cartoons, and I couldn't see what connected the two," you give the writer information useful for revision. (And if you try to articulate feedback in this way, you start to look at your own writing just as carefully.)

If you are asked to give feedback to the main argument, say first what you think the main argument is.

You may be seeing a different main argument from what the writer intends, and the writer needs to know; the writer can then reshape the argument to fit the original intention or can reshape it to pull out what you see. But if you give feedback on a different argument than what the writer intends, the writer will be revising at cross (and confusing) purposes.

PART 6
REVISING
WITH STYLE

REVISING YOUR WRITING

TWO ASPECTS OF REVISION

When you revise, you attend to large-scale persuasive aspects of a text: You focus on your argument and how well readers understand your argument. You will most strengthen your writing if you don't get distracted by grammar, spelling, and mechanics now but instead let yourself be open to large changes:

1 **ORGANIZATION.** Are your paragraphs arranged so that readers understand why one paragraph follows the next? Can they follow the steps of your argument?

  → We cover these aspects of writing a persuasive paper in Part 4, pages 54–78.

2 **STYLE.** Here in Part 6 we help you revise your writing so that it is clear, concise, and coherent; puts emphasis where you want emphasis; and engages your readers. Style is not about being fancy; it is about the detailed choices you make to design your ideas for your audience.

WHAT REVISING IS NOT

Revising is different from editing and proofreading. In editing, you attend to sentences and other large details: *Are sentences readable? Have you documented all your sources?* In proofreading, you check spelling, punctuation, and other mechanics.

  → See pages 202–203 for more on editing and proofreading.

TO REVISE, ASK YOURSELF:

❑ Am I clear about my argument? Can I state it as a thesis statement?
  → See pages 69 and 81–82.

❑ Did I offer well-supported and accurate evidence for each of my claims?
  → See pages 76–77.

❑ Have I been fair and respectful toward the differing positions one could take on my arguments?
  → See pages 64–74.

❑ Will my writing engage readers?
  → See pages 108–122.

❑ Does my introduction engage readers with my argument and initial concerns?
  → See page 110.

❑ Can I say why my paragraphs are ordered as they are? Can I describe the steps of my argument?
  → See pages 81–82.

❑ Will my readers understand the purpose of each paragraph?
  → See pages 83–89.

❑ Do my transitions help readers move from one paragraph to the next?
  → See page 111.

❑ Does my conclusion sum up my argument and end memorably for readers?
  → See page 109.

DEVELOPING A REVISION PLAN

After you receive feedback to a draft, make time to develop a revision plan for yourself. A revision plan is informal—just for you. Below, Jamie's plan lays out how she understands the feedback she received and how she plans to respond.

→ See Jamie's revised paper on pages 126–135.

Well, given the feedback I received, I can see that I need to make my argument clearer to myself before I can make it clear to anyone else! When I read over my draft, I see how important _time_ is: time for leisure, to think, to decide how we want to live (and _not_ time spent taking care of stuff!).

So I guess I do need to revise my thesis statement, now that writing the draft has helped me know better what I want:

> Having more time helps us lead the good life; therefore, having fewer possessions helps us lead a good life.

That means my warrant—which is how I need to start my paper and what I think my readers already believe—is something like "Having fewer possessions gives people more time (because they have less stuff to take care of)." And having fewer possessions is minimalism, so I can still start the paper pretty much the same way (just with a shorter story)—but then I need to revise what happens in the body.

I also need to:
- Write with a more formal tone. (I can't say "stuff"!)
- Use some of the other academic sources I found, so my argument about owning stuff and the good life is better supported. I also need to figure out formatting quotes!
- Figure out if I need the thrift–frugal distinction. It seemed so cool, but it doesn't seem to get me where I need to go.

→ See Jamie's draft on pages 96–101.

→ See the feedback she received on pages 103–104.

Thesis statements and arrangement
→ See pages 81–82.

Tone of voice and other matters of style
→ See Part 6.

Formatting quotations
→ See Part 4 pages 58–59.

STYLING PARAGRAPHS

The strategies below help writers compose engaging paragraphs:

VARY SENTENCE PATTERNS

In Part 9 we describe the four patterns of sentences. (→ See page 247.) Varying a paragraph's sentence patterns can keep readers engaged:

In the thirties, Harold Gray's comic strip *Little Orphan Annie* had 47 million readers. Then it languished until the 1970s when Martin Charnin thought it would make a good stage musical. It did. For the film, fresh songs and scenes were added, and 8,000 girls auditioned for the part of Annie. Director John Huston wanted "a girl who can sing, dance and act, with tons of personality, so that for two hours audiences won't take their eyes off her." Aileen Quinn's high spirits in the role have caused children to say, after seeing the film, that they too want to be orphans.

You don't have to use all four patterns in every paragraph. Just be aware that, if a paragraph's sentences sound repetitive to you, try varying the patterns.

VARY SENTENCE ORDER

In English, readers expect sentences to have the order of subject-verb-object. (→ See pages 248–250.) Because this expectation is so widespread, you can create emphasis in a paragraph by reversing the word order in its most important sentence. Just be careful to do this infrequently, only when you want to create special emphasis. The following paragraph would be less strong if the first sentence were *Potential homebuyers should check basements first.*

Basements are where potential homebuyers should go first. The most expensive home repairs come up from weak and shaky foundations, and after you buy a house you do not want the surprise of thousands of dollars in bills for digging out and replacing the stone or cement block that is supposed to support your house. Only a detailed inspection by a foundation specialist can tell you whether a crack results from simple settling or the foundation breaking in two.

VARY PARAGRAPH LENGTH

Audiences expect different paragraph lengths, depending on medium and genre. For example, because many people are still becoming accustomed to reading online, paragraphs in online genres such as newspapers are often much shorter— only two or three sentences each—than paragraphs in print. Paragraphs in academic genres, on the other hand, can extend over a page or two in a 20-page paper. (In a paper shorter than 10 pages, readers expect paragraphs to be shorter than a whole page.)

In general, all the paragraphs in any text will have similar length—just long enough to develop and clarify the concept the writer needs to make. But when you want to emphasize one point, you can use a paragraph that is much shorter than the others. Readers will see visually, and through a change in reading rhythm, that what the short paragraph discusses matters.

CONCLUDING PARAGRAPHS

Why talk about concluding paragraphs before introductory paragraphs? Because you cannot have a shining, strong introductory paragraph until you know the exact end toward which that paragraph points readers.

FUNCTIONS OF CONCLUDING PARAGRAPHS FOR READERS

1 Concluding paragraphs are logical: They sum up the arguments of the paper.

2 Concluding paragraphs carry emotional weight: Because readers read them last, concluding paragraphs are often what readers remember most.

STRATEGIES FOR CONCLUDING

You cannot separate the two functions of concluding paragraphs. As you read the following examples, look for how they mix functions. Also try to imagine what preceded the conclusion.

SUMMARIZING YOUR ARGUMENT

Provide a crisp summary, not a rote repetition. You can include a question, quotation, or recommended action:

In sum, the globalization of English does not mean that if we English-speakers just sit back and wait, we'll soon be able to exchange ideas with anyone else anywhere: We can't count on much more than a basic ability to communicate. Outside of certain professional fields, if English-speaking Americans hope to exchange ideas with people in a nuanced way, we should do as people elsewhere are doing: Become bilingual.

RECOMMENDING ACTION

The problem is so huge it requires a response like our national mobilization to fight—and win—World War II. To move our nation off of fossil fuels, we need inspired, Churchillian leadership and sweeping statutes like the Big War or the Civil Rights Movement. So, frankly, I feel a twinge of nausea each time I see that predictable "10 Things You Can Do" sidebar in a well-meaning magazine or newspaper article. In truth, the only list that actually matters is the one we should all be sending to Congress now, full of 10 clean-energy statutes that would finally do what we say we want: Rescue our life-giving Earth from climate catastrophe.

SUGGESTING MORE QUESTIONS FOR RESEARCH

Suggestions about technical writing courses must remain suggestions and not firm recommendations until we know more about engineers' composing processes. Additional research on composing might reveal how Nelson, his firm, and his subdiscipline are and are not typical. It might show how his composing habits are more or less efficient than those of his colleagues. It might suggest that some tasks call for very different composing habits and skills than others, or it might imply that technical writers should develop several composing styles to fit different composing situations. One thing seems certain, however: Only when more research is completed will teachers know how to better prepare students for the kinds of writing they will do at work.

INTRODUCTORY PARAGRAPHS

FUNCTIONS OF INTRODUCTORY PARAGRAPHS FOR READERS

1 Introductory paragraphs engage readers with the topic.

2 Introductory paragraphs focus readers' attention on the particular aspects of the topic that matter to you.

WHAT TO AVOID

• **Introductions that are broad and vague.** *From the beginning of time, humans have . . . or Life is amazing.* If you see similar phrases in your introduction, make your introduction more focused by stating as explicitly as you can what matters to you in this writing.

• **Starting with a dictionary definition.** Readers will think you are not confident enough about your own arguments to put them in your own words.

• **Excuses.** Don't make excuses about not being an expert. Readers don't expect experts to be writing college papers; instead, they expect students to develop well-researched arguments that acknowledge other possible positions.

STRATEGIES FOR INTRODUCTIONS

BE DIRECT AND EXPLICIT

In the following pages I argue that, even though many people consider microcredit capable of ending poverty, it instead can exacerbate poverty, especially for women and for the most poor.

USE A QUOTATION

In the 1820s, Fanny Trollope, that perceptive, sharp-tongued traveler, described North America as "a vast continent, by far the greater part of which is still in the state nature left it, and a busy, bustling, industrious population, hacking and hewing their way through it." That hewing, hacking, and shooting was to cause a lot of environmental damage.

USE A QUESTION

Millionaire Steve Fossett has been missing since last Monday, when he took off from a Nevada airstrip on a short flight. Rescue crews have yet to find the famous adventurer or his plane, but according to news reports they've discovered at least six uncharted wrecks across a 17,000-square-mile swath of the Sierra Nevada. Why are there so many undocumented crash sites in the Sierra Nevada?

MAKE A SURPRISING CLAIM

Strange but true: Energy-efficient lightbulbs and hybrid cars are hurting our nation's efforts to fight global warming.

MAKE A COMPELLING CLAIM

The number of visits to a doctor's office that resulted in a diagnosis of bipolar disorder in children and adolescents has increased by 40 times over the last decade, reported researchers funded in part by the National Institutes of Health (NIH). The cause of this increase needs determining.

TRANSITIONS BETWEEN PARAGRAPHS

In Part 5, we discussed creating coherence *within* paragraphs; here we discuss creating coherence *between* paragraphs.

Most writers need to learn how to provide transitions between paragraphs, and learning how to do this will help your writing be confident and effective. When you use the strategies we discuss here, you tell readers why one paragraph follows another; you enable readers to follow and so better understand your arguments.

STRATEGIES FOR BUILDING TRANSITIONS

- Repeat crucial words, phrases, or concepts from one paragraph to the next.
- Repeat crucial concepts by using synonyms for major concepts in later sentences after you introduce them.
- Use linking words to show relationships between paragraphs.
  → See page 85.

LINK THE LAST SENTENCE OF ONE PARAGRAPH TO THE FIRST SENTENCE OF THE NEXT

In constructing transitions from one paragraph to the next, choose the most important words, phrases, or concepts of the last sentence of a paragraph, and then weave those words, phrases, or concepts into the first sentence of the next paragraph.

AN EXAMPLE

The writer of the paragraphs below uses the first paragraph to discuss connections between pollution in Mexico City and the city's geography; in the second paragraph, he turns to discussing how the city's size contributes to its pollution problems. By beginning the second paragraph with *Furthermore*, he tells readers that additional information is being added; the repetition of *city* and *pollution* carries the topic from one paragraph to the next.

Ozone levels in Mexico City have exceeded the country's air-quality standards 284 days per year, on average. Geography doesn't help: Mexico City lies on a broad basin ringed by tall mountains that can block the movement of air masses that might clear out pollution.

Furthermore, the city's rapid spread in recent decades has aggravated its pollution problems. Mexico City now covers about 1,500 square kilometers—about 10 times as much as it occupied just 50 years ago.

STYLING PARAGRAPHS
PASSIVE VOICE

Passive voice is a feature of individual sentences (➜ We define passive voice on page 213.). Even though *passive voice* is a feature of sentences, we discuss it here because it is in paragraphs that passive voice has its largest effects. Readers will rarely notice the use of passive voice in one or two sentences within several paragraphs or sections; when a whole paragraph is in passive voice, however, what readers take from the paragraph will be affected because the whole sense of the paragraph is affected.

PASSIVE VOICE IN SCIENTIFIC AND TECHNICAL WRITING

The behavior of fiber reinforced polymer (FRP) strengthened reinforced concrete beams subject to torsional loads has not been well understood, compared to other loads. Interaction of different components of concrete, steel, and FRP in addition to the complex compatibility issues associated with torsional deformations have made it difficult to provide an accurate analytical solution. In this paper an analytical method is introduced for evaluation of the torsional capacity of FRP-strengthened RC beams.

PASSIVE VOICE—OR NOT?—IN WRITING FOR NONSCIENTIFIC AUDIENCES

Compare this paragraph—

During the last couple weeks, American snouts have increased dramatically in my garden and the surrounding area. But that is nothing like the masses that were recorded farther south in Texas a few weeks ago. An estimated 7.5 million snouts were reported in the Alamo area of the Lower Rio Grande Valley on September 5. And there is a chance that our numbers will continue to build over the next few weeks, at least until the really cold weather sets in.

—with this:

In the last few weeks, I thought American snouts had taken over my garden. On September 5, however, observers farther south in Texas recorded numbers that make my garden seem empty: They saw almost 7.5 million snouts in the Alamo area of the Lower Rio Grande Valley. And until the cold weather sets in, these small butterflies might very well overwhelm us with their numbers.

When they wish to sound scientific—which requires longer and less direct grammatical constructions—writers often carry the patterns of passive voice into their other sentences, making all of them longer and more complex than they need to be.

If an occasional passive voice sentence supports your purposes, be alert to keeping your other sentences in the active voice.

STYLING SENTENCES
ACADEMIC SENTENCES

CHECKLIST FOR FORMAL, ACADEMIC SENTENCES

❏ Your sentences have positive structures.
→ See the pattern box to the right.

❏ Each sentence fits one of the four sentence patterns.
→ See page 247.

❏ You use no sentence fragments— except, rarely, for emphasis.
→ See pages 214–217.

❏ Your sentences do not shift among grammatical forms.
→ See pages 204–207 to learn about shifts in person and number.

→ See pages 208–209 to learn about shifts in verb tense.

→ See page 213 to learn about shifts in voice.

→ See page 212 to learn about shifts in direct and indirect discourse.

→ See page 212 to learn about shifts in levels of formality.

❏ Your sentences are easy to read.
→ See page 114.

THE PATTERNS

SENTENCES DO NOT USE DOUBLE NEGATIVES

In formal writing, convention requires using only one negative in a sentence.

NEGATIVES: *barely hardly neither no not never none nothing scarcely*

Sometimes there will be more than one way to fix a double negative:

✗ Bob did not have no solution.
NEGATIVE   NEGATIVE

✓ Bob had no solution.
NEGATIVE

✓ Bob did not have a solution.
NEGATIVE

SENTENCES ARE POSITIVE, NOT NEGATIVE

The following two sentences are both grammatically correct—but the second sentence is easier to read and understand because it presents its information in a straightforward, positive manner.

Classic gangster films were not without a message, showing audiences that if a gangster's life had no order, it was because society had no order.

Classic gangster films had a message, showing audiences that the chaos of a gangster's life mirrored the chaos of society.

SENTENCES THAT ARE EASY TO READ

Easy-to-read sentences have the following six qualities:

SENTENCES ARE NOT WORDY

Due to the matter of the final report, which was turned in after the due date, I did not acquire the grade I hoped for in class and now therefore I appeal for a second chance to succeed.

Because of a late final report, I failed the class; I hope to retake the class.

SENTENCES AVOID EXPLETIVES

An expletive is a phrase that adds length but no meaning to a sentence, such as *There is . . .*, *There are . . .*, or *It is necessary . . . .* Using one or two such phrases in several pages of writing is not a disaster, but learn to be on the lookout for expletives and replace them:

If we are to end global warming, one thing that is necessary is that people get out of their cars and walk.

To end global warming, people need to get out of their cars and walk.

SENTENCES USE FEW PREPOSITIONAL PHRASES

One argument of the parents from the neighborhood was that all parks in the city should be child-friendly.

Neighborhood parents argued that all city parks should be child-friendly.

SENTENCES USE FEW RELATIVE PRONOUNS

The relative pronouns *who, which, whom, whose,* and *that* can slow readers:

Children who are breast-fed usually have stronger immune systems.

Breast-fed children usually have stronger immune systems.

SENTENCES FOCUS ON ACTION

A carefully chosen active verb can make sentences come alive for readers:

The never-ending war brought on a reduction in the morale of citizens.

The never-ending war demoralized citizens.

SENTENCES AVOID NOMINALIZATIONS

When you change a verb or an adjective into a noun, you nominalize the verb or adjective:

difficult → difficulty

destroy → destruction

investigate → investigation

analyze → analysis

Nominalizations shift a sentence's focus from verbs and adjectives to abstract nouns—and thus deaden sentences.

Change nominalizations back to verbs or adjectives to enliven sentences:

My observation was of the locals' table in a busy local restaurant.

I observed the locals' table in a busy local restaurant.

STYLING SENTENCES

PARALLELISM

If you want readers to see similarities between two or more ideas, use sentence structure: Parallel grammatical form makes the ideas look and sound similar. Readers will take that similarity away with them.

First we heard whispers, then giggles, then screams of laughter.

Under the eclipse's brief false night, birds cease their singing, cows head for the barn, and people get weak in the knees.

THE PATTERN

Build parallelism by repeating the same grammatical structure in a list of words, prepositional phrases, sentences, or any other grammatical unit.

She finished the work by not eating, drinking, or sleeping.
PARTICIPLE   PARTICIPLE   PARTICIPLE

My sister liked to eat chocolate and to avoid broccoli.
PREPOSITION + VERB + NOUN   PREPOSITION + VERB + NOUN

Empty stores are signs of a fading past; empty schools are a sign of a fading future.
"Empty"+ NOUN + "are a sign of a fading"+ NOUN   "empty"+ NOUN + "are a sign of a fading"+ NOUN

One way to check that you are building parallelism is to stack the parts on top of each other, to see that they follow the same grammatical structure:

For your final draft, pay close attention to proofreading your words,
                                    being sure you've cited all sources,
                        and formatting your works-cited list.

AVOIDING FAULTY PARALLELISM

Faulty parallelism, a common writing error, occurs when a writer builds a list that does not have parallel grammatical structures; fix faulty parallelism by giving each list element the same grammatical structure as the others.

✗   If you have trouble sleeping, try cutting out coffee after lunch, getting rid of the TV in your room, and to fall asleep at the same time every night.

✓   If you have trouble sleeping, try cutting out coffee after lunch, getting rid of the TV in your room, and falling asleep at the same time every night.

USING COORDINATION AND SUBORDINATION

- When the ideas are equal, they are **COORDINATE**.
- When one idea is less important than another, it is **SUBORDINATE**.

As you build sentences with independent clauses, you relate the clauses through coordination or subordination.

Both coordination and subordination are signs of formal, academic writing.

TO COORDINATE OR TO SUBORDINATE?

It's up to you: What understanding do you want readers to take from a sentence?

For example, if you want readers to consider knitting's traditional role to be equal to its more recent role, use **coordination**:

Knitting has traditionally been a domestic activity for women, and in the last decades it has been turned into a fine art.

Knitting has traditionally been a domestic activity for women; moreover, in the last decades it has been turned into a fine art.

If, however, you want to emphasize the recently growing importance of knitting over its past role, use **subordination**:

Although knitting has traditionally been a domestic activity for women, in the last decades it has been turned into a fine art.

→ To learn more about independent and dependent clauses, see pages 253 and 217 .

→ To learn more about conjunctions, see pages 242–245.

COORDINATION

1 | independent clause | + **;** + | coordinating conjunction | + | independent clause | ●

COORDINATING CONJUNCTIONS: *and, but, for, nor, or, so, yet*

Stone is bad insulating material, but it makes a tight wall that radiates stored heat for hours.

2 | independent clause | + **;** + | conjunctive adverb | + **,** + | independent clause | ●

CONJUNCTIVE ADVERBS: *consequently, furthermore, however, moreover, otherwise, therefore, thus, nevertheless*

Stone doesn't insulate well; nonetheless, it makes a tight wall that radiates stored heat for hours.

SUBORDINATION

There is one pattern for building a sentence that uses subordination, but you can put the independent clause at the beginning or the end:

| independent clause | + **,** + | subordinating conjunction | + | dependent clause | ●

| subordinating conjunction | + | dependent clause | + **,** + | independent clause | ●

SUBORDINATING CONJUNCTIONS: *after, although, as, because, before, if, since, that, though, unless, until, when, where, whether, which, while, who, whom, whose*

After she placed a doily on top of a cupcake, my grandmother would sift sugar on top to make a lacy pattern.

My grandmother would sift sugar on top of a cupcake to make a lacy pattern, after she had placed a doily on top of the cupcake.

STYLING SENTENCES

USING INCLUSIVE LANGUAGE

HOW DO YOU SHOW RESPECT TO YOUR READERS?

Ethnicity, gender, sexual orientation, age, religion, and mental and bodily ability are characteristics about which many are sensitive. Anytime you refer to such characteristics, check that your word choice is necessary—and respectful of those to whom you refer. Educate yourself about why people care about these issues, because knowing the reasons helps you make good decisions about communicating.

Given how she finished the race before so many others who had two real legs, you would almost think she was a real athlete.

In her short leather skirt, the prime minister addressed the financial relations between our countries.

He has two children and another girl adopted from China.

Equally important, how are readers likely to regard the person who wrote these sentences?

AVOIDING RACISM

- Have you been careful not to assume that your readers have the same ethnicity, beliefs, or experiences as you?

- Have you been as specific as you can in naming an ethnic group? To avoid stereotyping, use (for example) *Ojibwa* or *Cherokee* instead of *American Indian*.

- Have you *not* used hyphens in multiword names? In current usage, write *Japanese American*, not *Japanese-American*, because the hyphen implies dual citizenship (which may not be the case) and that one is not completely American.

- Have you avoided phrases that use ethnically tied terms? Some phrases that might seem to you just part of language, such as *Latin lover* or *Jewish mother*, are stereotypes.

- Have you capitalized ethnicities? For example, write *Polish American*.

AVOIDING SEXISM

- Have you used unequal terms to refer to men and women in equal positions? To write of *the team* and *the girls' team* implies the first is the standard and the second a deviation.

- Have you used *man, men, he,* or *him* to refer to groups that might include women? Substitute gender-neutral nouns for *man* or *men* or words that include them. For example, instead of *chairman*, use *chairperson*. Make a sentence plural so that you can change *he* and *him* to the gender-neutral *they* and *them*.

AVOIDING ABLEISM

- **Have you emphasized the person, not the disability?** This practice, known as *person-first language*, is called for by the 1990 Americans with Disabilities Act (ADA) and asks us to use language that treats all people as having strengths, abilities, and skills: Describe the person before the disability, writing *person with AIDS* rather than *AIDS sufferer* or *child who uses a wheelchair* rather than *wheelchair-bound child*.

- **Have you avoided asking your readers to think of the person as deserving only sympathy?** If you use emotional words to describe someone with a disability (*the poor child with the limp* or *the helpless quadriplegic*), you ask your readers to see the person as incapable of doing anything but passively accepting our concern.

AVOIDING AGEISM

- **Have you used ageist terms to describe others?** Terms to avoid for people who are older: *geriatrics, over the hill, old-timers, matronly, well-preserved*. Terms to avoid for young people: *punk, gangbanger, juvie*.

- **Have you used terms that patronize people because of their age?** Treat older—and younger—people with the same respect, using the same titles. The standard in Anglo culture in the United States, then, is not to call an old man *Grandpa* (unless he really is your grandfather) or to refer to an older woman as *Honey, Dear,* or *Auntie*: These terms imply a level of familiarity you wouldn't assume with people of other ages.

AVOIDING HETEROSEXISM

- **Have you used *sexual orientation* rather than *sexual preference?*** *Sexual preference* implies that sexuality is the result of conscious choice, a view that neither scientific research nor the reported experiences of lesbians, gays, or heterosexuals support.

- **Have you avoided assuming heterosexuality?** To write *Employees are encouraged to bring their wives* assumes that all employees are married, heterosexual males. *Employees are encouraged to bring their partners or significant others* includes employees of all genders and sexual orientations—as well as those who are not married.

AVOIDING RELIGIOUS DISCRIMINATION

- **When you write about religion in general, have you used terms that reflect a range of religions?** If you are writing about how communities construct special buildings for religious observances, you should not write, *All over the world, people build churches for practicing their religions*; instead, write *All over the world, people build houses of worship for their religions*. Similarly, be alert to the names religions use for their members and leaders. *Rabbi, priest, reverend, imam,* and *bishop* are only some of the possibilities. Doing a little research helps you show respect.

- **Have you acknowledged the broad beliefs held by people in the same religion?** When you write about a religion, do not assume all its members hold the same beliefs. Catholics, for example, like Muslims, Jews, or Baptists, hold a range of views on abortion, the death penalty, birth control, and the status of women.

STYLING WORDS

DICTIONARY DEFINITIONS AND ASSOCIATIONS WITH WORDS

The dictionary defines cancer as *A malignant growth of cells caused by their abnormal and uncontrolled division.* Chances are, however, that you cannot read the word *cancer* without some fear; it's possible you read the word with memories of someone close to you who has had cancer.

The definition of *cancer* is what we call the **denotation** of the word. The denotation of any word is simply its analytic definition, what we can count on others to know or be able to look up in a dictionary.

Connotation, on the other hand, is what individuals bring to a word because of their personal or cultural background. Connotation describes the ideas or mental pictures that come to people's minds—unbidden from their memories and experiences—when they hear a word.

As you choose words, consider what associations—the ideas and mental pictures—your readers are likely to have. Do you want your readers to have positive or negative associations?

Most importantly—and especially if you are writing for an audience you do not know very well—you want to avoid using words that will have associations opposite to those that will help you achieve your purposes.

THE NAMES WE USE

If the problem were called *Atmosphere cancer* or *Pollution death,* the entire conversation about what's happening with the climate would be different.

The writer of the above sentence is discussing global warming, and argues that we might, as individuals and as a culture, be less sanguine about global warming if the concept had been named more compellingly.

The words used to name a condition, a syndrome, or a place carry considerable weight through their connotations. Consider how the following terms ask readers to think about the person or position named:

pro-choice	pro-abortion
right-wing	conservative
heterosexual	straight
gun rights	gun control
affirmative action	racial preferences
illegal alien	undocumented immigrant

Readers respond to the names you use based on how they interpret the names. Someone in favor of affirmative action, for example, will likely be less amenable to writing that uses the expression *racial preferences*.

ACTION VERBS

Jump. Giggle. Estimate. Play. Clarify. Balance. Sing. Compare. Interpret.

Those are action verbs: They name actions readers can imagine themselves taking. (This is connotation at work again.) Because action verbs encourage readers to imagine doing what a sentence describes, action verbs help readers connect with writing.

He is enjoying performing.

He revels in performing.

The second sentence uses an action verb instead of *is*. *Revels* carries associations of energetic delight, and so will likely convey that emotion to readers.

The wasp put her stinger through the roach's exoskeleton and directly into its brain.

The wasp slipped her stinger through the roach's exoskeleton and directly into its brain.

The second sentence helps a reader understand more precisely what the wasp did—and makes the wasp's action scarier and more compelling.

CONCRETE NOUNS

When you read the word *it*, what picture comes into your head? Any?

In the sentence *After he ordered his lunch, he had to wait 30 minutes for it to be delivered*, it clearly refers to *his lunch*—and readers can make concrete connections with the word. But when you read the sentence below, what associations can you make with the *it* at the beginning?

It is wasteful of their energies if full-grown orangutans move randomly through trees looking for food.

It in the sentence above refers to nothing. Here is a revised sentence:

Full-grown orangutans can't afford to lumber along randomly through the trees, hoping to blunder upon food.

The replacement of *is wasteful* with *can't afford to* and the movement of *full-grown orangutans* to the front of the sentence make this sentence concretely descriptive and so clearer and more engaging.

When you want readers to have concrete (and hence compelling) pictures in their heads, start sentences with words referring to specific people, animals, or objects.

TIP: REPLACING "IS"

When you want your writing to connect with readers, underline every use of **is** (including its variations, such as *are* and *was* and *will be*) in your writing, and if you see more than a few, replace those words with action verbs.

TIP: REPLACING "IT IS"

Sometimes you need to use *it is* (or *there are*). But when you want your writing to connect with readers, underline every use of *is*, *it is*, and *there are*; if you see more than a few, replace those phrases with concrete nouns and verbs.

STYLING WORDS, continued

CLICHÉS

Playing with fire. No place like home. Have a field day. From bad to worse. Bad hair day.

Clichés are phrases that once stood out because they were—at one time—new and funny or compelling. Because they were new and stood out, however, people used them, and used them . . . and used them until they stopped being new and compelling. Because clichés have been used so much, they have become just part of language—and so they come to mind easily when you write. Readers notice them, however, and because they've seen them before, the writing will seem tired and boring.

TOO MANY WORDS

As far as we can see, it is a fact that there are a whole lot of ways you can end up with way too many words in your sentences and, as a result, you make your readers bored or make it too hard for them to figure out your purpose.

Sentences like the above are signs that a writer isn't sure what to say and is fumbling to say something. The sentence above is characterized by both **empty words** (words adding nothing to the sentence's purpose) and **redundant words** (words repeating uselessly what has already been said).

   If we modify the sentence, we can make a more concise and hence clearer sentence:

There are many ways to have too many words in a sentence, boring your readers and getting in the way of their understanding.

To compose focused sentences, ask yourself, *What is it exactly that I want readers to take from this sentence?*

JARGON

Jargon can describe the specialized language of an organization or a profession; it can also describe fancy-sounding words that you don't understand. Jargon, then, is useful when you write to those inside your profession and need to be precise; it is bad to use outside the profession because readers won't follow the writing.

In architecting our software, build systems, and engineering processes, we have given considerable thought to how our code will be able to evolve alongside the Mozilla code, without forking it.

Most readers know *architect* and *fork* as nouns, not verbs, and probably do not know what *a build system* or *Mozilla* is. A general audience is more likely to understand this sentence:

In developing our software and engineering processes, we considered how our code will evolve alongside the existing code with which it must work and which it cannot mess up.

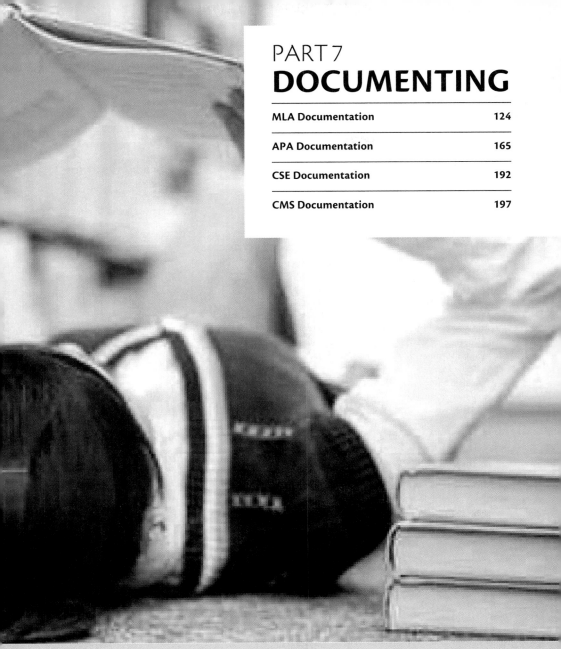

PART 7
DOCUMENTING

MLA DOCUMENTATION

GUIDE TO MLA DOCUMENTATION EXAMPLES

TIP: CAN'T FIND THE EXACT CITATION EXAMPLE YOU NEED?

→ Construct your citation following the patterns on pages 144–146—but also read page 148.

PAPER IN MLA FORMAT

The Modern Language Association (MLA) is an organization of scholars and teachers of languages and literature. The MLA publishes the *MLA Handbook for Writers of Research Papers*, which is now in its eighth edition and from which we take the formatting used here. The MLA style is used primarily in English studies, comparative literature, languages, literary criticism, and other humanities fields.

To the right is a paper in MLA style, showing MLA conventions.

MLA FORMATTING

To format in MLA style, use the margins we have shown in blue to the right and:

- Double-space the paper throughout (To fit the sample paper on these pages, we could not use double spacing.).

- Put your last name at top right of every page, with the page number.

- Center the title above the paper's body on the first page.

- Use a readable typeface (like Times or Arial) in a readable size, such as 12 point.

- Look through the pages of Jamie's paper shown here to see how to format quotations and citations as well as how to create the final page of works cited.

How you can read this paper

Try reading this paper all the way through first, without reading any of the comments. Then analyze the paper for yourself: *How persuasive do you find it? Which of Jamie's main strategies (the order of her arguments, her questioning tone of voice, her use of evidence) are most—or least—persuasive for you? Why?*

Using personal experience as evidence?

Jamie starts with a personal experience, which she knows her readers appreciate (→ see page 104). Using such anecdotes can lead to a too informal style, however, as Jamie's teacher noted (→ see page 103). Writing less formally—and using "I" in the writing—may or may not help you meet an assignment's expectations. If you have any questions about the level of formality to use, check with your teacher.

What is the argument of the paper?

Notice how Jamie gives readers a good idea of the focus of her paper, without revealing exactly what her argument will be.

MLA style: using long quotations?

In MLA style, any quotation that will use more than four lines in a final paper should be formatted as a "block quotation" (→ see page 59). Note how the left edge of a block quotation is formatted one half-inch from the left edge of the writing (or one-and-one-half inches from the left edge of the paper). Double-space block quotations, and do not put any additional space before or after them.

MLA style: no page number for a source?

In-text citations for print sources would show a page number here (→ see page 58). Because Jamie is citing a webpage that has no page or section numbers, she cannot put a page number here and leaves this space blank.

1"

Jamie Garza

Professor Lynch

ENG 101

5 April 2016

Choosing More by Choosing Less

Someone in our apartment building started giving away his possessions. It started with old clothes and textbooks, but soon he was giving away clothes that looked barely worn, cool kitchen equipment, and nice framed pictures. Curious (and a bit worried about him), my roommates and I asked him what he was doing. He explained that he was choosing a "minimalist lifestyle." Minimalism, he said, is about living with as little as possible in order to save money and, importantly, save time by not having to take care of so many things. He suggested a Google search to learn more if we were interested.

1"

This paper grows out of my research into minimalism. I learned that most people seek minimalism because they want more time and that they want more time because they believe it helps them get closer to the "good life." In this paper, then, I explore how one gets from having fewer possessions to having a "good life."

Leo Babauta, who writes the "Minimalist" blog and has become well-known for his writing on minimalism, defines "minimalism" this way:

> It's a way to escape the excesses of the world around us—the excesses of consumerism, material possessions, clutter, having too much to do, too much debt, too many distractions, too much noise. But too little meaning. Minimalism is a way of eschewing the non-essential in order to focus on what's truly important, what gives our lives meaning, what gives us joy and value.

1 1/2"

In her "Minimalist Student" blog, Jessica Dang defines minimalism as "about being able to go almost anywhere at any time because you don't have many possessions to carry." Dang claims having fewer possessions brings happiness because it brings freedom. In a post titled "21 Benefits of Owning Less," the authors of the "Becoming Minimalist" blog list among the benefits spending less, having less stress because there is less to worry about, damaging the environment less, having more time, being able to care for what matters most, having fewer distractions, and being more productive.

1"

How to achieve a formal academic style?

Compare Jamie's tone in this final draft to her first draft (→ see pages 96–101). Jamie's teacher asked her to write more formally. Do you think Jamie's writing has become more formal? What qualities shift the formality from the first draft to the last?

As you read the paper to the right, look closely at how Jamie integrates the words of others into her writing, always making clear when she is using the words or ideas of others.

Note also how she follows MLA style for showing the authors and titles of cited works and for showing page numbers of sources in parentheses. This style has been designed to keep the parenthetical citations as unobtrusive as possible so that readers can read easily.

→ See pages 136–139 to learn how to create such in-text citations.

How can you help readers follow the argument?

Notice how in this paragraph Jamie reminds readers of what she presented in the previous paragraph by offering a quick summary. Notice, too, that she points out the main point she would like her readers to take from that paragraph, in order to ask a question that leads into the main part of her writing.

How can you help readers move from one paragraph to the next?

Notice how, in the first sentence of this new paragraph, Jamie repeats the main concepts of the preceding paragraph, to show how new evidence (from the Kasser article) connects to the ideas she has been building. With such repetitions, Jamie keeps readers oriented in her argument.

Look at the beginnings of all of Jamie's other paragraphs in this final draft: What other strategies has she used to help readers understand why she moves them from one paragraph to the next?

→ See page 111 about transitions between paragraphs.

How to use summaries and paraphrases?

Throughout this paragraph about the Kasser article, Jamie quotes from the article—but she also follows the quotations with summaries and paraphrases of the article and of the points she most wants her readers to remember.

→ See pages 55–57 about summaries and paraphrases.

Those definitions make clear that popular understandings of minimalism offer a range of reasons for being minimal—but all share the basic understanding that minimalism is about owning less and that owning less opens up more time. All the writers also write as though owning less automatically makes one happier. Can that be?

On the surface, it would make sense that owning fewer things means that one puts less time into caring for things or carrying them around: this would create more time in general. But does having more time automatically make one more happy—meaning then that fewer possessions automatically creates happiness? The research considered in this paper suggests that the answer could be "yes," although probably one does need to make conscious choices toward happiness, including being clear about what brings happiness.

The automatic link between having fewer things and being happier is supported by the research of Tim Kasser, a psychologist at Knox College in Illinois. In his essay, "Changes in Materialism, Changes in Psychological Well-Being: Evidence from Three Longitudinal Studies and an Intervention Experiment," Kasser acknowledges that "an on-going meta-analysis of over 200 independent samples revealed that the negative association between materialism and well-being is robust across different operationalizations of the constructs and across different personal and cultural characteristics" (2), meaning that 200 different studies show that people who are more materialistic are less happy. Kasser argues, though, that most of these studies look at this connection at just one moment in a person's life. Kasser describes how, in response, he pulled together four studies carried out by other researchers (as well as himself): he looked at studies of young adults in the United States and of adults in Iceland who were interviewed over differing amounts of time ranging from two months to twelve years; these other studies show that "decreasing one's focus on materialistic aims is associated with improvements in one's psychological well-being over time" (18). In other words, people who place considerable weight on making money and having possessions are less mentally healthy and have less "well-being" than people who care less (or learned to care less) about those material goals. Kasser's study seems to show that people who care less about owning things simply automatically feel better about life and themselves.

TIP: **LEARN FROM ANOTHER'S PROCESS**

The paper to the right is the final draft of Jamie's paper, which we've shown developing throughout this book.

→ On page 10 in Part 1 you can see Jamie's very first thoughts on this assignment.

→ Pages 14, 17, and 32 in Part 2 show Jamie's initial research on the topic of minimalism.

→ In Part 3, you can see how Jamie found, evaluated, and tracked sources in her initial work toward this paper.

→ In Part 4, we show Jamie's annotated bibliography for two of her sources. We also show her putting two of her sources in dialogue with each other. If you look back at Jamie's earlier writing, you can see how she used that writing in her drafts.

→ In Part 5, you can see how Jamie developed a thesis statement for organizing her paper. You can also see her statement of purpose that she developed through studying her audience.

→ Also in Part 5, pages 96–101 show Jamie's first draft and the feedback from some of her readers. Look for differences between the two drafts to learn choices you can make to strengthen your writing.

→ On page 107 of Part 6, you can see Jamie's revision plan for her first draft.

How to use distinctions?

Jamie first uses the Kasser source to make a distinction between *owning fewer possessions* and *caring less about owning*. Once she has that distinction in place, she can move on to the Evans source, to show her readers a further distinction (between *being thrifty* and *being frugal*) growing out of the original. At each step, these distinctions help Jamie help her readers understand more about what matters with minimalism.

→ See page 75 to learn about distinctions.

How to introduce and use sources?

In the highlighted passage, notice how Jamie has told her readers about the writer she quotes as well as the title of the source. Once she has done that, she quotes from the source, careful to give the page citation at the end of the quotation.

→ See pages 58–59 and 292–293 to learn about quotations in MLA style.

How to choose tone of voice?

How would you characterize Jamie's tone in this paragraph? How would this paragraph be different if Jamie had not included "perhaps" in her first sentence? Try restating this paragraph in a more forceful, lecturing tone: How might such a tone shape a reader's response?

What Kasser's article seems to show, then, isn't that *owning less stuff* automatically leads to well-being. Instead, Kasser's study shows that *caring less about stuff* is what leads to well-being. In these studies, it was the people who didn't want to make lots of money or own lots of expensive things who had "well-being." The way to well-being seems to be through values rather than possessions—and through particular values.

For example, because being minimal and so owning fewer possessions means that one needs to think carefully about spending, being minimal seems to require the values of being thrifty or being frugal. The distinction between being thrifty and being frugal perhaps seem unimportant, but the difference demonstrates something important about the values involved in being minimal. The distinction between the two values is the focus of sociologist David Evans's article "Thrifty, Green, or Frugal: Reflections on Sustainable Consumption in a Changing Environmental Climate." Evans defines "thrift" as "doing more (consumption) with less (money) and so thrifty practices are practices of savvy consumption, characterized by the thrill and skill of 'the bargain'" (551). Being thrifty is about spending carefully: for example, one might decide to spend less on clothes in order to go on a big trip. Someone who is frugal, on the other hand, "values work over leisure; saving over spending; restraint over indulgence; deferred over immediate gratification and the satisfaction of 'needs' over the satisfaction of wants and desires" (552). Evans argues that thrift continues to be about consuming; it is about caring for those with whom you live and helping them have better lives by being careful about where your money goes. Frugality, on the other hand, is about trying to consume as little as possible because one cares about the environment and how the shape of the environment affects everyone, not just those with whom one lives most closely.

What the distinction between being thrifty and being frugal demonstrates, then, is that perhaps part of what connects owning less to "the good life" are the choices one consciously makes in deciding to own less. If one decides to become minimal, one chooses what to value. To follow Evans, being thrifty can be about caring for one's family, while being frugal can be about caring for others and the world. In either case, one decides whether to most value personal satisfaction or something larger than the personal.

REFLECTIVE WRITING ABOUT THIS PAPER

In class on the day Jamie turned in this paper, her teacher asked everyone to write informally in response to these questions: *What made them proud of their papers? What helped them make the revisions they did? What will they do differently on a next paper—or what do they want to remember from this writing?* Here is Jamie's writing:

Right now, I'm happy with this paper. I worked hard, paying attention to feedback and looking hard for new sources and, probably what most paid off, really figuring out what I wanted to argue. I am also proud that this really feels like MY paper. I figured this out. I made this thinking happen.

I learned a lot from sticking with the research and finding new sources. I am proud of how I reworked my original thesis statement and really made it make sense in the paper (or so it looks like to me now).

I made the revisions I did (and I've never revised any writing so much!) because I wanted to figure this out. Not only did I need to figure out my argument, but I had to work hard on making the writing more academic. I worked on making my sentences have more complex patterns. I also worked hard on the transitions; the Writing Center helped me hear how my words sound to others.

I want to remember the satisfaction from the hard work. And how to write for readers.

How to order sources?

At the beginning of her paper, Jamie used popular sources to help her define her main term, "minimalism." Then she used two academic sources to help her make careful distinctions about why people become minimalist, enabling her to bring up the values at work in minimalism. Finally, Jamie uses one more academic source—the Skidelsky book—to deepen her considerations of the values that can underlie minimalism. Jamie has thus used her sources to go from what is more simple (definition) to what is more complex (distinctions, and the values implied by those distinctions).

Following a plan

Earlier, Jamie developed an organizational plan for this paper (→ see pages 81–82) based on her thesis statement, and she followed that plan more with this final version than with her initial draft. Do you think the organization of the final version works more effectively than the organization of her draft (→ on pages 96–101)? Why or why not?

Concluding

Compare this last paragraph to the last paragraph of Jamie's original draft (→ see page 101). Do you think she has made her argument clearer in this version? How do you think her readers might respond to her last points?

Similar concerns come up in the book *How Much is Enough? Money and the Good Life*, by two economists. The book describes how people used to be taught to think about how they used their time and about how to compose a "good life." To show how societies and governments turned from supporting "the good life" and how we all came to value being consumers and owning more, the book gives a history of economics as a discipline. In discussing some problems of increased consumption and the environment, the book also gives some history of the idea of "happiness" to show that this is not the same as "the good life." At the end, the authors argue that having "a good life" depends on having certain basic needs met; those basic needs are health, security, respect from and for others, personality (which means being able to express one's self freely), harmony with nature, friendship, and leisure. "Leisure" is the time to pursue interests such as art, reading, hobbies—as well as just time to think. Notice, too, how time for friendship is separated out from this, as are "harmony with nature" and having respect back-and-forth in one's relationships in the world, to show how important are those wider values.

What all this research about connections between owning less and having a "good life" demonstrates, then, is that owning less probably connects with time in two ways. First, one doesn't have to spend so much time thinking about what to buy, taking care of it once it is bought, or moving it around. Second, the time one could be involved with possessions is time one can spend with friends and family and seeking "harmony with nature"—but is also time one can use to think. Time for thinking is necessary for one to decide what values to hold and whether one's actions are supporting those values.

The connections between owning less stuff and having a "good life," then, seem to work like this: When one decides to own less, that decidion already demonstrates that one values something other than being material. But when one decides to own less, one does free up time, and that time can be used for being with friends and family and in nature—and to think even more about what makes life worth living. One might very well start seeking something bigger than one's self—and seeking something bigger than ourselves seems to be what is most important in building a "good life."

A WORKS-CITED PAGE IN MLA FORMAT

The last page or pages in a paper written in MLA style will look like the page to the right.

❑ Put the works-cited list after the last page of the paper.

❑ The works-cited list starts on its own page.

❑ Use the same margin measurements as the rest of the paper (→ see pages 127 and 129).

❑ Number each works-cited page at the top right of the page (as you do each page in MLA format; → see page 127). The number on the first page of the works-cited list follows the number of the last page of the paper. For example, if the last page of the paper is 8, the first page of the works-cited list will be 9.

❑ **Works Cited** is centered at the top of the page.

❑ The listings are arranged alphabetically by the author's last name. (If a listing starts with the title of a source, place it into the whole list alphabetically, using the first letter of the title. If the title begins with **A**, **An**, or **The**, alphabetize by the second word of the title.)

❑ If you list two or more sources by the same author, alphabetize them by the source titles. List the author only once; start all subsequent entries by the same author with three hyphens and a period.

❑ If you have two authors with the same last name, alphabetize by the first name.

❑ Double-space the entries.

→ Starting on page 140, we show you how to make the individual listings that go on such a page.

NOTE!
Only include on your works-cited list those sources you cited in your paper. Do not include sources that you read but did not cite.

Works Cited

Babauta, Leo. "Minimalist FAQs." *mnlist.com,* mnmlist.com/minimalist-faqs. Accessed 17 Mar. 2016.

Becker, Joshua. "21 Benefits of Owning Less." *Becoming Minimalist,* 2015, www.becomingminimalist.com/minimalism-benefits.

Dang, Jessica. "Why Minimalism Brings Happiness." *Minimal Student,* 2014, www.minimalstudent.com/why-minimalism-brings-happiness. Accessed 6 Mar. 2016.

Evans, David. "Thrifty, Green, or Frugal: Reflections on Sustainable Consumption in a Changing Environmental Climate." *Geoforum,* vol. 42, 2011, pp. 550–57. *Science Direct*, doi:10.1016/j.geoforum.2011.03.008.

Kasser, Tim, et al. "Changes in Materialism, Changes in Psychological Well-being: Evidence from Three Longitudinal Studies and an Intervention Experiment." *Motivation and Emotion*, vol. 38, no. 1, 2014, pp. 1–22. *Springer Link*, doi:10.1007/s11031-013-9371-4.

Sidelsky, Robert and Edward Sidelsky. *How Much is Enough? Money and the Good Life.* Other Press, 2012.

Use hanging indentation

So that readers can scan the alphabetic list easily and quickly, MLA style asks for a 1/2 inch indent of all lines underneath the first line of each entry.

Enough support?

Do you think Jamie used enough sources to make her overall argument? If not, how many more—and what kinds of sources—would you recommend?

MLA DOCUMENTATION FOR IN-TEXT CITATIONS

In-text citations guide readers to the works-cited page to learn the information that helps them find the source itself.

Garza 4

David Evans defines "thrift" as "doing more (consumption) with less (money) and so thrifty practices are practices of savvy consumption, characterized by the thrill and skill of 'the bargain'" (551). Being thrifty is about spending carefully: for example, one might decide to spend less on clothes in order to go on a big trip. Someone who is frugal,

indulg

satisfa

consu

lives b

about

and ho

lives r

that pe

Garza 5

Works Cited

Becker, Joshua. "21 Benefits of Owning Less." *Becoming Minimalist*, 2015, www.becomingminimalist.com/minimalism-benefits.

Dang, Jessica. "Why Minimalism Brings Happiness." *Minimal Student*, 2014, www.minimalstudent.com/why-minimalism-brings-happiness. Accessed 6 Mar. 2016.

Evans, David. "Thrifty, Green, or Frugal: Reflections on Sustainable Consumption in a Changing Environmental Climate." *Geoforum*, vol. 42, 2011, pp. 550–57. *Science Direct*, doi:10.1016/j.geoforum.2011.03.008.

THE PATTERN

IN-TEXT CITATIONS IN MLA STYLE

In-text citations in MLA style generally contain two elements:

1

The name of the author of the words or ideas being quoted, summarized, or paraphrased. The name can appear within the sentence containing the quotation or within parentheses at the sentence's end.

2

The page number(s) of or some other reference to the words or ideas being cited. The number of the page from which quoted words come goes at the end of the sentence, in parentheses.

In her article on two nineteenth-century women preachers, Patricia Bizzell argues that "a conjunction between the female sex and moral activism is traditional in Methodism" (379).

or

One writer on nineteenth-century women preachers argues that "a conjunction between the female sex and moral activism is traditional in Methodism" (Bizzell 379).

VARIATIONS ON THE MLA IN-TEXT CITATION PATTERN

NO AUTHOR IS NAMED

If no author is named, use the work's title:

To "watch the rejects crash and burn" is why we watch *American Idol,* according to *Rolling Stone* magazine ("Idol Worship" 7).

→ If a company name or government organization is listed as author, see pages 150 and 151.

YOU CITE TWO OR MORE SOURCES BY THE SAME AUTHOR

When you use two or more works by the same author, each in-text citation should give the particular work's name in your sentence or in the parenthetical reference.

If you give the work's name in the parenthetical reference, do not use the full title, to save space; instead, use the title's first main noun and any adjectives that come before it (but not articles).

Here is a citation for a first source:

That meat from cows fed on grass is more nutritious than that from corn-fed cows is just one of the many arguments Pollan makes (*Omnivore's Dilemma* 68).

Here is how the second source is cited:

Because his research shows just what chemicals go into a commercial potato, Pollan cannot bring himself to eat one (*Botany* 235).

If you need to put the author's name, the work's title, and a page number into the parenthetical citation, put a comma between the author's name and the title and put a space between the title and page number:

(Pollan, *Botany* 235)

YOU CITE SOURCES BY AUTHORS WITH THE SAME LAST NAME

So that readers can find the right citation in your works-cited list, either use authors' full names in your sentences or use each author's first initial and full last name in the parenthetical citation. (If both authors have the same first initial, use their full first names instead.)

Here are examples from the same paper:

Richard Rorty argues that our understanding of what knowledge is has changed over two hundred years.

Amélie Oksenberg Rorty shows how Aristotle's *Rhetoric* draws on understandings of how people communicate, the psychology of audiences, the character of communicators, and politics.

These examples avoid ambiguity through their parenthetical citations:

Some philosophers argue that our understanding of what knowledge is has changed over the last two hundred years (R. Rorty).

Aristotle's *Rhetoric* draws on understandings of how people communicate, the psychology of audiences, the character of communicators, and politics (A. Rorty).

THE SOURCE YOU CITE HAS TWO AUTHORS

List the names in the order they are given in the source. Use *and* between the two names, whether you use the names in your sentence or in parentheses at sentence end:

As "much an activist as an analytical method" is how Moeller and Moberly describe McAllister's approach to computer games.

Reviewers describe McAllister's approach to computer games as as "much an activist as an analytical method" (Moeller and Moberly).

THE SOURCE YOU CITE HAS THREE OR MORE AUTHORS

If the work you cite has three or more authors, use only the first author's name, followed by the expression *et al.*, putting a period after *al*. (*Et al.* is Latin for *and others*.)

Fine et al. offer a two-year study of such a class in "Before the Bleach Gets Us All."

or:

When a ninth-grade world literature class is offered at high honors level for everyone, without tracking, students "who never expected to be seen as smart" come to see themselves as capable and sharp (Fine et al. 174, 175).

THE SOURCE YOU CITE HAS A CORPORATE AUTHOR OR IS A GOVERNMENT DOCUMENT

If there are common abbreviations for terms in the author name, use them in the parenthetical citation. If a name is long and can't be abbreviated, putting it in the sentence will read less awkwardly than putting it within the parentheses.

According to a booklet published by the Keweenaw National Historical Park, in the early twentieth century, in the copper mines of Michigan's Upper Peninsula, the "division of labor often followed ethnic lines" (United States, Dept. of the Interior, National Park Service).

Because the writer explains the quotation is from a booklet, readers do not expect a page number; they will look in the works-cited list under *United States, Dept. of the Interior.*

Also notice that, in the parenthetical citation, each of the governmental units is mentioned, in order, just as they would be in the works-cited list.

→ See pages 150 and 151 on the works-cited list entries for corporate and government authors.

THERE IS NO PAGE NUMBER

Some print sources have no page numbers. If the paragraphs or sections are numbered, include them in the citation; otherwise, make the author or source title clear

The Museum of Modern Art's pamphlet, "The Changing of the Avant-Garde," argues that architecture following World War II was influenced by "pop culture, the first stirrings of the information age, and the radical politics of the 1960s."

The words make clear the source is a pamphlet; readers won't expect a page number and will look for "The Changing of the Avant-Garde" in the works-cited list.

Some online sources, like e-books, have location numbers; these numbers change from device to device, so do not use them. Instead, if such a source has chapters, use them:

Linden describes people born without an ability to feel pain, which sounds like a wonderful ability—but he notes that without an ability to feel pain "we do not learn to recoil from sharp blades, boiling liquids, or damaging chemicals" (ch. 6).

Here is the works-cited entry for the above in-text citation; note that the citation does not tell what kind of book was cited:

Linden, David J. *Touch: The Science of Hand, Heart, and Mind.* Viking, 2015.
     E-BOOK

YOU CITE TIME-BASED MEDIA, LIKE TELEVISION OR VIDEO

Cite the time or range of times of the passage you reference. Give the hours, minutes, and seconds as displayed in your media player, separating the numbers with colons:

In her TED Talk on "How Humans Could Evolve to Live in Space," Lisa Nip suggests we can use "synthetic biology to change the genetic makeup of any living organisms"—including humans (00:11:09).

YOU CITE PART OF AN EDITED COLLECTION OR ANTHOLOGY

Use the name of the author who wrote the words you quote—*not* the name of the collection's editor. For example, if you cite an article by Tania Modleski in a collection edited by Amelia Jones, use Modleski's name in your in-text citations:

Tania Modleski's article "The Search for Tomorrow in Today's Soap Operas" examines the different pleasures women find in soap opera narratives.

One scholar examines the different pleasures women find in soap opera narratives (Modleski).

YOU CITE TWO OR MORE SOURCES IN ONE SENTENCE

Your first option, if you refer to the different sources in different parts of the sentence, is to put a citation after each reference:

While some research finds a link between violent games and aggressive behavior in children (Provenzo 12), many recent studies challenge the idea of a direct connection between gaming and real-world behaviors (Jones 144).

Your second option, if your sources support one main point, is to put them all into the parentheses, separated by semicolons:

Although there is agreement that hundreds of languages were spoken in the Americas before Europeans arrived, there is disagreement over the number of linguistic families into which the languages fit (Crystal 403-08; Wade 113-18).

YOU REFERENCE AN ENTIRE SOURCE

If you need to refer to an entire source in your writing, do not include page numbers. Instead, put only the author's and the work's names, or refer to the source in the parentheses at the end of the sentence.

Oliver Sacks's *Seeing Voices* argues that sign languages are indeed real languages, so when people who are deaf learn to sign, they gain the same neurological benefits as people who can hear gain when they learn to speak.

An increase in childhood sports injuries seems related to increased competition (Gorman).

YOU CITE AN ENCYCLOPEDIA OR DICTIONARY

If you cite a reference work that has a named author, then set up your citation and works-cited entry just as you would for a part of a book, using the author's name.

If you cite a reference work with no listed author, put the citation into your works-cited list alphabetically by the title. Because reference work sections are usually arranged alphabetically, you do not need to give a page number; readers can find what you are referencing without the page number.

Mad cow disease, the popular name for bovine spongiform encephalopathy (a fatal neurological disorder), appears to be transferable to humans, in whom it is called Creutzfeldt-Jakob disease; mad cow disease spreads when cows are fed the processed remains of cattle who have the disease ("Bovine Spongiform Encephalopathy").

YOU QUOTE WORDS THAT ANOTHER WRITER QUOTED

Use **qtd. in** (for *quoted in*) before the source reference to show where you found the quoted words:

Elizabeth Durack argues that *Star Wars* "and other popular media creations take the place in modern America that culture myths like those of the Greeks or Native Americans did for earlier peoples" (qtd. in Jenkins 153).

Readers will look for the corresponding works-cited item under *Jenkins*.

MLA DOCUMENTATION FOR WORKS CITED

These pages show you how to create the individual citations for the Works Cited list that goes at the end of all research papers written in MLA style.

MLA STYLE FOR CHANGING MEDIA

In 2016, the MLA revised its approach to documenting sources, publishing its changes in the eighth edition of the *MLA Handbook*. Because how we read, write, publish, and exchange texts has changed with the Internet, the MLA states that writers "need a system for documenting sources that begins with a few principles rather than a long list of rules" (8).

The new principles help writers figure out how to document any source, old or new, without needing to be told the exact format for a new source: "A work in a new medium thus can be documented without new instructions" (3).

MLA PRINCIPLES FOR DOCUMENTATION

1 **"Cite simple traits shared by most works"** (3)
Citations grow out of the features *all* sources share: an author and a title. Then other information—shared by different kinds of sources—is added to the citation.

2 **"Remember that there is often more than one correct way to document a source"** (4)
When writers need to decide whether to include more or less information, the MLA says that the writer's purposes should guide the decision.

3 **"Make your documentation useful to readers"** (4)
Following the MLA guidelines helps readers because the guidelines help readers find sources.

AN IMPORTANT CONCEPT: "CONTAINERS"

→ See pages 000–000 on this concept used in MLA citations.

WORK CITED ABOVE

MLA Handbook. 8th ed., Modern Language Association of America, 2016.
BOOK—CORPORATE AUTHOR AND PUBLISHER ARE THE SAME

TO MAKE MLA WORKS CITED PAGES

1
COLLECT THE INFORMATION YOU NEED FOR EACH OF YOUR SOURCES.

To know what information to collect, you need to know whether your source is a stand-alone source, is a source inside a container—or is a source inside a container inside a container.

→ See pages 142–143 about stand-alone sources and containers.

→ See pages 41–49 for the information to collect for your source.

2
CONSTRUCT A CITATION FOR EACH SOURCE, FOLLOWING THE MLA PATTERN.

Follow the pattern to construct your listing element by element, starting with the author, moving on to the title, and so on, step by step, until you have a full citation.

→ The pattern is on pages 144–145.

→ The pattern for sources in containers is on page 146.

3
CONSTRUCT YOUR WORKS CITED PAGE

When you have all your individual citations, put them together into the Works Cited page.

→ See pages 134–135 for how to format the Works Cited page.

CONCEPTS NECESSARY FOR MLA CITATIONS: "**STAND-ALONE SOURCES**" AND "**SOURCES IN CONTAINERS**"

STAND-ALONE SOURCES

A stand-alone source exists as a self-contained whole, such as:

SOURCES IN CONTAINERS

Some sources exist only inside other texts that contain them:

A scholarly article...

can have an online journal as its **container**:

A television episode...

can have a series as its **container**:

 Look across these three categories to determine which fits your source; knowing the category of your source helps you build your source's citation.

SOURCES IN CONTAINERS, IN CONTAINERS

Some sources exist only inside other texts that in turn are contained in other texts:

A scholarly article...

↓
can have
a journal as its **container**...

↓
which can have
an online database as its **container**.

A video...

↓
can have
a series as its **container**...

↓
which can have
a website as its **container**.

THE PATTERN FOR MLA CITATIONS

The pattern to the right lists the nine elements—in the order they go into a citation—that can be included in an MLA works-cited citation. All citations will include—minimally—a title, a publication date, and some of the other elements. Almost no citations require all the elements listed.

Read the information about each element linked from the opposite page to learn how to include the element.

Note, too, that the pattern shows the punctuation that follows each element. However, all citations end with a period, even if they do not end with a location.

The citations below show how different citations use different elements of the pattern shown to the right; the pattern elements are underlined:

Brown, James. *Ethical Programs: Hospitality and the Rhetorics of Software.*
₁   ₂

   U of Michigan P, 2015.
    ₇   ₈

   BOOK

Young, Vershawn Ashanti. "Readings on Rhetoric and Performance."
₁   ₂

   Text and Performance Quarterly, vol. 31, no. 4, 2011, pp. 451-53.
   ₃   ₆   ₈   ₉

   ARTICLE, IN SCHOLARLY JOURNAL

Weingarten, Judith. "Writing Tablets from Ancient Palmyra." *Zenobia: Empress*
₁   ₂   ₃

   of the East, 30 Mar. 2016, judithweingarten.blogspot.com/2016/03/
    ₈   ₉

   writing-tablets-from-ancient-palmyra.html.

   POST, ON BLOG

ABOUT THE BLUE SUBTITLES UNDER CITATIONS IN THESE PAGES

The blue subtitles describe the kind of source being cited—but if the blue subtitles contain a comma, the information following the first comma indicates the source's container; the information following a *second* comma indicates a second container.

1 **AUTHOR.**

→ Pages 148–150 explain how to format author names and work with differing kinds of authors.

2 **SOURCE TITLE.**

→ Pages 152–155 show how to format source titles.

3 **CONTAINER TITLE,**

→ Pages 152–155 show how to format container titles.

4 **OTHER CONTRIBUTORS,**

→ Page 156 explains when and how to list other contributors.

5 **VERSION,**

→ Page 157 explains when and how to include a version.

6 **NUMBER,**

→ Page 158 explains when and how to include a number.

7 **PUBLISHER,**

→ Page 159 explains when and how to include publisher information.

8 **PUBLICATION DATE,**

→ Pages 160–161 explain how to include publication date information.

9 **LOCATION.**

→ Pages 162–163 explain what a "location" is and when and how to include a location.

IF YOUR SOURCE IS INSIDE A CONTAINER THAT IS INSIDE ANOTHER CONTAINER

THE PATTERN FOR MLA CITATIONS WITH TWO CONTAINERS

START WITH THE CITATION FOR THE FIRST SOURCE AND ITS CONTAINER, put a period, and then add (in order) whichever of the following elements is necessary to describe the second container:

3 **SECOND CONTAINER TITLE,**

4 **OTHER CONTRIBUTORS,**

5 **VERSION,**

6 **NUMBER,**

7 **PUBLISHER,**

8 **PUBLICATION DATE,**

9 **LOCATION.**

→ The information that goes into elements 3–9 is formatted exactly as for the basic MLA pattern on pages 144–145.

For example, if you found the second source listed on page 144 (whose first container is a journal) inside an online database, the citation would look like this:

Young, Vershawn Ashanti. "Readings on Rhetoric and Performance."

1   2

Text and Performance Quarterly, vol. 31, no. 4, 2011, pp. 451-53.

3   6   8   9

Communication & Mass Media Complete, doi: 10.1080/10462937.2011.604426.

3   9

ARTICLE, IN SCHOLARLY JOURNAL, IN DATABASE

Note that for such citations you put a period after the citation for the first source and its container; then begin the citation for the new container.

MLA WORKS CITED
WHAT SOURCES NEED WHICH ELEMENTS?

Very few sources will use all nine elements of the basic MLA citation pattern. Remember that a source *inside a container inside another container* will also need all the second container's elements.)

- ■ You *probably* will find this element for a source of this kind; *most* citations for a source of this kind will include the blue elements noted.

- ■ You *might* find this element for a source of this kind, or you can include information here if it fits your purposes.

Source	AUTHOR, pp. 148–150	SOURCE TITLE, pp. 152–155	CONTAINER TITLE, pp. 152–155	OTHER CONTRIBUTORS, p. 156	VERSION, p. 157	NUMBER, p. 158	PUBLISHER, p. 159	PUBLICATION DATE, pp. 160–161	LOCATION, pp. 162–163
ARTICLE IN JOURNAL, MAGAZINE, OR NEWSPAPER	■	■	■			■		■	■
BLOG, ENTIRE	■	■	■				■	■	■
BLOG, SINGLE ENTRY	■	■	■					■	■
BOOK	■	■		■	■		■	■	
COMIC OR GRAPHIC NOVEL PUBLISHED AS PART OF SERIES	■	■	■	■	■	■	■	■	
COMIC OR GRAPHIC NOVEL PUBLISHED AS STAND-ALONE	■	■		■	■	■	■	■	
ESSAY OR OTHER PART IN BOOK	■	■	■	■			■	■	■
MOVIE		■		■			■	■	
PODCAST	■	■	■				■	■	
SOCIAL MEDIA POST	■	■	■					■	■
SONG	■	■	■				■	■	■
TELEVISION EPISODE	■	■	■	■			■	■	
TELEVISION SERIES	■	■	■			■	■	■	
VIDEO ONLINE	■	■	■					■	■
WEBPAGE	■	■	■					■	■
WEBSITE	■	■					■	■	■

MLA WORKS CITED
FIGURING OUT A CITATION
IF THERE ISN'T A MODEL

If you cannot find—here or in the MLA Handbook*—a model for the citation you need, what do you do?*

Follow the MLA's advice, given on page 3 of the *Handbook*: "The writer examines the source and records its visible features, attending to the work itself and a set of universal guidelines. A work in a new medium thus can be documented without new instructions" (3).

Below we describe how we followed the MLA's "universal guidelines," as a suggestion for how you can do similarly should you need to.

EXAMPLE: AN ADVERTISEMENT

The *MLA Handbook* does not give a citation example for an adverisement in a magazine.

And so we turned to the guidelines we've taken from the MLA and have described throughout these pages, and we were able to develop this citation, which should enable any reader to find the source:

Walgreens. Advertisement for Vitamin Angels program. *O: The Oprah Magazine*. Apr. 2016.
    pp. 44–45. Advertisement.
    ADVERTISEMENT, IN MAGAZINE
    UNTITLED SOURCE
    UNEXPECTED SOURCE

Here's how we came up with a citation:

1 An advertisement does not usually list any single person as author, but the *MLA Handbook* does describe how a text "may be created by a corporate author—an institution, an association, a government agency, or another kind of organization" (25). We believe we can therefore use the corporation behind the advertisement as the author.

2 An advertisement does not have a title. The *MLA Handbook* does state, however, "When a source is untitled, provide a generic description of it, neither italicized nor enclosed in quotation marks, in place of a title. Capitalize the first word of the description and any proper nouns in it" (28–29). In the citation above, you can see the description we came up with for this advertisement, based on the information in the advertisement.

3 The advertisement appears in *O: The Oprah Magazine*, so our citation lists that magazine as our source's container, adding to the citation the information one includes about a magazine: its date and the source's page numbers.

4 The MLA states that for "unexpected" kinds of texts, a writer can add a description at the end of the citation: To help our readers know exactly what sort of text we cite, we add **Advertisement.** to the end of our citation.

1 AUTHOR.

The author pattern is consistent for citations of all texts in all media. Keep in mind that *author* can mean a single person, several people, or an organization; when an organization—any group, committee, or business—is responsible for a text, you have a *corporate author*.

THE PATTERN FOR WHEN AUTHORS ARE PEOPLE

The first author listed is written with the last name first, followed by a comma, and then the first name.

Last Name, First Name.   Singh, Amardeep.

If the writer you cite uses a middle name or initials, those follow the first name.

Phelps, Louise Wetherbee.   Mitchell, W. J. T.

If your source has more than one author, list the authors as they are listed in the source; see below for how to format differing numbers of authors.

In a citation, there is a period after the author's name or the list of authors' names.

NO AUTHOR NAMED

If you cannot find an author's name, start the citation with the source's title. (Consider, though, whether there might be a corporate author.)

"Revenant." *Merriam-Webster Dictionary*. www.merriam-webster. com/dictionary/revenant. Accessed 2 Apr. 2016.
DICTIONARY—ONLINE
ONLINE SOURCE—NO SOURCE DATE, SO ACCESS DATE GIVEN

"Io in Motion." *NASA on The Commons*. 2 Apr. 2007. www.flickr. com/photos/nasacommons/5278071978. Photograph.
PHOTOGRAPH—NO AUTHOR NAMED

ONE AUTHOR

Chernysheva, Natalia. *Le retour*. 2015, vimeo.com/63082999.
VIDEO ONLINE

Peacay. "1930s Modern Publicity." *Bibliodyssey*, 24 Apr. 2014, bibliodyssey.blogspot.com/2014/04/1930s-modern-publicity.html.
POST UNDER PSEUDONYM, ON BLOG

TWO AUTHORS

Add the second author as shown to a one author pattern.

Ahern, Kati Fargo, and Jordan Frith. "Speaking Back to Our Spaces: The Rhetoric of Social Soundscaping." *Harlot*, no. 9, 2013, harlotofthearts.org/index.php/harlot/article/ view/150/122.
ARTICLE, IN SCHOLARLY JOURNAL ONLINE

Author *information continues on the next two pages.*·······>

THREE OR MORE AUTHORS

Use the name of the first author followed by a comma. Then put **et al.** (meaning "and others").

Fine, Michelle, et al. "Before the Bleach Gets Us All." *Construction Sites*, edited by Lois Weiss and Michelle Fine, Teachers College, 2000, pp. 161-79.
ESSAY, IN EDITED COLLECTION

Nelson, Scott, et. al. "Crossing Battle Lines: Teaching Multimodal Literacies through Alternate Reality Games." *Kairos*, vol. 17, no. 3, 2013, http://kairos.technorhetoric.net/17.3/praxis/nelson-et-al/index.html.
ARTICLE, IN SCHOLARLY JOURNAL ONLINE

PSEUDONYM

Use the pseudonym as the author's name, spelled exactly as the pseudonym appears. If you know the name of the person using a pseudonym, you can add it in parentheses.

In citing a tweet, include the @ symbol.)

Alice Addertongue (Benjamin Franklin). Letter to the editor. *The Pennsylvania Gazette*, 12 Sept.1732. *The Papers of Benjamin Franklin*, vol. 1, American Philosophical Society / Yale University, franklinpapers.org/franklin/framedVolumes.jsp?vol=1&page=243a.
LETTER TO THE EDITOR
SOURCE WITH TWO PUBLISHERS

@manwhohasitall. "TODAY'S DEBATE: What unique skills do men bring to the boardroom?" 22 Mar. 2016, 4:00 p.m. twitter.com/manwhohasitall/status/712383569415397376.
TWEET

A CORPORATE AUTHOR

Start with the corporate author's name exactly as listed in the source (but omit **A, An,** or **The**).

If the same organization is both author and publisher, begin the entry with the work's title and put the organization only as publisher.

Some sources (like advertisements) may seem to have no author, but the organization responsible for the source can be listed as author.

→ If you have a government author, see the opposite page.

Hunter College Women's and Gender Studies Collective. *Women's Realities, Women's Choices: An Introduction to Women's Studies*. 4th ed., Oxford UP, 2015.
BOOK—CORPORATE AUTHOR

Médecins Sans Frontières (MSF). 2016, www.msf.org.
WEBSITE—CORPORATE AUTHOR

"Six Extinctions In Six Minutes." *Shelf Life*, American Museum of Natural History, episode 10, 21 Dec. 2015. www.youtube.com/watch?v=AZuwOgcS1W0
VIDEO—CORPORATE AUTHOR AND PUBLISHER ARE THE SAME

The Changing of the Avant-Garde: Visionary Architectural Drawings from the Howard Gilman Collection. Museum of Modern Art, 2002.
BOOK—CORPORATE AUTHOR AND PUBLISHER ARE THE SAME

Wisconsin League of Conservation Voters. "The Nelson Award." *Wisconsin Gazette*. 24 Mar. 2016, p. 25. Advertisement.
ADVERTISEMENT—CORPORATE AUTHOR

A GOVERNMENT AUTHOR

Begin the entry with the name of the country or state; then put a comma and the name of the government agency. Between the country or state and the agency names, list (separated by commas) the organizational units of which the agency is a part. Arrange the names from the largest government entity to the smallest. (Note that you omit The from the names.)

United States, Census Bureau. "Veteran Statistics: Alabama." 10 Nov. 2015. www.census.gov/library/infographics/veterans-statistics.html. Chart.
GOVERNMENT DOCUMENT—FEDERAL
CHART

United States, Department of the Interior, National Park Service. "Cape Lookout National Seashore." 2007. Brochure.
GOVERNMENT DOCUMENT—FEDERAL
BROCHURE

Montana, Department of Fish, Wildlife, and Parks. "2016 Montana Fishing Regulations." 2016. Booklet.
GOVERNMENT DOCUMENT—STATE
BOOKLET

United Nations High Commission for Refugees." Global Appeal 2016–2017." www.unhcr.org/pages/49c3646c4b8.html.
GOVERNMENT DOCUMENT—INTERNATIONAL

AN EDITED COLLECTION

Put editor (or editors for multiple editors) after the names that begin the citation.

If the book has more than two editors, follow the pattern for a book with multiple authors.

Le Faye, Deirdre, editor. *Jane Austen's Letters*. 3rd ed. Oxford UP, 1995.
BOOK—EDITED

Bechdel, Alison, editor. *Best American Comics 2011*. Houghton Mifflin, 2011.
BOOK—EDITED
GRAPHIC NOVEL—EDITED COLLECTION

Hocks, Mary, and Michelle Kendrick, editors. *Eloquent Images: Word and Image in the Age of New Media*. MIT P, 2003.
BOOK—EDITED WITH TWO EDITORS

COMICS, GRAPHIC NOVELS, FILM, TELEVISION, AND OTHER MEDIA PRODUCED BY MANY PEOPLE

If you wish to focus on a particular person's contribution, start with that person's name followed by a label describing the person's contribution; otherwise, omit an author and begin with the source title.

Coates, Ta-Nehisi, writer. *Black Panther: A Nation Under Our Feet, Book 1*. Illustrated by Brian Stelfreeze, Marvel, 2016.
COMIC BOOK—WITH FOCUS ON WRITER AND ADDITION OF OTHER CONTRIBUTOR

Cheadle, Don, actor, director, and writer. *Miles Ahead*. Bifrost Pictures, 2015.
FILM—WITH FOCUS ON CONTRIBUTION OF ONE PERSON

Miles Ahead. Bifrost Pictures, 2015.
FILM

Bela, Dalila, actor. "Trials and Tubulations." *Odd Squad*, season 1, episode 29, 1 Sept. 2015.
TELEVISION EPISODE—WITH FOCUS ON CONTRIBUTION OF ONE PERSON

2 SOURCE TITLES

3 CONTAINER TITLES

To follow MLA conventions accurately, you need to understand the following distinction:

STAND-ALONE SOURCES

→ Pages 142–143 also explain about stand-alone sources and sources in containers.

Sometimes you cite a whole book, a whole website, a film, an album, or a computer game.

In such cases, you have **a stand-alone source**.

Stand-alone sources do not have containers: they are self-contained.

In such cases, your citation will include element 2 from the MLA pattern for works-cited lists but not element 3.

SOURCES IN CONTAINERS

→ Pages 142–143 also explain about stand-alone sources and sources in containers.

Some sources live within larger texts:

- A journal article is contained within a journal.
- A webpage is contained within a website.
- An essay is contained within a collection.
- Poems are generally contained within a printed or online collection of many poems.
- A television episode is contained within a series.
- A song is contained within an album.

In such cases, you have **a source in a container**. In such cases, your citation will include both element 2 and element 3 from the MLA pattern for works-cited lists.

Your citation needs to include only one title, that of the stand-alone source:

2 SOURCE TITLE.

Your citation needs to include a source title followed by the container title:

2 SOURCE TITLE.

3 CONTAINER TITLE,

THE PATTERN FOR FORMATTING STAND-ALONE SOURCE TITLES AND CONTAINER TITLES

ITALICIZE STAND-ALONE AND CONTAINER TITLES.

Put **a period** after stand-alone source titles:

WHOLE BOOKS:	*Crow Lake.*	*Autobiography of a Face.*
FILMS:	*1916: The Irish Rebellion.*	*In Jackson Heights.*
ALBUMS:	*Marvin Gaye: What's Going On.*	*Music in Exile.*
GAMES:	*The Elder Scrolls V: Skyrim.*	*Minecraft.*

Put **a comma** after container source titles:

NEWSPAPERS:	*Washington Post,*	*Daily Mining Gazette,*
JOURNALS:	*Journal of Experimental Medicine,*	*Journal of American History,*
MAGAZINES:	*TIME,*	*National Geographic,*
TELEVISION SHOWS:	*Buffy the Vampire Slayer,*	*Shots Fired,*
WEBSITES:	*The Mary Sue,*	*Anime News Network,*

THE PATTERN FOR FORMATTING SOURCES IN CONTAINERS

PUT QUOTATION MARKS AROUND THE TITLES OF SOURCES THAT ARE IN CONTAINERS.

Put a period after the last word of the title, inside the final quotation mark. (If the title ends with a question mark or exclamation point, use that.)

ESSAY IN A BOOK:	"Meno."
SONG FROM AN ALBUM:	"Me Voy Enamorando."
ARTICLE IN A NEWSPAPER:	"The Global Journey of the Zika Virus."
ARTICLE IN A JOURNAL:	"Cloudshine: New Light on Dark Clouds."
ARTICLE IN A MAGAZINE:	"My Guide to a Better Night's Sleep."
TELEVISION EPISODE:	"Trials and Tubulations."
WEB PAGE ON A WEBSITE:	"A Bookling Monument."

MLA

THE PATTERN FOR CAPITALIZING TITLES

ALL TITLES FOR ALL SOURCES IN ALL MEDIA HAVE THIS PATTERN:

1 Capitalize all the words of the title except for:

articles (*a, an, the*)

prepositions (*to, at, by, for, from, in, of, with*)

conjunctions (*and, but, for, or*)

the word **to** when it is part of an infinitive (as in *to read* or *to write*)

2 Capitalize the first and last words, even if the words are one of the exceptions above.

3 If there is a subtitle, put it after a colon and capitalize it as you would the title.

Scribbling the Cat: Travels with an African Soldier • *The Quick and the Dead: Artists and Anatomy*

"Lucky Catch: Tongue Fishhook Injuries" • "Like a Thesis: A Postmodern Reading of Madonna Videos"

TITLES FOR STAND-ALONE SOURCES

Note that the titles are always italicized and followed by a period. Also note that sometimes no author is cited, because stand-alone sources produced by many people (such as a film, television show or website) do not have a single author. However, if the purpose of your writing about such a source is to focus on one of the people involved, you can put that person's name in the author position, as in the example to the right about the film *In Jackson Heights*.

Marvin Gaye. *Marvin Gaye: What's Going On*. Tamla Records, 1971.
ALBUM

Lawson, Mary. *Crow Lake*. Delta Trade, 2002.
BOOK

The Elder Scrolls V: Skyrim. Bethesda Game Studios, 2011.
COMPUTER GAME

Frederick Wiseman, director. *In Jackson Heights*. Moulins Films, 2015.
FILM WITH FOCUS ON DIRECTOR

Cosmos: A Spacetime Odyssey. Cosmos Studios, 2014.
TELEVISION SERIES

@paulaakpan and @harrietevs. *The "I'm Tired" Project*. 2016. www.instagram.com/theimtiredproject.
WEBSITE—INSTAGRAM

All Day. allday.com. Accessed 25 Mar. 2016.
WEBSITE—WITH NO DATE OF PRODUCTION

TITLES FOR STAND-ALONE SOURCES IN CONTAINERS

Bruegel, Pieter, the Elder. *The Triumph of Death*. Museo Nacional del Prado, 1562–1563, www.museodelprado.es/coleccion/obra-de-arte/el-triunfo-de-la-muerte/d3d82b0b-9bf2-4082-ab04-66ed53196ccc.
PAINTING, ONLINE

TITLES FOR SOURCES IN CONTAINERS—AND THEIR CONTAINER TITLES—AND *THEIR* CONTAINER TITLES (IF THERE IS ONE)

Ahmad, Leila. "Self-Driving Cars Will Eliminate Accidents." *Daily Cardinal*, 28 Mar. 2016, p. 5.
ARTICLE, IN NEWSPAPER PUBLISHED DAILY

Owens, Jill. "Ethan Canin: The Powells.com Interview." *Powells. com Blog*, 21 Mar. 2016, www.powells.com/post/interviews/ethan-canin-the-powellscom-interview.
INTERVIEW, ON BLOG

"Ingrid Bergman in *Gaslight*, 1944." *George Cukor papers*, 1944. *Margaret Herrick Library Digital Collections*, digitalcollections. oscars.org/cdm/singleitem/collection/p15759coll13/id/12/rec/13.
PHOTOGRAPH, IN ARCHIVE, IN ONLINE COLLECTION
PHOTOGRAPH—UNTITLED

Goodman, Robert B. "Men blast granite to build tunnels for a hydroelectric project in Australia, 1963." *Found*, National Geographic, 21 Aug. 2015, natgeofound.tumblr.com.
PHOTOGRAPH, ON TUMBLR

Bragg, Melvyn. "Bedlam." *In Our Time*, BBC, 17 Mar. 2016, www. bbc.co.uk/programmes/b0739rfg#in=collection:p01dh5yg.
PODCAST, FROM WEBSITE

Kilwein Guevara, Maurice. "Pets." *Poema*, U of Arizona P, 2009, p. 48.
POEM, IN BOOK BY ONE AUTHOR

Simone, Nina. "Please Don't Let Me Be Misunderstood." *The Lady Has the Blues*, Tomato Records, 2003.
SONG, ON ALBUM

UNTITLED SOURCES

If you need to cite an e-mail, use the subject as the title. Capitalize the title as in the pattern on page 153.

If you need to cite a tweet, put the whole tweet within quotation marks as the title.

If you cite an utitled review of a book or other text, follow the model shown to the right.

Bill Gates. "Windows Usability Systematic Degradation Flame." Received by Jim Allchin. 15 Jan. 2003.
E-MAIL

@CDCGov. "The best way to prevent #Zika is to prevent mosquito bites. http://1.usa.gov/1QbHwpF." 23 Mar. 2012, 12:00 p.m. twitter.com/CDCgov/status /712685452298289153.
TWEET

Haas, Christina. Review of *Literacy and Racial Justice: The Politics of Learning after* Brown v. Board of Education, by Catherine Prendergast. *African American Review*, vol. 38, no. 3, Fall 2004, pp. 537-39.
REVIEW OF BOOK, IN JOURNAL

4 OTHER CONTRIBUTORS,

A PIECE FROM AN EDITED COLLECTION

Because the people who edit collections play central roles in producing the collections, their roles are always entered in citations.

Lebowitz, Fran. "Pointers for Pets." *Living with the Animals*, edited by Gary Indiana. Faber, 1994, pp. 61-64.
ESSAY, IN EDITED COLLECTION

Chen, Lynn. "You Are What You Eat." Art by Paul Wei. *Secret Identities: The Asian American Superhero Anthology*, edited by Jeff Yang et al. New Press, 2009, pp. 100–106.
GRAPHIC NOVEL, IN EDITED COLLECTION

Colby, Richard. "Writing and Assessing Procedural Rhetoric in Student-produced Video Games." *Computers and Composition*, edited by Carl Whithaus, special issue on multimodal assessment, vol. 31, pp. 43–52. *Science Direct*, doi:10.1016/j.compcom.2013.12.003.
ARTICLE, IN SCHOLARLY JOURNAL, IN DATABASE
ARTICLE, IN SCHOLARLY JOURNAL—SPECIAL ISSUE

A TEXT TRANSLATED FROM ANOTHER LANGUAGE

Like editors, translators play central roles in the production of these texts, and their roles are noted in citations, as shown to the right.

Mina, Hanna. "On the Sacks." *Literature from the "Axis of Evil,"* translated by Hanadi Al-Samman. New Press, 2006, pp. 179-206.
SHORT STORY, IN EDITED BOOK
SHORT STORY—TRANSLATED

Grossman, David. *See Under: Love.* Translated by Betsy Rosenberg. Washington Square, 1989.
BOOK—TRANSLATED

OTHER KINDS OF CONTRIBUTORS

Include other contributors relevant to your purposes. Examples of other kinds of contributions include:

Adapted by
Directed by
Illustrated by
Introduction by
Narrated by
Performance by
Uploaded by

Dillard, Annie. *The Abundance: Narrative Essays Both Old and New.* Foreword by Geoff Dyer. HarperCollins, 2016.
BOOK—WITH CONTRIBUTOR FOREWORD

Keegan, Marina. *The Opposite of Loneliness: Essays and Stories.* Introduction by Anne Fadiman. Scribner, 2014.
BOOK—WITH CONTRIBUTOR INTRODUCTION

Moore, Alan, writer. *Watchmen.* Illustrated and lettered by Dave Gibbons, colored by John Higgins, DC Comics, 1987.
GRAPHIC NOVEL

5 VERSION,

If, in collecting citation information about your source, you discover that there are multiple versions of the source, identify the particular version you cite.

In a citation that includes version information, the version information usually begins with a lowercase letter. However, if the version information follows directly behind an italicized title with a period, the version information begins with a capital letter.

If your source is an edited version, in your citation note that with **ed.,** as in the different versions below. Also see below for examples of the different versions sources can have.

VERSIONS IN PRINT

Print sources (including those you find online) can appear in different editions, labeled by a date, number, or other descriptor.

The Bible. Introduction and notes by Robert Carroll and Stephen Prickett, authorized King James Version, Oxford UP, 1998.
BIBLE—KING JAMES VERSION

Coutin, Anne-Sophie. *Essential Obstetric and Newborn Care.* 2015 ed., Médecins Sans Frontières, 2015, http://refbooks.msf.org/ msf_docs/en/obstetrics/obstetrics_en.pdf.
BOOK—ONLINE
BOOK—VERSION BY YEAR

Macchiavelli, Niccolo. *The Prince.* Translated by Harvey C. Mansfield, 2nd ed., Chicago UP, 1998.
BOOK—TRANSLATED
BOOK—SECOND EDITION

Norman, Don. *The Design of Everyday Things.* Revised and expanded ed., Basic Books, 2013.
BOOK—REVISED AND EXPANDED EDITION

Hugo, Victor. *Les Misérables.* Abridged ed., Fawcett, 1982.
BOOK—ABRIDGED EDITION

VERSIONS IN OTHER MEDIA

Note that the titles are always italicized and followed by a period.

Morrison, Van. *Moondance.* Expanded ed., Rhino, 2013.
ALBUM—EXPANDED EDITION

Watchmen. Director's cut, Warner Home Video, 2009
FILM—DIRECTOR'S CUT

Martin, Alan C. *Tank Girl One.* Illustrated by Jamie Hewlett, anniversary ed., Titan Books, 2009.
GRAPHIC NOVEL—ANNIVERSARY EDITION

6 NUMBER,

PERIODICALS: VOLUME AND ISSUE NUMBERS

Periodicals—magazines and journals that are published regularly every month or season—often track their publications by year: *Volume 1* is all the issues published in the periodical's first year, *Volume 2* in the second year, and so on. The *Number* of an issue then refers to when in the year it was published: *Number 1* appeared first, *Number 2* second, and so on.

If you find only a volume number or only a number, give whichever you find.

→ Page 45 shows where to find volume and issue information.

French, R. M. "Using Guitars to Teach Vibrations and Acoustics." *Experimental Techniques*, vol. 29, no. 2, 2005, pp. 47-48.
ARTICLE, IN SCHOLARLY JOURNAL

Borrero, Luis Alberto. "Moving: Hunter-gatherers and the Cultural Geography of South America." *Quaternary International*, vol. 363, 30 Mar. 2015, pp. 126–33. *Science Direct*, doi:10.1016/j.quaint.2014.03.011.
ARTICLE, IN SCHOLARLY JOURNAL, IN DATABASE

Kampf, Ronit and Esra Cuhadar. "Do Computer Games Enhance Learning about Conflicts? A Cross-national Inquiry into Proximate and Distant Scenarios in Global Conflicts." *Computers in Human Behavior*, vol. 52, Nov. 2015, pp. 541–49. *Social Sciences Full Text*, doi:10.1016/j.chb.2014.08.008.
ARTICLE, IN SCHOLARLY JOURNAL, IN DATABASE

"Vaccination: A Jab in Time." *Economist*, vol. 418, no. 8982, 26 Mar. 2016, p. 67.
ARTICLE, IN POPULAR MAGAZINE PUBLISHED WEEKLY

NUMBER INFORMATION FOR OTHER KINDS OF TEXTS

Television shows have season and episode numbers; graphic novels and comic books can have volumes and numbers.

Whenever you cite a source number, precede it with a descriptive term (like **vol.**, **no.**, **season**, or **episode**).

"eps1.7_wh1ter0se.m4v." *Mr. Robot*, season 1, episode 7, Universal Cable, 12 Aug. 2015.
TELEVISION EPISODE

Liu, Marjorie, writer and Sana Takeda, illustrator. *Monstress*. No. 4, Image Comic, 2015.
COMIC BOOK

Vaughan, Brian K., writer, and Fiona Staples, illustrator. *Saga*. Vol. 5, 2015.
COMIC BOOK

TIP: Vol. or vol.? No. or no.?
If the number information follows an element ending in a period, capitalize the first letter. If it follows a comma, the number information starts with lower case.

7 PUBLISHER,

A publisher does the work of taking the author's words, pictures, or sounds and getting them to readers: This can be a traditional press, a museum, a production company, a library...

PATTERNS FOR PUBLISHERS' NAMES

- From the publisher's name, omit any business words like *Company (Co.)*, *Corporation (Corp.)*, *Incorporated (Inc.)*, or *Limited (Ltd.)*.
- If your source was published by an academic press, in the press's title you can replace *University* with *U* and *Press* with *P*:

  University of California Press → U of California Press   MIT Press → MIT P
  Kent State University Press → Kent State UP   Syracuse University Press → Syracuse UP

- Otherwise, put the publisher's name into your citation exactly as you find the name in your source:

  Random House • HarperCollins • Penguin Press • Riverhead Books • Picador • Verso

→ Page 42 shows where to find the publisher information in a book; page 47 shows where to look for publisher information in a website.

TWO OR MORE PUBLISHERS

If you find two or more names given as the publisher, and they both seem equally responsible, include both, formatted as shown at right.

Sherman, Claire Richter. *Writing on Hands: Memory and Knowledge in Early Modern Europe.* Trout Gallery / Folger Shakespeare Library, 2001.
BOOK—TWO PUBLISHERS

Invisible Man: Gordon Parks and Ralph Ellison in Harlem. Steidl /The Gordon Parks Foundation / The Art Institute of Chicago, 2016.
BOOK—THREE PUBLISHERS
BOOK—CORPORATE AUTHOR AND PUBLISHER ARE THE SAME

PUBLISHERS FOR NON-PRINT MEDIA

For films, television series, or other sources produced by several companies, the MLA recommends to name as publisher the company with primary responsibility.

A blog network serves as the publisher of the blogs it hosts.

What Happened, Miss Simone? Directed by Liz Garbus, Moxie Firecracker Films, 2015.
FILM

Greg Laden. "Are Engineers More Likely To Be Terrorists, And If So, Why?" *Greg Laden's Blog: Culture as Science, Science as Culture,* Science Blogs, 2016, scienceblogs.com/ gregladen/2016/03/25/are-engineers-more-likely-to-be-terrorists-and-if-so-why.
POST, ON BLOG, PUBLISHED BY BLOG NETWORK

8 PUBLICATION DATE,

A date in a citation helps readers judge the relevance of a source and also find the source. Because different kinds of sources are produced under different time frames, different kinds of sources need different formats for how the publication is presented.

SOURCES THAT NEED A YEAR IN THE CITATION

A book's citation generally only needs to show a year to help readers find the particular edition you cite. Similarly, some journals only need a year for date information because the number information focuses in on a specific issue.

Austen, Jane. *Pride and Prejudice.* Scribner's, 1918. *Google Books,* books.google.com/books/about/Pride_and_Prejudice.html?id=s1gVAAAAYAAJ.
BOOK, IN GOOGLE BOOKS

Sengupta, Somini. *The End of Karma: Hope and Fury Among India's Young.* W.W. Norton, 2016.
BOOK

Hawhee, Debra. "Rhetoric's Sensorium." *Quarterly Journal of Speech,* vol. 101, no. 1, 2015, pp. 2–17.
ARTICLE, IN SCHOLARLY JOURNAL

SOURCES WITH A YEAR PLUS A MONTH OR SEASON IN THE CITATION

Because periodicals—journals, magazines, newspapers—are published regularly (as often as daily or weekly), readers need a date in the citation if they are to find your source.

Different kinds of periodicals will need different kinds of dates in citations: You can't go wrong if you use the date as you find it listed in the source.

Wortham, Jenna. "We're More Honest with Our Phones Than with Our Doctors." *New York Times,* 23 Mar. 2016, www.nytimes.com/2016/03/27/magazine/were-more-honest-with-our-phones-than-with-our-doctors.html.
ARTICLE, IN NEWSPAPER PUBLISHED DAILY—ONLINE

Cobb, Jelani. "The Matter of Black Lives." *New Yorker,* vol. 92, no. 5, 14 Mar. 2016. www.newyorker.com/magazine/2016/03/14/where-is-black-lives-matter-headed.
ARTICLE, IN POPULAR MAGAZINE PUBLISHED WEEKLY

"Saving Africa's Rhinos: Pooches v. Poachers." *Economist,* vol. 418, no. 8976, 13 Feb. 2016, p. 40.
ARTICLE, IN POPULAR MAGAZINE PUBLISHED WEEKLY

Miklósi, Adám. "The Science of a Friendship: How Dogs Became Our Closest Animal Companions." *Scientific American Mind,* May–June 2015.
ARTICLE, IN POPULAR MAGAZINE PUBLISHED BI-MONTHLY

Ken, Stephanie Wong. "Blood on the Tracks: An Interview with Living Legend Buffy Sainte Marie." *Bitch,* no. 68, Fall 2015, pp. 73–75.
ARTICLE, IN POPULAR MAGAZINE PUBLISHED SEASONALLY
INTERVIEW

SOURCES WITH A DATE AND TIME IN THE CITATION

If you cite an online source that includes a time as well as a date, put both in your citation. Choose either a consistent twelve- or twenty-four-hour format for times.

Werner, Sarah. Comment on "How to Destroy Special Collections with Social Media." *Wynken de Worde*, 2 Aug. 2015, 10:59 a.m., sarahwerner.net/blog/2015/07/how-to-destroy-special-collections-with-social-media.

COMMENT, ON BLOG POST

"19,300 Women Transformed by Fistula Surgery Since 2009." *Fistula Foundation*, 5 Mar. 2016, 5:30 p.m., *Facebook*, www.facebook.com/fistulafoundation/photos/a.138870922878394.26855.13875 4956223324/907569836008495/?type=3&theater. Graph.

CHART, ON FACEBOOK

INCLUDING THE DATE YOU ACCESSED A SOURCE

Online sources can be changed or deleted; sometimes they appear without publication dates. Giving the date you accessed the source helps readers understand the source's time period and the version you cite. When you include an access date, put it at the end of your citation; do still include any information you have about the source's publication date.

sunagainstgold. "FAQ." *I am a Food Blog*, iamafoodblog.com/faq. Accessed 27 Mar. 2016.

ONLINE SOURCE—NO DATE
POST, ON BLOG—UNDATED

A. C. Smith. "The Waif." *A Selection of Australian Poetry and Prose*, librivox.org/a-selection-of-australian-poetry-and-prose. Accessed 2 Apr. 2016. Audiobook.

AUDIOBOOK
ONLINE SOURCE—NO DATE
POEM, IN COLLECTION, ONLINE

"Bovine Spongiform Encephalopathy (BSE)." *Encyclopædia Britannica*, www.britannica.com/science/bovine-spongiform-encephalopathy. Accessed 2 Apr. 2016.

ARTICLE, IN ONLINE REFERENCE WORK
ONLINE SOURCE—NO DATE

THE PATTERN FOR FORMATTING DATES

The MLA's convention for formatting a date is to use no commas by putting the date in the order of day–month–year:

1 Jan. 2017	29 Feb. 2016	1 Mar. 1963	15 Apr. 1984	18 May 1926
22 July 1929	23 Aug. 1961	22 Sept. 1955	10 Nov. 1956	3 Dec. 1951

If a month's name is longer than four letters, abbreviate it in your works-cited list. The MLA's preferred abbreviations are shown here:

Jan.	Feb.	Mar.	Apr.	May	June
July	Aug.	Sept.	Oct.	Nov.	Dec.

9 LOCATION.

Location information depends on the kind of source; check these pages for the information to include for your source. (Some citations—generally stand-alone sources where the publisher information is all readers need to find the source—do not need locations.)

TWO OPTIONS EXIST FOR ONLINE SOURCE LOCATIONS

DOI

DOI stands for **digital object identifier.** The DOI system gives a publication a unique identifying number—the DOI—that provides a persistent link to the source. DOIs are more stable and shorter than URLs; if you have both a DOI and a URL, use the DOI.

In a citation, put **doi:** and then the DOI information.

→ See pages 48–49 on finding DOIs in sources.

Stell, Gerald. "Uses and Functions of English in Namibia's Multiethnic Settings." *World Englishes,* vol. 33, no. 2, 2014, pp. 223-41. *Education Research Complete,* doi:10.1111/weng.12082.
ARTICLE, IN SCHOLARLY JOURNAL, IN DATABASE

United States, Department of the Interior, U. S. Geological Survey. "Geologic Map of Alaska." Scientific Investigations Map 3340, 2015, doi:10.3133/sim3340.
MAP
GOVERNMENT DOCUMENT—FEDERAL

URL (OR A PERMALINK)

As you enter URLs into reference lists, first remove **http://** or **https://**. Then make sure your word processor does not automatically hyphenate the URL: This can "break" the URL, since a reader will try to use the hyphen as part of the URL. Instead, if you have a long URL and need to break it across lines, break it before a slash or other hyphenation.

You do not need to list a URL in a reference if you provide the DOI for your source.

Friedman, Jane. "Four Lessons for Authors on the Current State of Publishing." 14 Mar. 2016, janefriedman.com/4-lessons-publishing.
BLOG POST—INDIVIDUAL BLOG

"Ōmi Kuni-ezu." 1837. *Stanford Digital Depository,* Stanford University Libraries, purl.stanford.edu/hs631zg4177. Accessed 25 July 2016. Map.
MAP, IN ONLINE LIBRARY SPECIAL COLLECTION
REPUBLISHED SOURCE—SHOWING ORIGINAL PUBLICATION DATE

A permalink is a stable web address, usually available on blogs and sometimes given with databases; if you can find a permalink for a source, use it instead of a URL.

→ See pages 48–49 for an example of a stable URL for a journal in a database.

SOURCES WITH LOCATIONS THAT ARE NUMBERED PAGES

If your source is part of a book or is a journal article, include the page numbers in your citation, following the pattern below.

Saulitis, Eva. "Wondering Where the Whales Are." *Leaving Resurrection: Chronicles of a Whale Scientist*, Boreal Books, 2008, pp. 140–52.
ESSAY, IN COLLECTION OF ONE AUTHOR'S WRITING

Russell, Joshua Kahn. "Anger Works Best When You Have the Moral High Ground." *Beautiful Trouble: A Toolbox for Revolution*, edited by Andrew Boyd, OR Books, 2012, pp. 96–97.
ESSAY, IN EDITED COLLECTION

SOURCES THAT NEED TWO LOCATIONS

If your source is inside a container inside another container, your citation might include two locations. This generally will happen for sources where you need to give an article's page numbers and then a **URL** or **doi** for the online container.

"Traveling Notes in Italy: Pompei." *The Builder*, vol. 7, no. 309, 6 Jan. 1849, pp. 2–4. *Internet Library of Early Journals–Bodlein Library*, www.bodley.ox.ac.uk/cgi-bin/ilej/image1.pl?item=page &seq=1&size=1&id=bu.1849.1.6.7.x.x.2.
ARTICLE, IN POPULAR MAGAZINE, IN ONLINE ARCHIVE

Hoel, Aud Sissel. "Measuring the Heavens: Charles S. Peirce and Astronomical Photography." *History of Photography*, vol. 40, no. 1, 2016, pp. 49–66. *Taylor & Francis Online*, doi: 10.1080/03087298.2016.1140329.
ARTICLE, IN SCHOLARLY JOURNAL, IN DATABASE

LOCATIONS FOR OTHER KINDS OF SOURCES

If you cite a live performance or lecture, or a physical object in a museum or other space, include the name of the venue and the city. (If the city name is in the venue name, you do not have to repeat it.)

Turrell, James. *One Accord*. 2001, Live Oak Friends Meeting House, Houston.
ARTWORK—PHYSICAL OBJECT

Lupton, Carter. "Beyond the Veil: Diversity in Arab and Muslim Women's Clothing." Lunch and Lecture Series, 5 May 2014, Milwaukee Public Museum.
LECTURE

D'Angelo. 7 Feb. 2015, Apollo Theater, New York.
MUSICAL PERFORMANCE—LIVE

THE PATTERN FOR PAGE NUMBERS FOR PERIODICAL ARTICLES

Place a comma after the date of the periodical and then put the page number or numbers. End the citation with a period. Give the page numbers for the entire article, even if you refer to only a small portion of an article. Use **p.** for *page* and **pp.** for *pages*.

p. 52.   pp. 721-86.   pp. 237-58.   p. B5.   pp. 21-28.   pp. 237-358.

(Note that if the ending page is above 100, you list only the last two digits of the page number unless more are necessary for clarity.)

CITING SOURCES WHEN YOUR PROJECT ISN'T A RESEACH PAPER

According to *the MLA Handbook*, how to cite sources in a research project that does not take the form of a paper "is not yet a settled matter" (128). Nonetheless, the MLA states that you should still offer citation information "that enables a curious reader, viewer, or other user to track down your sources and giving credit to those whose work influenced yours" (128). To those ends, the MLA has some suggestions:

CITING SOURCES IN RESEARCH PROJECTS YOU PUT ONLINE
The suggested options include:

• Putting links to sources in your project itself, when a source is named.

• Putting a full works-cited list, with links to sources, at the end of the project or on a linked webpage.

CITING SOURCES IN A SLIDE PRESENTATION
The suggested options include putting citations on:

• Any slide that uses anyone else's written or visual sources.

• A works-cited slide at the end of the presentation.

• A printed works-cited handout for your audience.

• A works-cited webpage, for which you provide the URL.

CITING SOURCES IN A VIDEO
The suggested options include putting citation information:

• At the bottom of any screen that uses anyone else's written or visual sources. Such information might be the name of the person being interviewed, the producer and title of a video clip, the name and title of any photographs.

• In a full works-cited listing in your closing credits.

APA DOCUMENTATION

GUIDE TO APA DOCUMENTATION MODELS

PAGES FROM A PAPER IN APA FORMAT

Nonverbal Power Displays by Doormen
Christine Wysocki
University of San Diego

Abstract

This paper reports the results of a study conducted by a research team into the nonverbal behavior of doormen and security personnel at eight establishments within the city limits of San Diego. The initial hypothesis was that doormen are likely to speak with strong, stern voices, have a large physical appearance, use direct body orientations, and adopt or adapt various artifacts that signal or exert the power necessary to establish and maintain their authority and control over approaching patrons. The results of the study mostly confirmed the initial hypothesis, with two exceptions: The doormen did not uniformly employ a strong, stern tone of voice, and the doormen did not use the advantage of a higher plane of orientation in order to establish and maintain relations of power.

Title page

Approximately halfway down your title page, center the following information without bolding or italicizing it: your paper's title, your name, and your institution. (In a paper to be published, you would also include an "author note"; see the APA *Publication Manual*.)

Abstract

The APA requires a separate abstract page for papers going to publication; if your teacher asks you to include it, put it on a separate page (following the title page and numbered as page 2). Abstracts average 150–250 words but can be shorter. An abstract is a summary of the paper, reporting (without evaluation) what was studied, why it was studied, and the results of the study.

Running Head

At the top left of every page—including the title page—put a running head containing your title in all capital letters. The running head title should be no more than fifty characters; if you have a title that has two phrases separated by a colon, only put the part of the title before the colon into the running head. *Only on the title page* should the running head be preceded by "Running head:"

Repeat your title

Center your title above the body of your paper. Do not bold or italicize it.

1"

NONVERBAL POWER DISPLAYS BY DOORMEN   3

1"   1"

Nonverbal Power Displays by Doormen

According to some researchers, nonverbal cues may contribute up to 65% of what we understand in any communication exchange (Knott, 1979). Even before people speak, they transmit nonverbal messages, so that verbal and nonverbal communication are always entwined in any given situation. Understanding the roles the nonverbal—or what is often referred to as "paralanguage"—plays in overall communication can help us to become better communicators.

Although people control only a part of the nonverbal messages they send, it is possible to extend the conscious control one has of what one nonverbally projects—the nonverbal signals one sends—in any given situation. In other words, those who seek to project an image of power can learn to take on certain behaviors and appearances in order to affect others.

This paper reports on a study of a group of people, doormen at nightclubs, whose work necessitates that they project an image of po[wer] enters a club, doormen need others to accept their authority. Through observations and in[terviews] behaviors doormen use, and do not use, to d[...]

1½" The perceived or actual social distances be[...] in interactive behaviors (Carney & LeBeau, 200[...]

The content of the introduction: How does your research relate to others' research?

In an APA paper, the introduction lays out the problem under consideration, saying why the problem is worth addressing and how it relates to previous research—which you can see here as Christine first describes other research to situate her own work and then states this paper's specific focus.

Power relations are also present in bodily orientation—or proxemics. If a person moves close to another, or violates another's personal space, the other can become stressed and react in a variety of ways, including but not limited to, increased anxiety, discomfort, and aggressiveness (May, 2000). Likewise, standing in the center of a small space, such as a doorway, or blocking others' access to a destination signals to others that movement is not possible without negotiation or struggle (Nadler, 1986). Perceived power can also be influenced by posture and the plane of interaction: Elevation provides the most power, followed by postural orientation and rank (Schwartz, Tesser, & Powell, 1982). Conversely, as Tiedens and Fragale's study on body orientation mimicry and posture shows, a complimentary (open/closed versus closed/closed) posture results in higher likeabil

Finally, what one wears or carries—consi

example, wearing a uniform can deliver authori

conditioned [in our society] to regard with awe

some way, its authority can be enhanced (Cohe

Based on this intial research, we hypothesize that, to establish and maintain their authority and control over approaching patrons, doormen are likely to speak with strong, stern voices; have a large physical appearance; use direct body orientations; and use various artifacts that signal or exert power.

> **The content of the introduction: What is your hypothesis?**
>
> After you have introduced the problem on which your paper focuses and have provided background for it, state your hypothesis or the main question guiding your research.

Method

Three research methods were used in the collection of data.

The first method was based on a series of observations conducted by four researchers at eight establishments in the city of San Diego. The eight establishments studied were Pacific Beach Bar & Grill, The Field, Cabo Cantina, Typhoon, Tavern, The Marble Room, Stingaree, and San

recorde

doorme

Researc

> **THE METHOD SECTION**
>
> In this section you describe in detail how you conducted your study. You give this information so readers can evaluate the appropriateness of your approaches, which then enables them to judge the validity of your results.
>
> Describe in detail who or what you studied, by characteristics, number, and place where you performed your study. When you describe the characteristics of a group, emphasize the characteristics that might bear on your results.

Beach Bar & Grill, The Field, Cabo Cantina, Typhoon, Tavern, The Marble Room, Stingaree, and Sandbar. The researchers unobtrusively observed doormen at these different locations and recorded in detail the interactions between doormen and patrons. Data was collected about the doormen's use of vocal tones, haptics, physical appearance, body orientation, and use of artifacts. Researc[h]

ensure the greatest degree of

The second method of d

researchers and the doormen

insights into the ways the do

authority, and it allowed for a more direct conection of data.

Passive voice

Because the APA style reports research that any researcher anywhere should be able to replicate, the identity of the person doing the research shouldn't matter—and so passive voice is used to put emphasis on what was done rather than on who did it.

→ See pages 112 and 213 for more on passive voice.

The last method of data collection was face-to-face interviews conducted with individual doormen at four of the different establishments. The interviewers gathered data about the degree to which doormen were cognitively aware of their behaviors in establishing power.

Results

Based on our observations, we drew the following results.

In terms of vocal tones, four out of five of the doormen used softer vocal tones with females. Speaking with men, six out of eight doormen used mo[re]

In their physical appearance, five out of eight

It was observed that doormen also responded to pa[trons]

were perceived as a possible threat due to physical s[...]

address the male member of a male-female couple, [...]

height was closer to, or taller than, theirs.

THE RESULTS SECTION

In this section, summarize the data you collected and whatever analysis you performed that supports your conclusions. If you have results that run counter to your initial hypothesis, be sure to mention this.

The body orientation of doormen was shown through how six doormen stood on the same level as the patrons, while only one sat on a stool and one stood on a raised platform.

[...]n wore some sort of attire that signified the particular

[...]e sample wore jackets with writing that announced their

[...]), and the other half wore all-black clothing. Three out of

Formatting in APA style

- Double-space the paper throughout, including titles and quotations.
- The "preferred" typeface for APA papers is Times New Roman, in 12-point size. Use the same typeface throughout the entire paper.

A REFERENCE LIST PAGE
IN APA FORMAT.

- ❑ Put the reference list at the very end of the paper, starting on its own page.
- ❑ Use the same margin measurements as the rest of the paper (➔ see pages 166 and 167).
- ❑ Put the running head and page number on each reference list page at the top (as on every APA formatted page; ➔ see page 167). The number on the first page follows the number of the paper's last page. For example, if the last page of the paper is 7, the first page of the reference list will be 8.
- ❑ **References** is centered, top.
- ❑ Listings are arranged alphabetically by authors' last names. (If a listing starts with a source title, insert it into the reference list using the title's first letter. If the title begins with **A, An**, or **The**, alphabetize by the second word of the title.)
- ❑ Double-space the entries.
   - ➔ See pages 174–191 for creating individual entries.
- ❑ So readers can scan the list easily, indent by 1/2 inch all lines underneath the first of each entry. This is called *hanging indent*.

NONVERBAL POWER DISPLAYS BY DOORMEN   8

References

Carney, D., Hall, J., & LeBeau, L. (2005, Summer). Beliefs about the nonverbal expression of social power. *Journal of Nonverbal Behavior, 29*(2), 105–123. doi:10.1007/s10919-005-2743-z

Cohen, H. (1980). *You can negotiate anything*. New York, NY: Bantam Books.

Dunbar, N., & Abra, G. (2008, May). *Observations of dyadic power in interpersonal interaction*. Paper presented at the annual meeting of the International Communication Association, Montreal, Canada. Retrieved from http://www.icahdq.org/

Dunbar, N., & Burgoon, J. (2005, April). Perceptions of power and interactional dominance in interpersonal relationships. *Journal of Social & Personal Relationships, 22*(2), 207–233. doi:10.1177/0265407505050944

Knott, G. (1979, October). Nonverbal communication during early childhood. *Theory into practice, 18*(4), 226. Retrieved from http://search.ebscohost.com.ezproxy.lib.uwm.edu/ login.aspx?direct=true&db=a9h&AN=5201824&loginpage=Login.asp&site=ehost-live

Krumhuber, E., Manstead, A., & Kappas, A. (2007, Spring). Temporal aspects of facial displays in person and expression perception: The effects of smile dynamics, head-tilt, and gender. *Journal of Nonverbal Behavior, 31*(1), 39–56. doi:10.1007/s10919-006-0019-x

1/2"

May, S. (2000, Winter). Proxemics: The hula hoop and use of personal space. *Communication Teacher, 14*(2), 4–5. Retrieved from http://search.ebscohost.com.ezproxy.lib.uwm.edu/ login.aspx?direct=true&db=ufh&AN=31746491&loginpage=Login.asp&site=ehost-live

- ❑ If you list two or more sources by the same author, order them by the date, with the earliest first. If there are multiple authors, alphabetize subsequent sources for these authors by the second author's name.

APA DOCUMENTATION FOR IN-TEXT CITATIONS

THE PATTERN

IN-TEXT CITATIONS IN APA STYLE

Whether you are citing books, periodicals, or electronic sources, in-text citations in APA style generally contain three elements:

1

The name of the author of the words or ideas being quoted, summarized, or paraphrased. The name can appear within a sentence containing quoted words, or it can appear in parentheses at the sentence's end.

2

The date when the source being cited was published.

3

The page number(s) of or some other reference to the cited words or ideas. The number of the page from which quoted words come goes at the end of the sentence, in parentheses. Note that **p.** goes before the page number.

You can arrange these three APA elements in two ways to create an in-text citation:

In writing about two nineteenth-century women preachers, Bizzell (2006) argues that "a conjunction between the female sex and moral activism is traditional in Methodism" (p. 379).

One writer on nineteenth-century women preachers argues that "a conjunction between the female sex and moral activism is traditional in Methodism" (Bizzell, 2006, p. 379).

→ Pages 172–173 list variations on this pattern for APA in-text citations.

PUNCTUATION IN APA IN-TEXT CITATIONS

- The parentheses that contain page numbers go at a sentence's end, followed by the punctuation that ends the sentence.
- When you include an author's name in the parentheses with the year and page number, put a comma between each element.
- If the words you quote run across several pages, use **pp.** to cite them like this: (pp. 23–25) (**pp.** stands for *pages*).
- If the words you quote are from nonconsecutive pages, cite them like this: (pp. 45, 76).

VARIATIONS ON THE APA PATTERN FOR IN-TEXT CITATIONS

NO AUTHOR IS NAMED

If no author is named, use the work's title:

To "watch the rejects crash and burn" is why we watch *American Idol*, according to *Rolling Stone* magazine ("Idol Worship," 2007, p. 7).

THERE IS NO PAGE NUMBER

Give a paragraph or part number (if there is one); otherwise, give the author's name.

The World Health Organization identifies obstetric fistulas as a global problem; over 2 million women suffer from them (2006, para. 64).

(Readers will look in the references for a listing under *World Health Organization*.)

YOU CITE TWO OR MORE SOURCES BY THE SAME AUTHOR

Give the date of each source in your citation.
This cites the first source from an author:

That meat from cows fed on grass is more nutritious than that from corn-fed cows is one of Pollan's many arguments (2006, p. 211).

This cites a second source by the author:

Because his research shows what chemicals go into a commercial potato, Pollan cannot bring himself to eat one (2001, p. 98).

A SOURCE HAS TWO AUTHORS

List the names in the order they appear in the source. Use *and* between the names in an in-text citation, but use an ampersand (**&**) in parenthetical references:

As "much an activist as an analytical method" is how Moeller and Moberly (2006) describe McAllister's approach to computer games.

As "much an activist as an analytical method" is how reviewers describe McAllister's approach to computer games (Moeller & Moberly, 2006).

YOU CITE TWO AUTHORS WITH THE SAME LAST NAME

Include the authors' initials in your citations so that readers know which citation to check in the reference list.

R. M. Rorty (1979) argues that we ought no longer to think of our minds as "mirrors" that only reflect what is already in the world.

A. O. Rorty (1996) shows how Aristotle's *Rhetoric* brings together understandings of communication contexts, the psychology of audiences, communicators' character, and politics.

These examples use their parenthetical citations to avoid ambiguity:

Some philosophers argue that our understanding of what knowledge is has changed in the last 200 years (R. M. Rorty, 1979).

Aristotle's *Rhetoric* brings together understandings of communication contexts, the psychology of audiences, the character of communicators, and politics (A. O. Rorty, 1996).

A SOURCE HAS THREE, FOUR, OR FIVE AUTHORS

The first time you cite the source, list each author's name. After that, list the first author's name followed by **et al.** (Latin for *and others*.) Put a period after *al*.

What happens when a ninth-grade class is offered at the honors level for all students, without tracking? Fine, Anand, Jordan, and Sherman (2000) offer a two-year study of such a class.

Later in the same paper:

As a result of their study, Fine et al. (2000) argue that students "who never expected to be seen as smart" come to see themselves as capable and sharp (pp. 174, 175).

A SOURCE HAS SIX OR MORE AUTHORS

Include only the first author's name, followed by *et al.* (Latin for *and others*.) Put a period after *al*.

Statistical data is "easily misinterpreted" (Walpole et al., 2006, p. 217).

Walpole et al. (2006, p. 217) argue that statistical data is "easily misinterpreted."

A SOURCE HAS A GROUP OR CORPORATE AUTHOR OR IS A GOVERNMENT DOCUMENT

Write out the name of the group author.

When organizing catalogs, librarians typically follow a set of guidelines established by the American Library Association (2004).

When organizing catalogs, librarians typically follow established guidelines (American Library Association, 2004).

YOU CITE TWO OR MORE SOURCES IN ONE SENTENCE

List the sources (separated by semicolon) in alphabetical order by author's last name.

The words used to describe race and ethnicity shape the way people respond to calls for diversity or justice (Adams, 2000; Fletcher, 2007).

Adams (2000) and Fletcher (2007) argue that language plays a vital role in shaping how people respond to calls for diversity and justice.

YOU CITE A CLASSICAL SOURCE, SACRED TEXT, OR OTHER SOURCE WITH NO DATE LISTED

Use the author's name followed by a comma and **n.d.** (for *no date*).

Early in its history, rhetoric was defined as the use of the available means of persuasion (Aristotle, n.d.).

You can also use the date of translation, if known, preceded by *trans*.

Early in its history, rhetoric was defined as the use of the available means of persuasion (Aristotle, trans. 1954).

If you cite a sacred text such as the Bible or the Koran, you do not need to provide a reference list entry. The first time you cite the work, identify the version you are using.

John 11:7 (Revised Standard Version)

YOU CITE ELECTRONIC SOURCES

If your source includes paragraph numbers, use that number preceded by *para*.

Some researchers have used a concept of "virtual wives" to describe technology in personal life (Clark-Flory, 2007, para. 12).

If the source does not number paragraphs, cite the nearest main heading and number the paragraph of your quotation relative to that heading.

Some researchers have used a concept of "virtual wives" to describe technology in personal life (Clark-Flory, 2007, Introduction, para. 1).

Because personal e-mails cannot be retrieved by readers, do not include them in a reference list. Cite them in your text only.

Austin's famous Congress Avenue bats first appeared in 1980 (E. C. Lupfer, personal communication, March 17, 2003).

APA DOCUMENTATION FOR REFERENCE LIST ENTRIES

The following pages show you how to format entries in the reference list that goes at the end of any APA-style paper. The essential pattern is shown here:

THE PATTERN

Four elements make up any citation in the reference list of an APA-style paper:

Author's Name. (Date of Publication). *Title of text.* **Publication information.**
1   2   3   4

The publication information about a text includes who published a text and where. For example, here is a citation for a book:

Boo, Katherine. (2012). *Behind the Beautiful Forevers: Life, Death, and Hope in a*
1   2   3

        Mumbai Undercity. **New York: Random House.**
                    4

(Note the indenting in the example: This is standard when formatting your list of references, as we describe on page 170.)

The APA distinguishes works to be cited as periodicals and nonperiodicals. (Nonperiodicals are books and any other kind of source not published on a regular schedule.) We follow the same distinction in the pages that follow.

Note that when you cite a book, periodical, or webpage, the format of the citation—the capitalization of the title of a book, the inclusion of a periodical's issue number, or the listing of a URL—tells a reader what kind of text you are citing. When you cite a text that isn't a book, periodical, or webpage, you may also need to indicate what kind of text it is.

TO MAKE APA REFERENCE LISTS

1 MAKE AN INDIVIDUAL LISTING FOR EACH WORK YOU ARE CITING

Do you know the kind of source you have?

YES   NO ·· ▶ Go to pages 22–27.

Have you collected the expected citation information for your source?

YES   NO ·· ▶ Go to pages 41–49.

Go to the page with the citation pattern for the kind of source you have.

PERIODICAL   NONPERIODICAL

Page 176   Page 178

- Follow the pattern to construct your listing part by part, starting with the author, moving on to the title, and so on.
- If a part of your citation varies from the pattern, follow the page references to see the format for the variation.

2 CONSTRUCT YOUR REFERENCE LIST
When you have all your individual citations, put them together into the reference list.
→ See page 170 for details on how to format the reference list.

APA DOCUMENTATION FOR REFERENCES LIST ENTRIES
FOR PERIODICAL SOURCES

1 ARE YOU SURE YOU ARE WORKING WITH A PERIODICAL?
See pages 22–27 to check.

2 DO YOU HAVE ALL THE NEEDED INFORMATION FOR YOUR CITATION?
See pages 44–45 to check.

3

THE PATTERN

Here is a sample APA citation for an article from a periodical, followed by a detailed pattern.

Jeffries, M. P. (2014) Hip-hop urbanism old and new. *International Journal of Urban and Regional Research*, 38(2), 706–715 doi: 10.1111/1468-2427.12106

Author's Name. (Date). Title of article.

The pattern for an author's name is on page 180.

WHAT TO DO WHEN YOU HAVE:

- no author named: page 180
- one author: page 180
- two to seven authors: page 180
- eight or more authors: page 181
- two or more works published by the same author in the same year: page 181
- a government author: page 181
- a corporate author: page 181
- a work signed *Anonymous*: page 181

The pattern for date of publication is on page 182.

WHAT TO DO WHEN YOU HAVE:

- a monthly magazine article: page 182
- a daily newspaper article: page 182

The pattern for the article title is on page 184.

WHAT TO DO WHEN YOU HAVE:

- a letter to the editor: page 186
- a review: page 186

WHAT COUNTS AS A PERIODICAL?

A periodical is a publication published at regular intervals: every week, every month, every season. Journal, magazine, or newspaper articles, *including those published online,* are periodicals.

Periodical Name, Volume(Issue), Pages. doi:

If the periodical name begins with **A** or **The**, you can leave off those words.

Italicize the periodical name.

The pattern for the volume and issue numbers is on page 187.

WHAT TO DO WHEN YOU HAVE:

- no issue number: page 187
- only a date: page 187
- a daily newspaper: page 187
- a weekly or biweekly journal or magazine: page 187

Include a digital object identifier (**doi**) if you see one with your source. See page 188.

Give the inclusive page numbers: **37–52** or **121–145**.

If you cite a newspaper article, put **p.** (for single-page articles) or **pp.** (for multipage articles) before the page numbers: **p. J3** or **pp. C2–C5**. If the pages are discontinuous, put a comma between the numbers: **pp. B1, B4**.

FOR NONPERIODICAL SOURCES

1
ARE YOU SURE YOU ARE WORKING WITH A NONPERIODICAL?
See pages 22–27 to check.

2
DO YOU HAVE ALL THE NEEDED INFORMATION FOR YOUR CITATION?
See pages 42–43 to check.

3

THE PATTERN

Here is a sample APA citation for a nonperiodical, followed by a detailed pattern.

Berger, J. (1992). *About looking.* New York, NY: Vintage.

Author's Name. (Date). *Source title.*

The pattern for an author's name is on page 180.

WHAT TO DO WHEN YOU HAVE:

- no author named: page 180
- one author: page 180
- two to seven authors: page 180
- eight or more authors: page 181
- an edited collection: page 181
- a government author: page 181
- a corporate author: page 181
- a work signed *Anonymous*: page 181

The pattern for titles is on pages 184–185.

WHAT TO DO WHEN YOU HAVE:

- an essay or chapter in a book: page 185
- an essay in an online collection: page 185
- an article from a reference book: page 185

Put the year in parentheses, followed by a period. If you have no publication date, put **n.d.** (for *no date*) inside the parentheses, without quotation marks.

WHAT COUNTS AS A NONPERIODICAL?

Nonperiodical sources include books, parts of books (such as essays and chapters in books), films, videos, CDs, audio recordings, and reports—*including those that are published online.*

Place of publication: Publisher.

The pattern for the place of publication is on page 183.

WHAT TO DO:

- about the state where the source was published: page 183
- when the source was published in another country: page 183

From the publisher's full name, you can leave off words such as *Press* or *Company*.
 Note that a colon precedes the publisher's name and that a period follows it.

IF YOUR SOURCE IS ONLINE:
The pattern for online sources is on pages 188–189.

YOU MAY NEED TO INCLUDE ADDITIONAL INFORMATION HERE IN YOUR CITATION IF:

- you are citing a report from the Education Resources Information Center (ERIC): page 186
- the work is translated: page 186
- a book is a second (or later) edition: page 186
- the work is in more than one volume: page 186
- the work is a review: page 186
- you are citing software, visual sources such as charts or photographs, film and television shows, interviews, conference papers, or sound recordings: pages 188–191

AUTHOR'S NAME

The pattern for author names is consistent across differing texts and differing media.

THE PATTERN

The first author listed is always written with the last name first, then a comma, and then the initials. (If an author's first name is hyphenated, include the hyphen with the initials.)

Last Name, Initials.   Singh, A. R.   Chen, K.-H.

If a work you are citing has more than one author, list the additional names in the order in which they are given in the source. All authors are cited last name first. Use an ampersand (&) before the last author's name.

Phelps, L. W., & Emig, J.   Fine, M. T., Weis, L., Pruitt, L. P., & Burns, A.

Note that, in a reference list entry, there is a period after the author's name or the list of authors' names.

NO AUTHOR NAMED

If you cannot find an author's name, start the entry with the name of the book or article.

Idol worship. (2007, February 8). *Rolling Stone*, 1016, 7.
MAGAZINE ARTICLE

Ultimate visual dictionary (Rev. ed.). (2002). New York, NY: Dorling Kindersley.
REFERENCE WORK

ONE AUTHOR

Xavier, J. (2007, June 11). Timo Veikkola (Nokia): A vision for the future. Message posted to http://julianax.blogspot.com /2007/06/timo-veikkola-nokia-vision-of-future.html
BLOG POST

Fletcher, M. A. (2007). At the corner of progress and peril. In K. Merida (Ed.), *Being a black man: At the corner of progress and peril.* New York, NY: Public Affairs.
ESSAY, IN EDITED BOOK

TWO TO SEVEN AUTHORS

In reference list entries, include the names of up to seven authors. Separate names and initials with commas, and use an ampersand (&) before the last author.

Levitt, S. D., & Dubner, S. J. (2006). *Freakonomics: A rogue economist explores the hidden side of everything.* New York, NY: HarperCollins.
BOOK

DeVoss, D. N., Cushman, E., & Grabill, J. T. (2005). Infrastructure and composing: The when of new-media writing. *CCC, 57,* 14–44.
ARTICLE, IN ACADEMIC PERIODICAL

EIGHT OR MORE AUTHORS

List the first seven names, insert an ellipsis, and then list the last author's name.

Liu, X., Zhang, L., You, L., Yu, J., Zhao, J., Li, L., Wang. Q., . . . Wu, H. (2011). Differential toxicological effects induced by mercury in gills from three pedigrees of manila clam ruditapes philippinarum by nmr-based metabolomics. *Ecotoxicology, 20*(1), 177–186.
ARTICLE, IN ACADEMIC PERIODICAL, MORE THAN EIGHT AUTHORS

TWO OR MORE WORKS PUBLISHED BY THE SAME AUTHOR IN THE SAME YEAR

List the works in alphabetical order by title, and use lowercase letters (**a**, **b**, **c**, etc.) following the year to distinguish the works.

Helfand, G., & Walker, C. J. (Eds.) (2001a). *Mastering APA style: Instructor's resource guide.* Washington, DC: American Psychological Association.
BOOK

Helfand, G., & Walker, C. J. (Eds.) (2001b). *Mastering APA style: Student's workbook and training guide.* Washington, DC: American Psychological Association.
BOOK

Your in-text citations will also need the lowercase letters you added so readers know which of the two sources you are citing.

ANONYMOUS AUTHOR

Use **Anonymous** as the author only if the work is so signed.

Anonymous. (2007). How to be an anarchist. Retrieved from WikiHow: http://www.wikihow.com/Be-an-Anarchist
WIKI POST

A CORPORATE AUTHOR

A corporate author is an organization, corporation, or association. Start with the name of the corporate author exactly as it is listed (but omit **A**, **An**, or **The**).

American Counseling Association. (2007). *Basic facts about clinical depression* [Brochure]. Alexandria, VA: Author.
BROCHURE

Employee Benefit Research Institute. (2007). *How are retirees doing financially in retirement?* (Issue Brief No. 302). Washington, DC: Author.
REPORT FROM A PRIVATE ORGANIZATION

A GOVERNMENT AUTHOR

National Center for Educational Statistics. (2005). *Comparative indicators of education in the United States and other G8 countries: 2004.* Washington, DC: U.S. Department of Education Center for Educational Studies.
REPORT

AN EDITED COLLECTION

Adams, M. (Ed.). (2000). *Readings for diversity and social justice: An anthology on racism, sexism, antisemitism, heterosexism, classism, and ableism.* New York, NY: Routledge.
BOOK, EDITED

If you are citing only a piece from an edited collection and not the whole collection, create the citation following the pattern for an essay or chapter in a book shown on page 185.

DATE OF PUBLICATION

The pattern for date of publication is consistent across differing texts and differing media.

THE PATTERN

Place the copyright date or year of publication in parentheses, followed by a period.

(Year of Publication).   (2007).

If you find more than one copyright date for a book, use the most recent one.

For monthly magazines, newspapers, and newsletters, give the year, then the month.

(2006, July).

Include the day for periodicals published daily, like newspapers: **(2007, August 23)**.

A BOOK THAT HAS BEEN REPUBLISHED

Use the standard book pattern, but add the original publication date at the end.

Johnson, S. (2002). *Emergence: The connected lives of ants, brains, cities, and software.* New York, NY: Touchstone-Simon. (Original work published 2001)
BOOK, REPUBLISHED

A BOOK THAT HAS NO PUBLICATION DATE

Put **n.d.** (for *no date*) where the year of publication usually goes in a citation.

Baudrillard, J. (n.d.). *Simulations.* New York, NY: Semiotext(e).
BOOK, NO PUBLICATION DATE

MAGAZINE ARTICLE

Include the month of publication following the year.

Ehrenreich, B. (2000, April). *Maid to order: The politics of other women's work. Harper's,* 59–70.
ARTICLE, IN POPULAR MAGAZINE

NEWSPAPER ARTICLE

For newspapers and other daily periodicals, include the month and day of publication following the year.

Lipton, E. (2007, September 2). Product safety commission bears heavy scrutiny. *Austin American Statesman,* p. A11.
ARTICLE, NEWSPAPER

Rood, L. (2011, March 5). More information on attorney discipline. *Des Moines Register.* Retrieved from http://www.DesMoinesRegister.com/article/20110306/NEWS/103060335/More-information-on-attorney-discipline?odyssey=tab|topnews|text|News
ARTICLE, NEWSPAPER, ONLINE

APA

PLACE OF PUBLICATION

The pattern for place of publication is consistent across differing texts and differing media.

APA

THE PATTERN

Put the place of publication after the title of the book, followed by a colon.

Place of Publication: Boston, MA: Cambridge, England: Santa Monica, CA: Calumet, MI:

If more than one place of publication is listed, use the first one.

EXAMPLES

Merrell, F. (1991). *Unthinking thinking: Jorge Luis Borges, mathematics, and the new physics.* West Lafayette, IN: Purdue University Press.
BOOK

Wardlow, G. D. (1998). *Chasin' that devil music: Searching for the blues.* San Francisco, CA: Miller Freeman.
BOOK

INCLUDE THE STATE
The convention for adding the state is to use the two-letter abbreviation used by the U.S. Postal Service.

Eisner, W. (1996). *Graphic storytelling and visual narrative.* Tamarac, FL: Poorhouse.
BOOK

Hargittai, I., & Hargittai, M. (1994). *Symmetry: A unifying concept.* Bolinas, CA: Shelter Publications.
BOOK

Harris, S. L. (1990). *Agents of chaos: Earthquakes, volcanoes, and other natural disasters.* Missoula, MT: Mountain Press.
BOOK

A BOOK PUBLISHED IN ANOTHER COUNTRY
Put the name of the city of publication, a comma, and then the country name.

Yanagi, S. (1989). *The unknown craftsman: A Japanese insight into beauty.* Tokyo, Japan: Kodansha.
BOOK, PUBLISHED IN ANOTHER COUNTRY

Bourriaud, N. (2004). *Relational aesthetics.* Dijon-Quetigny, France: Les Presses du Réel.
BOOK, PUBLISHED IN ANOTHER COUNTRY

TITLES

The pattern for titles is consistent across differing texts and differing media.

THE PATTERN

BOOK TITLES

1 Capitalize only the first word of the title and the first word of the subtitle.

2 Capitalize any proper nouns within a title.

3 Italicize the entire title. If you are not using a computer, underline the title.

4 Put a period after the title. (If the title ends with a question mark or exclamation point, use that instead.)

The title of the book.

Crow Lake.

The diving bell and the butterfly.

If the book has a subtitle, put the subtitle after a colon and capitalize its first word.

Scribbling the cat: Travels with an African soldier.

The quick and the dead: Artists and anatomy.

A country doctor's casebook: Tales from the north woods.

THE PATTERN

TITLES OF BOOK PARTS, PERIODICAL ARTICLES, AND WEBPAGES

1 Capitalize only the first word of the title and the first word of the subtitle.

2 Do not italicize or put quotation marks around the title.

3 Put a period after the last word. (If the title ends with a question mark or exclamation point, use that instead.)

4 Follow the pattern below for finishing:

PARTS OF BOOKS

List the chapter title, followed by the word **In** and the editor's name, followed by (**Ed.**) and the book's title.

At the corner of progress and peril. In K. Merida (Ed.), *Being a black man: At the corner of progress and peril.*

JOURNAL ARTICLES

Put the name of the journal—in italics—after the article title.

Article title. *Journal Name*

Will the next election be hacked? *Rolling Stone*

WEBPAGES

Put the name of the website—in italics—after the name of the webpage.

Article title. *Website name.*

Project description. *The Nora Project.*

A BOOK	Petherbridge, D., & Jordanova, L. (1997). *The quick and the dead: Artists and anatomy*. Berkeley, CA: University of California Press.
	BOOK
	Vaillant, J. (2012). *The tiger: A true story of vengeance and survival*. Retrieved from /www.barnesandnoble.com
	BOOK ON AN E-READER

A WEBSITE

Austin City Connection: The Official Web Site of the City of Austin. (n.d.). *Childhood lead poisoning prevention program*. Retrieved from http://www.ci.austin.tx.us/health/education.htm

WEBSITE, ENTIRE SITE

AN ESSAY OR CHAPTER IN A BOOK

Makhan, J. (1998). Island ecology and cultural perceptions: A case study of Lakshdweep. In B. Saraswatie (Ed.), *Lifestyle and ecology*. New Delhi, India: Indira Gandhi National Centre for the Arts. Retrieved from http://www.ignca.nic.in/cd_08012.htm

ESSAY, IN ONLINE BOOK

Plato. (1961). Meno (W. K. C. Guthrie, Trans.). In E. Hamilton & H. Cairns (Eds.), *The collected dialogues of Plato* (pp. 353–385). Princeton, NJ: Princeton University Press.

ESSAY, IN EDITED BOOK
ESSAY, TRANSLATED

Parry, D. (2012). The digital humanities or a digital humanism. In Matthew K. Gold (Ed.). *Debates in the digital humanities* (pp. 429–437). Minneapolis, MN: Minnesota University Press.

ESSAY, IN EDITED BOOK

AN ESSAY IN AN ONLINE COLLECTION

Badger, M. (2004, June). Visual blogs. In L. J. Gurak, S. Antonijevic, L. Johnson, & J. Reyman (Eds.), *Into the blogosphere: Rhetoric, community, and culture of weblogs*. Retrieved from http://blog.lib.umn.edu/blogosphere/visual_blogs.html

ESSAY, IN ONLINE COLLECTION

AN ARTICLE FROM A REFERENCE BOOK

Reference works rarely give the names of the people who wrote the articles. Put the title in place of the author in these cases.

Islam. (1989). In *The New York Public Library desk reference*.

ARTICLE, IN REFERENCE BOOK

Bovine spongiform encephalopathy. (2007). In *Encyclopaedia Britannica*. Retrieved from Encyclopaedia Britannica Online: http://www.search.eb.com/eb/article-9002739

ARTICLE, IN ONLINE REFERENCE BOOK

APA

ADDITIONAL INFORMATION

REPORT FROM THE EDUCATION RESOURCES INFORMATION CENTER (ERIC)

Polette, N. (2007). *Teaching thinking skills with picture books, K–3*. Portsmouth, NH: Teacher Ideas Press. Retrieved from ERIC database. (ED497152)

REPORT, FROM ERIC

A WORK WITH A TRANSLATOR

Burgat, F. (2008). *Islamism in the age of al-Qaeda* (P. Hutchinson, Trans.). Austin, TX: University of Texas Press.

BOOK, TRANSLATED

A BOOK IN A SECOND OR LATER EDITION

Rubenstein, J. M. (2004). *The cultural landscape: An introduction to human geography* (8th ed.). Upper Saddle River, NJ: Prentice Hall.

BOOK, IN A SECOND OR LATER EDITION

WORK IN MORE THAN ONE VOLUME

Goldman, B. A., & Mitchell, D. F. (2007). *Directory of unpublished experimental mental measures* (Vol. 9). Washington, DC: American Psychological Association.

BOOK, MULTIVOLUME

A BOOK REVIEW

Julius, A. (2007, September 2). A people and a nation [Review of the book *Jews and power*, by R. R. Wisse]. *The New York Times Book Review*, p. 27.

REVIEW, OF BOOK

AN ABSTRACT

Lacy, E., & Leslie, S. (2007). Library outreach near and far: Programs to staff and patients of the Piedmont Healthcare System. *Medical Reference Services Quarterly, 26(3):* 91–103. Abstract obtained from Library, Information Science & Technology Abstracts database.

ABSTRACT, JOURNAL ARTICLE

LETTER TO THE EDITOR

Delaney, J. (2007, August 28). Helping the world's sexually abused children [Letter to the editor]. *The Washington Post*, p. A12.

LETTER TO THE EDITOR

PERIODICAL VOLUME AND ISSUE

THE PATTERN

VOLUME AND ISSUE NUMBER

The volume number, italicized, follows the name of the periodical; there is a comma between the two. If there is an issue number, put it in parentheses after the volume number, with no space before the parentheses. Issue numbers are not italicized.

Volume(Issue)   5(2)   27(11)

EXAMPLE

Watts, S. (1995, June). Walt Disney: Art and politics in the American century. *The Journal of American History, 82*(1), 84–110.
ARTICLE, IN ACADEMIC PERIODICAL

WHEN THERE IS NO ISSUE NUMBER

Lawrence, R. (2000). Equivalent mass of a coil spring. *Physics Teacher, 38*, 140–141.
ARTICLE, IN A PERIODICAL PAGINATED BY VOLUME

WHEN THERE IS ONLY A DATE

Many popular magazines only list a date.

Birnbaum, C. A. (2007, September). Cultivating appreciation. *Dwell*, 196+.
ARTICLE, IN POPULAR MAGAZINE

A DAILY NEWSPAPER

Daily newspapers do not have volumes and issues; they are cited only by the date.

Rozek, D. (2006, November 10). Girls' squabble over iPod over: And in the end, neither will get music player. *Chicago Sun-Times*, p. 3.
NEWSPAPER ARTICLE

A WEEKLY OR BIWEEKLY JOURNAL OR MAGAZINE

If a weekly or biweekly journal or magazine does not have volume and issue numbers, cite only the date.

Gorman, C. (2006, September 18). To an athlete, aching young. *Time, 168*(12), 60. Retrieved from Expanded Academic ASAP database.
ARTICLE, IN WEEKLY JOURNAL, RETRIEVED FROM ONLINE DATABASE

Schlei, R. (2007, September 6). Faithful comrade: A monumental affair [Review of the book *Loving Frank*]. *Shepherd Express*, 48.
REVIEW, OF BOOK, IN WEEKLY JOURNAL

FOR ONLINE TEXTS

The APA recommends that reference list entries for online sources include all the same information as for print sources, in the same order—but with the addition at the citation's end of information that enables readers to find electronic sources.

THE APA GIVES TWO OPTIONS:

1 GIVE THE SOURCE'S URL.

As you find and track sources, copy a source's URL from your browser and paste it into your working bibliography list (→ see pages 50–51).

When you put the URL into your reference list, create the citation as you would following the patterns on pages 176–179, then put **Retrieved from**, followed by the URL.

> Moeller, R. M., & Moberly, K. (2006). [Review of the book *Game work: Language, power, and computer game culture*]. *Kairos, 10*(2). Retrieved from http://english.ttu.edu/kairos/ 10.2/binder.html?reviews/moeller_moberley/index.html
> REVIEW OF BOOK, ONLINE

As you enter URLs into reference lists, make sure that your word processor does not automatically hyphenate them: This can "break" the URL, since a reader will try to use the hyphen as part of the URL. Instead, if you have a long URL and need to break it across lines, break it before a slash or other hyphenation. (Always keep **http://** together, however.) Do not put a hyphen at the break, and do not put a period after the URL.

2 GIVE THE SOURCE'S DOI.

DOI stands for **digital object identifier.** The DOI system was developed by a group of international publishers to help readers find sources. The publishers recognized that URLs can change and shift and so are not stable enough to ensure readers can find sources. With the DOI system, a publication is given a unique identifying number—the DOI—that provides a persistent link to the online source.

You can find DOIs at the top of journal articles or in the long citation information provided by databases. (→ See pages 48–49 on finding DOIs.)

To put a DOI into a reference list citation, create the citation as you would following the patterns on pages 176–179, then insert **doi:** followed by the DOI.

> Stell, G. (2014). Uses and functions of English in Namibia's multiethnic settings. *World Englishes 33*(2), 223-241. doi: 10.1111/weng.12082.
> ARTICLE, FROM DATABASE

You do not need to list a URL in a reference if you provide the DOI for your source.

CITING AN ENTIRE WEBSITE

Austin City Connection: The Official Web Site of the City of Austin. (n.d.). *Childhood Lead Poisoning Prevention Program*. Retrieved from http://www.ci.austin.tx.us/health/education.htm
WEBSITE

CITING ONLINE ARTICLES

Cite online articles as you would any other article, but include the URL or DOI if one exists. When you cite articles from databases, give either the DOI for the article or find the stable URL provided by the database (→ see pages 48–49); you do not need to provide the database name.

Flora, Carlin. (2005, November). Tough love. *Psychology Today*. Retrieved from http://www.psychologytoday.com/articles /200511/tough-love
ARTICLE, ONLINE VERSION OF PRINT SOURCE

Kelly, S., & Nardi, B. (2014). Playing with sustainability: Using video games to simulate futures of scarcity. *First Monday 19*(5). doi: http://dx.doi.org/10.5210/fm.v19i5.5259
ARTICLE, ONLINE ONLY

Franzen, L., & Smith, C. (2009). Acculturation and environmental change impacts dietary habits among adult Hmong. *Appetite*, 52(1), 173–183. doi: 10.1016/j.appet.2008.09.012
ARTICLE, FROM DATABASE

CITING E-MAIL, DISCUSSION LISTS, OR MAILING LISTS

Because your readers cannot retrieve personal e-mail, the APA says not to include it in a Reference list (→ see page 173 on in-text citations for e-mail). For retrievable postings— discussion groups, mailing lists— use the format shown right.

McLaughlin, B. (2007, September 4). Webinar for environmental benchmarking survey [Message posted to AAUP-L mailing list]. Retrieved from http://ucp.uchicago. edu/mailman/listinfo/aaup-l
DISCUSSION GROUP OR MAILING LIST POST

CITING BLOGS AND WIKIS

Xavier, J. (2007, June 11). Timo Veikkola (Nokia): A vision for the future. [Web log post]. Retrieved from http://julianax.blogspot. com/2007/06/timo-veikkola-nokia-vision-of-future.html
BLOG POST

Echidna catenata. (2014, May 25). Retrieved May 27, 2014, from Wikipedia: http://en.wikipedia.org/wiki/Echidna_catenata
WIKI POST

CITING PART OF AN ONLINE DOCUMENT

Sales, L. (2005). Part II. In *Hurricane Katrina: Reporter's diary*. Retrieved from http://www.abc.net.au/ news/newsitems/200509/s1460732
ONLINE DOCUMENT, A PART OF

FOR OTHER KINDS OF SOURCES

You may need to create references for other types of sources, including visual and multimedia sources. In APA style, a note or identifying description usually helps clarify the type of source you are citing.

As the examples on these two pages show, you can help readers by describing the medium of a source that is not usual:

Author's Name. (Year). *Title* [Medium.] Place of Publication: Publisher. Online
   information (if necessary).
   NONPERIODICAL

As the examples on these two pages show, you can add to the citation, in brackets, **Chart**, **CD**, **Computer software**, **Television series**, **Television episode**, **Motion picture**—whatever information will help readers know the source kind if it is not a print or online alphabetic text.

SOFTWARE

Cite software as you would a book without a named author (→ see page 180)—but include **Computer software** in brackets after the title. If there is a publisher, include the name and date of publication; for software you have downloaded, give the date of the download and the URL.

PsychMate (Version 2.0) [Computer software]. (2007).
   Philadelphia, PA: Psychology Software Tools.
   SOFTWARE

SOUND RECORDING

Camera Obscura. (2009). Away with murder. *On My Maudlin Career* [CD]. London, England: 4AD Records.
   MUSIC OR AUDIO RECORDING

TIP: WORKING WITH UNUSUAL SOURCES

The APA has this recommendation: "In general, a reference should contain the author name, date of publication, title of the work, and publication data." If you cannot find in these pages a sample exactly like what you need, the APA recommends that you "choose the example that is most like your source and follow that format. Sometimes you will need to combine elements of more than one reference format."

VISUAL SOURCES

Sander, N., Abel, G. J., & Bauer, R. (2014). *The global flow of people* [Chart.]. Retrieved from http://www.global-migration.info /?_ga=1.22066875.1833179927.1399505154
CHART, ONLINE

Cubitt, C. (2006). *Church* [Photograph]. Katrina: A gallery of images. Retrieved from http://www.claytoncubitt.com/ publish/katrina
PHOTOGRAPH, ONLINE

Adams, A. (ca. 1930). *Factory Building, San Francisco* [Photograph]. Santa Fe, NM: Museum of Fine Arts.
PHOTOGRAPH

CONFERENCE PRESENTATION OR LECTURE

Use this format if you need to cite a conference presentation or similar lecture or speech that has not been published.

Kleinberg, S. L. (2005, June). *The changing face of Texas in the twenty-first century: Perspectives on the new immigration.* Paper presented at Gateway on the Gulf, a Humanities Texas Institute for Texas Teachers, Galveston, TX.
PRESENTATION OR LECTURE

AN INTERVIEW YOU CONDUCT

The APA does not consider an unpublished interview to be checkable data and so an interview should not go in the reference list. You may, however, give an in-text citation for the interview.

Some music composers believe digital technologies slow down their composing processes because they offer so many options (M. Boracz, personal communication, October 18, 2015).

FILM AND TELEVISION

Gibney, A. (Director). (2005). *Enron: The smartest guys in the room* [Motion picture]. New York, NY: Magnolia.
FILM, VIDEOTAPE, OR DVD

Hanson, H. (Writer), & Yaltanes, G. (Director). (2005, September 13). Pilot [Television series episode]. In B. Josephson & H. Hanson (Producers), *Bones*. New York, NY: Fox Broadcasting.
TELEVISION SHOW OR SERIES

TIP: FINDING INFORMATION ABOUT FILMS
The *Internet Movie Database* (http://www.imdb.com) gives you access to all the information you need for citing films.

APA

CSE DOCUMENTATION

GUIDE TO CSE DOCUMENTATION MODELS

THE PATTERNS

CSE REFERENCES

FOR BOOKS

Number. Author's Last Name Followed by Initials. Title of the book. City of Publication (State): Publisher; Year.

19. Stewart J. Calculus. Boston (MA): Brooks/Cole; 2002.

FOR ARTICLES FROM PERIODICALS

Number. Author's Last Name Followed by Initials. Article title. Periodical. Date;Volume(Issue):Pages.

17. Richie DJ, Lappos VJ, Palmer PL. Sizing/optimization of a small satellite energy storage and attitude control system. JOSR. 2007 Jul-Aug;87(52):940-952.

FOR ONLINE SOURCES AND ELECTRONIC MEDIA

Number. Title of source [Kind of electronic medium]. Edition. Place of Publication: Publisher; date of publication [date updated; date cited]. Notes.

44. WebElements: chemistry nexus [Internet]. Sheffield (UK): University of Sheffield; c1993-2007 [cited 2007 Jun 18]. Available from: http://www.webelements.com/nexus/

When you cite a book, periodical, or webpage, the format of the citation—the punctuation of the title, the inclusion of a periodical's issue number, or the listing of a URL—tells readers what kind of text you are citing. When you cite a text that isn't a book, periodical, or webpage, indicate what kind of text you are citing, in brackets after the title (as in the pattern for online sources).

DETAILS OF THE PATTERNS

AUTHOR'S NAME

An author's name is listed last name first, with initials for first and middle names. If there are two initials, they are not separated by space or periods. A period separates the author's name from the title.

TITLES OF BOOKS AND PARTS OF BOOKS

1 Capitalize only the first word and any proper nouns.

2 Do not italicize or underline book titles.

3 Put a period after the title.

JOURNAL TITLES

Journal titles in CSE are always abbreviated according to the ISO (International Organization for Standardization). For example, the full title of the journal in the example numbered 17 to the left is the *Journal of Spacecraft and Rockets*. The CSE manual has guidelines for abbreviations. Your school's library has this manual.

DATES

If you cannot find a date but can figure it out from other information, set the date in brackets: [2002]. If only a copyright date is available, use that with a **c** for *copyright*: (**c1962**). If there is a publication date and a copyright date, with more than three years between them, give both dates: (**2007, c1962**). If there is no date of publication, use the words *date unknown* in brackets: [**date unknown**]. With a website, the copyright or publication date will be a span of years. In this case, use a dash: (**c1993–2007**). For multiple years of publication, separate the years by an en-dash: (**2004–2005**). (The box to the right explains en-dashes.)

ONLINE SOURCES AND ELECTRONIC MEDIA

References for Internet sources and electronic media do not differ significantly from what is required for print sources. There is still an author or organization who is responsible for the content, a title, a place of publication, and a date of publication. Additional information will be the URL and access date, and with some media, technical information.

Always put the medium (**Internet; CD-ROM; DVD**) in brackets after the title.

CSE also notes dates of updates (which are most applicable to websites) and dates accessed for Internet sources. In some cases, a date of update will not be provided, but you should always note the date of access, especially for materials that change frequently, such as a blog or wiki.

In a CSE citation, notes include URLs as well as technical information. See the examples for audio and video recordings and CD-ROMs for examples of technical notes.

→ See sample references on pages 195–196.

TIP: EN-DASHES

hyphen: -   en-dash: –

CSE style specifies that you use an en-dash (instead of a hyphen) in dates. On Macintosh computers, you can make an en-dash by holding down the Option key as you click the hyphen key; on Windows computers, hold down the ALT key while typing 0150.

CSE LIST OF REFERENCES

In CSE's citation-name system, writers complete the list of references and then create the in-text citations. The reference list (called *References*, *Cited References*, *Literature Cited*, or *Bibliography*) is arranged alphabetically by author and then numbered:

References

1. Amann RI, Ludwig W, Schleifer KH. Phylogenetic identification and in situ detection of individual microbial cells without cultivation. Microhi01 Rev. 1995;59:143-169.

2. Barns SM, Fundyga RE, Jeffries MW, Pace NR. Remarkable arched diversity detected in a Yellowstone National Park hot spring environment. Proc Natl Acad Sci USA. 1994;91:1609-1613.

3. Dojka, MA, Harris JK, Pace NR. Expanding the known diversity and environmental distribution of an uncultured phylogenetic division of bacteria. Appi Environ Microbiol. 2000;66:1617-1621.

→ See page 192 for information on how to format CSE style references.

CSE IN-TEXT CITATIONS

The numbers alphabetically assigned to these end references are then used for in-text references, regardless of the sequence in which the works appear in the text:

Early studies [2] used molecular methods to reveal remarkable microbial diversity in the sediment of Yellowstone hot springs.

or:

Early studies (2) used molecular methods to reveal remarkable microbial diversity in the sediment of Yellowstone hot springs.

In order to avoid ambiguity, citation numbers appear immediately after the relevant word, title, or phrase rather than at the end of a sentence. Usually, the citation number appears as a superscript, but it can also be set in parentheses. Set the citation number with one space both before and after, except when followed by a punctuation mark. This spacing makes the citation number easier to see.

When there are several in-text citations occurring at the same point in the text, put them in numerical order so that a reader can find them easily in the list of references. Separate the numbers by commas; if the numbers are consecutive, they can be joined by a hyphen:

Researchers have studied brucellosis for the better part of a century [3,5,16-18,43], finding that transmission. . .

CSE SAMPLE REFERENCES

NO AUTHOR NAMED
Start with the work's title.

8. Handbook of geriatric drug therapy. Springhouse (PA): Springhouse; c2000.

MORE THAN ONE AUTHOR

17. Sebastini AM, Fishbeck DW. Mammalian anatomy: the cat. 2nd ed. Burlington (NC): Carolina Biological; 2005.

A CORPORATION OR ORGANIZATION AS AUTHOR
Start with the abbreviated name of the corporate author as it appears in the source.

3. [CCPS] Center for Chemical Process Safety. Guidelines for safe and reliable instrumented protective systems. Indianapolis (IN): Wiley Publishing, Inc.; 2007.

AN EDITED BOOK
Put editor or editors after the name(s) at the start.

2. Brockman J, editor. What we believe but cannot prove: today's leading thinkers on science in the age of certainty. New York (NY): HarperCollins; 2006.

A GOVERNMENT AUTHOR
GPO stands for *Government Printing Office.*

6. [GPO] US Government Printing Office. Style manual. Washington (DC): The Office; 2000.

AN ESSAY OR CHAPTER IN A BOOK

8. Feynman RP. The making of a scientist. In: Leighton R, editor. Classic Feynman: All the adventures of a curious character. New York (NY): Norton; 2006. p. 13-19.

A REVISED OR LATER EDITION OF A BOOK
Add the edition after the title.

22. Tufte ER. The visual display of quantitative information. 2nd ed. Cheshire (CT): Graphics Press; 2001.

AN ONLINE BOOK

7. Ebert D. Ecology, epidemiology, and evolution of parasitism in Daphnia [Internet]. Bethesda (MD): National Library of Medicine (US), National Center for Biotechnology Information; 2005 [cited 2007 Sep 4]. Available from: http://www.ncbi.nlm.nih.gov/entrez/query.fcgi?db=Books

AN ARTICLE IN A DAILY NEWSPAPER

24. Revkin AC. Cooking up a fable of life on melting ice. New York Times. 2007 Jul 22;Sect. 2:11.

CSE

A VOLUME IN A SERIES
The series information goes in parentheses at the end.

9. Honjo T, Melchers F, editors. Gut-associated lymphoid tissues. Berlin (Germany): Springer-Verlag; 2006. (Current Topics in Microbiology and Immunology; vol. 308).

A TECHNICAL REPORT
Include the performing and/or sponsoring organization. (The example shows the performing organization [the group that performed the research], the University of Washington Department of Statistics; the sponsoring group funded the research.)

14. Krivitsky P, Handcock M, Raftery AE, Hoff P. Representing degree distributions, clustering, and homophily in social networks with latent cluster random effects models [Internet]. Seattle (WA): University of Washington Department of Statistics; 2007. No. 517. Available from: http://www.stat.washington.edu/www/research/reports/

Note: Often, the very end of the citation acknowledges the funding; for example: (Sponsored by the Nuclear Regulatory Commission). The report number goes at the end of the citation (before the URL if there is one). If there is a contract number, include it.

A CONFERENCE PRESENTATION
Include the location and dates.

2. Braun F, Noterdaeme JM, Colas L. Simulations of different Faraday screen configurations for the ITER ICRH Antenna. In: Ryan PM, Rassmussen D, editors. Radio frequency power in plasmas: 17th topical conference on radio frequency power in plasmas; 2007 May 7-9; Clearwater (FL). Melville (NY): [AIP] American Institute of Physics; 2007. p. 175-178.

A JOURNAL PAGINATED BY VOLUME

8. Gradstein FM, Og JG. Geologic time scale 2004—why, how, and where near! Lethaia. 2004;(37):175-181.

AN ONLINE ARTICLE

24. Spiesel S. Can a rollercoaster really scare you to death? and more. Slate [Internet]. Aug 28 [cited 2007 Sep 3]. Available from: http://www.slate.com/id/2172960/fr/flyout

A WEBPAGE

5. DNA Interactive [Internet]. Cold Spring Harbor (NY): Cold Spring Harbor Lab; c2003 [cited 2007 Aug 12]. Available from: http://www.dnai.org/

AN ONLINE DATABASE

3. Catalysts and catalysed reactions [Internet]. London (UK): RSC Publishing. 2002 [updated 2007 Aug; cited 2007 Sep 5]. Available from: http://pubs.rsc.org/Publishing/CurrentAwareness/CCR/CCRSearchPage.cfm

A BLOG POSTING

4. Diganta [screen name]. Pushing the limits of speciesism. In: Desicritics.org [Web log]. [posted 2007 Jun 18; cited 2007 Sep 2].

CMS DOCUMENTATION

GUIDE TO CMS DOCUMENTATION MODEL

CMS IN-TEXT CITATIONS AND FOOTNOTES

The sample sentence below contains a quotation as it would appear in the body of a paper, with a superscript number at its end. The footnote to that sentence follows, linked by the number. (This sample is numbered 12 because there are eleven source references before it.)

In *Marriage, a History*, Stephanie Coontz states that, "whether it is valued or not, love is rarely seen as the main ingredient for marital success."[12]

12. Stephanie Coontz, *Marriage, a History: From Obedience to Intimacy or How Love Conquered Marriage* (New York: Viking, 2005), 18.

SUBSEQUENT NOTE ENTRIES

After the first reference to a book or other source, CMS conventions say that writers should put into a footnote the following:

- the author's last name
- the title of the work (or a shortened version if the title is long)
- a page number

Some writers, however, use only the author's name and the page number if there will be no ambiguity as to which source is being cited. The footnote could thus read

10. Coontz, *Marriage*, 99.

or

10. Coontz, 99.

If a reference is to the same work as in the preceding note, you can use the abbreviation **Ibid**. (*Ibid.* is a shortened form of the Latin word *ibidem*, which means *in the same place*.)

11. Ibid., 103.

BIBLIOGRAPHY

If the writer of these sample citations were to include a bibliography listing at the paper's end, the citation would be:

Coontz, Stephanie. *Marriage, a History: From Obedience to Intimacy or How Love Conquered Marriage.* New York: Viking, 2005.

(Notice, in this case, that the listing has the same formatting as MLA style.)

CMS SAMPLE REFERENCES

BOOKS

For a footnote:

16. J. H. Plumb, *The Italian Renaissance* (New York: Mariner Books, 2001), 86.

In the bibliography:

Plumb, J. H. *The Italian Renaissance.* New York: Mariner Books, 2001.

AN ESSAY OR CHAPTER IN A BOOK

For a footnote:

8. F. J. Byrne, "Early Irish Society (1st–9th Century)," in *The Course of Irish History*, eds. T. W. Moody and F. X. Martin (Lanham, MD: Roberts Rinehart, 2002), 55.

In the bibliography:

Byrne, F. J. "Early Irish Society (1st–9th Century)." In *The Course of Irish History*, edited by T. W. Moody and F. X. Martin, 43–60. Lanham, MD: Roberts Rinehart, 2002.

ARTICLES FROM PERIODICALS

For a footnote:

13. Valerie A. Kivelson, "On Words, Sources, and Historical Method: Which Truth About Muscovy?" *Kritika: Explorations in Russian and Eurasian History* 3, no. 3 (2002): 490.

In the bibliography:

Kivelson, Valerie A. "On Words, Sources, and Historical Method: Which Truth About Muscovy?" *Kritika: Explorations in Russian and Eurasian History* 3, no. 3 (2002): 487–99.

A JOURNAL ARTICLE RETRIEVED FROM AN ELECTRONIC DATABASE

The citation should follow the same form for a journal, but the URL for the article is included.

For a footnote:

23. Bryon MacWilliams, "Yale U. Press Strikes Deal with Russian Archive to Open Stalin's Papers to Scholars," *Chronicle of Higher Education* 53, no. 44 (July 2007), http://web.ebscohost.com.ezproxy.lib.utexas.edu/ehost.

In the bibliography:

MacWilliams, Bryon. "Yale U. Press Strikes Deal with Russian Archive to Open Stalin's Papers to Scholars." *Chronicle of Higher Education* 53, no. 44 (July 2007), http://web.ebscohost.com.ezproxy.lib.utexas.edu/ehost.

ONLINE SOURCES (OTHER THAN DATABASES)

For a footnote:

4. Chris Johnson, "Statement from Human Rights Campaign President Joe Solmonese on Recent ENDA Developments," *Human Rights Campaign*, September 28, 2007, http://www.hrcbackstory.org/2007/09/statement-from-.html.

In the bibliography:

Johnson, Chris. "Statement from Human Rights Campaign President Joe Solmonese on Recent ENDA Developments." *Human Rights Campaign*, September 28, 2007. http://www.hrcbackstory.org/2007/09/statement-from-.html.

NO AUTHOR NAMED

Start the citation with the work's title.

For a footnote:

4. *Broad Stripes and Bright Stars* (Kansas City, MO: Andrews McMeel, 2002), 15.

In the bibliography:

Broad Stripes and Bright Stars. Kansas City, MO: Andrews McMeel, 2002.

TWO OR THREE AUTHORS

In a footnote, put all of the authors' full names. For subsequent references, give the authors' last names only. In the bibliography, give full names.

For a footnote:

2. Larry J. Reynolds and Gordon Hutner, eds., *National Imaginaries, American Identities: The Cultural Work of American Iconography* (Princeton, NJ: Princeton University Press, 2000), 56.

In the bibliography:

Reynolds, Larry J., and Gordon Hutner, eds. *National Imaginaries, American Identities: The Cultural Work of American Iconography*. Princeton, NJ: Princeton University Press, 2000.

FOUR OR MORE AUTHORS

In a footnote, give the name of the first author listed, followed by *et al.* List all the authors in the bibliography.

For a footnote:

3. James Drake et al., *James Drake* (Austin, TX: UT Press, 2008), 40.

In the bibliography:

Drake, James, Bruce Ferguson, Steven Henry Madoff, and Jimmy Santiago Baca. *James Drake*. Austin, TX: UT Press, 2008.

A CORPORATE AUTHOR

Start with the name of the corporate author as it appears in the source.

For a footnote:

5. Brady Center to Prevent Gun Violence, *Guns and Hate: A Lethal Combination* (Washington, DC: Brady Center to Prevent Gun Violence, 2009), 13.

In the bibliography:

Brady Center to Prevent Gun Violence. *Guns and Hate: A Lethal Combination*. Washington, DC: Brady Center to Prevent Gun Violence, 2009.

A GOVERNMENT AUTHOR

List the full agency or department name as author.

For a footnote:

11. Central Intelligence Agency, *The World Fact Book 2007* (Washington, DC: Potomac Books, Inc., 2007), 136.

In the bibliography:

Central Intelligence Agency. *The World Fact Book 2007*. Washington, DC: Potomac Books, Inc., 2007.

AN EDITED BOOK

Put *ed.* (or *eds.* for multiple editors) after the names that begin the citation.

For a footnote:

14. J. Peter Burkholder and Claude V. Palisca, eds., *Norton Anthology of Western Music*, Vol. 1, *Ancient to Baroque* (New York: Norton, 2005), 550.

In the bibliography:

Burkholder, J. Peter, and Claude V. Palisca, eds. *Norton Anthology of Western Music.* Vol. 1, *Ancient to Baroque.* New York: Norton, 2005.

AN ARTICLE FROM A REFERENCE BOOK

Well-known reference materials are not usually listed in a CMS bibliography, so you need to know only the footnote format. Start with the name of the reference work, and then list its edition. Put **s.v.** (*sub verba*, Latin for *under the word*) and then put the title of the entry you are citing in quotation marks:

9. *Riverside Dictionary of Biography*, 2004 ed., s.v. "Aaron, Hank (Henry Lewis)."

AN ARTICLE FROM AN ONLINE REFERENCE

The access date should be included in the citation only for sources that are frequently updated, such as Wikis. (And, as with reference works in print, there should be no listing in the bibliography.)

26. Wikipedia, s.v. "Deadwood, South Dakota," last modified http://en.wikipedia.org/wiki/Deadwood%2C_South_Dakota.

A RELIGIOUS TEXT

Citations for religious texts appear in the notes, but not in the bibliography.

12. Qur'an 18:16–20.

AN E-MAIL

If you reference e-mails in the text of your paper, you do not need to provide a note. E-mails are not listed in a CMS bibliography.

In an e-mail message to the author on November 6, 2006, Jason Craft noted. . . .

If you do need to include a footnote:

24. Jason Craft, e-mail message to author, November 6, 2006.

A WEBPAGE

For a footnote:

19. New York Historical Society, "Galleries," *New York Divided: Slavery and the Civil War,* http://www.slaveryinnewyork.org/tour_galleries.htm (accessed September 2, 2007).

In the bibliography:

New York Historical Society. "Galleries." *New York Divided: Slavery and the Civil War.* http://www.slaveryinnewyork.org/tour_galleries.htm (accessed September 2, 2007).

A BLOG POSTING

When you give the URL for a blog entry, give the permalink to the entry rather than the URL of that blog so a reader can go directly to the entry without having to scroll through the entire blog.

For a footnote:

8. Dooce [Screen name], "The Labor Story, Part 2," In the Dooce Blog, comment posted July 27, 2009, http://www.dooce.com/2009/07/27/labor-story-part-two (accessed August 3, 2009).

In the bibliography:

Dooce Blog. "The Labor Story, Part 2." http://www.dooce.com/2009/07/27/labor-story-part-two.

EDITING AND PROOFREADING

WHAT ARE REVISING, EDITING, AND PROOFREADING?

As you write a paper, you move through stages of development. In the initial stages, you are finding and arranging ideas and then arranging them into an overall argument. Once you have a full first draft, you move into the middle stage of writing—revision—and then into the later stages—editing and proofreading.

REVISING

When you revise, you attend to large-scale persuasive aspects of a text: organization and style. You start revising once you have close to a full draft.

→ See pages 106–107 for more on revising.

EDITING

When your overall argument is solid and unlikely to change, you focus on editing. In editing, you attend to sentences and other large details: Are sentences readable? Have you documented all your sources?

PROOFREADING

When proofreading, you check spelling, punctuation, and other mechanics. While you can pay attention to these details throughout the development of a paper, you also want to do this *as your very last step*. Whenever you revise or edit you can make mistakes, and you want to be sure to catch them once and for all.

TO EDIT, ASK:

Are my sentences easy to read? Will they engage readers?

❏ For easy-to-read sentences, see page 114.

❏ Are my verbs active? Are my nouns concrete? See page 121.

Are my sentences grammatically appropriate for my audience and purpose?

❏ A sentence's subject and verb agree in person and number. See pages 204–207.

❏ Verb tenses meet academic conventions. See pages 210–211.

❏ The tenses of verbs change only when necessary. See pages 208–209.

❏ The voice and level of formality are consistent. See pages 212–213.

❏ There are no sentence fragments, run-ons, or comma splices—except for ones I can justify rhetorically. See pages 214–219.

❏ Each pronoun has a clear antecedent with which it agrees in person and number. See pages 220–221.

❏ Modifiers in sentences are placed so readers can tell easily what is being modified. See pages 222–223.

Have I integrated my quotations of others' work into my writing—while making it clear when I am using others' ideas or words?

❏ See pages 55–59.

Have I documented my sources according to expected conventions?

❏ See Part 7 of this book.

Have I removed any biased language?

❏ See pages 118–119.

TO PROOFREAD, ASK:

Have I followed conventions for spelling, capitalization, and other mechanics?

❏ For spelling, see page 299.

❏ For capitalization, see page 300.

❏ For other details of mechanics, see pages 301–303.

Did I omit words?

Only careful proofreading helps you find words accidentally left out.

Have I used the right word?

Wrong words have one of two causes: A spellchecker suggests an incorrect replacement word (**their** instead of **there**) OR you are not yet familiar enough with the conventions of formal writing or of a discipline to know the expected word.

❏ For the first kind, use spellcheckers attentively and proofread carefully.

❏ For the second kind, find someone who knows your audience's expectations; ask that person to read for any such words.

Is my punctuation conventional?

❏ Check that you have apostrophes in possessives and contractions. See pages 224–225.

❏ Do you have commas before coordinating conjunctions in compound sentences? See pages 242 and 270–271.

❏ Are there commas after nonessential information at a sentence's beginning? See page 228.

Are quotations punctuated conventionally?

❏ Pages 292–293 offer a chart to help you punctuate quotations.

MAKING SUBJECT–VERB AGREEMENT

In sentences that fit with academic expectations, the subject has the same person and number as the verb.

The information to the right will help you figure this out.

THE PATTERN

SUBJECTS AND VERBS AGREE IN PERSON AND NUMBER.

✓ **He loves me.**
third person, singular | third person, singular

✗ **He love me.**
third person, singular | second person, singular

✓ **We are addicted to oil.**
first person, plural | first person, plural

✗ **We is addicted to oil.**
first person, plural | third person, singular

✓ **The senator and her brothers are going to jail.**
third person, plural | third person, plural

✗ **The senator and her brothers is going to jail.**
third person, plural | third person, singular

TIP: HOW TO EDIT FOR SUBJECT–VERB AGREEMENT: PERSON

1 Identify a sentence's subject. (See below.)

2 Determine the subject's person: Is it first, second, or third person? (→ See page 206.)

3 Find the sentence's verb, and identify its person: Is it first, second, or third person? (→ See pages 211 and 236–238.)

4 Do the subject and verb have the same person?

YES? Your sentence is fine.

NO? Use the information on pages 211 and 236–238 to create the appropriate form of the verb.

TIP: HOW TO EDIT FOR SUBJECT–VERB AGREEMENT: NUMBER

1 Identify a sentence's subject. (See below.)

2 Determine the subject's number: Is it singular or plural? (→ See page 206.)

3 Find the sentence's verb, and identify its number: Is it singular or plural? (→ See pages 211 and 236–238.)

4 Are the subject and verb the same number?

YES? Your sentence is fine.

NO? Use the information on pages 211 and 236–238 to create the appropriate verb.

IDENTIFYING A SENTENCE'S SUBJECT

The information on pages 250–251 can help you identify the subject of a sentence. Sentences that contain prepositional phrases, however, can confuse writers trying to identify the subject because they add nouns to the sentence in addition to the subject. The following steps will help you identify the subject.

1 Underline any prepositional phrases (→ see pages 240–241 and 252) or other descriptive phrases that come before the verb.

The boy with the gloves dances particularly well.

The record that he set for driving across country is thirty-one hours.

2 Rewrite the sentence *without* the phrases you underlined. This should put the subject next to the verb.

The boy dances particularly well.

The record is thirty-one hours.

Help with subject–verb agreement continues on the next page . . .

2 DETERMINING THE SUBJECT'S PERSON

Use the grid below to determine the person of the subject you've identified.

	singular	plural
First person	I	we
Second person	you	you
Third person	he, she, it	they
	All nouns are third person:	
	woman, dog	women, dogs
	The President of the United States	
	furniture, justice	

3 DETERMINING WHETHER THE SUBJECT IS SINGULAR OR PLURAL

Use the information about the plurals of nouns on page 225 to help you determine the number of the subject. Keep an eye out, however, for the following kinds of subjects, whose numbers might not be immediately obvious.

COMPOUND SUBJECTS JOINED BY *and*

Compound subjects joined by *and* are usually plural:

Leela and Joe work on their homework together.

There are exceptions:

- If the compound subject names what we consider to be one object or activity—as with *peanut butter and jelly* or *drinking and driving*—it is singular. (Company names using *and* are also singular, as with a law firm named *Black and Bland*.)

- If the compound subject refers to the same person or thing, then it is singular:

My best friend and advisor is my father.

- If the compound subject is preceded by *each* or *every*, then it is singular:

Each dog, cat, and pet ferret is to be registered.

Every girl and boy deserves health insurance.

COMPOUND SUBJECTS JOINED BY *or, nor, either . . . or,* OR *neither . . . nor*

The number of the subject is determined by the noun closest to the verb:

A dog or crows get into our garbage every week. Because **crows** is closest to the verb and is plural, the subject of this sentence is plural.

Crows or a dog gets into our garbage every week. Because *a dog* is closest to the verb and is singular, the subject of this sentence is singular.

SUBJECTS THAT USE INDEFINITE PRONOUNS

The indefinite pronouns (→ see page 232) **anybody**, **anyone**, **anything**, **each**, **everybody**, **everyone**, **everything**, **nobody**, **no one**, **someone**, **somebody**, and **something** are singular:

Everyone in my class is late with homework! • Everything has gone wrong.

The indefinite pronouns **both** and **many** are plural:

Both motorcycles were broken. • Many have visited our town.

The indefinite pronouns **all**, **any**, **none**, and **some** can be singular or plural, depending on the noun or pronoun to which they refer:

SINGULAR All my money goes to rent. Some of his dinner was overcooked.

PLURAL All my nieces go fishing. Some of his books were lost.

COLLECTIVE NOUNS

Nouns referring to collections of people—**audience**, **class**, **committee**, **crowd**, **family**, **group**, **public**, **team**—are usually singular, because the collection is usually described as acting as one unit.

The audience was delighted by the performance.

When such a noun refers to its members acting individually, however, it is plural:

The audience were looking at each other.

CLAUSES AND PHRASES

When a sentence's subject is a clause or a phrase, the subject is singular:

What frustrates me is my math homework.

Going to the dentist makes me nervous.

If the verb is a form of **be** and the word or words following it (which are called the **subject complement**) are plural, then the verb is plural even if the subject is singular:

What frustrates me are inconsiderate drivers.

WATCH OUT FOR THIS!

Phrases as such **along with**, **in addition to**, and **together with** can sound as though they build compound nouns—but they do not. The subject of the sentence below is **Hasan**; **together with Kim** is an adjectival phrase.

Hasan, together with Kim, is driving to Appleton.

USING VERB TENSES CONSISTENTLY

THE PATTERN

CONSISTENT VERB TENSES CREATE COHERENCE

If you shift verb tenses in a sentence, you shift from one sense of time to another. Readers can be confused by such shifts because readers might not then know if the actions of a sentence happened in the past, present, or future.

✓ Jenna wrote me about her Botswana trip; she saw new uranium mining.
  simple past tense   simple past tense

✗ Jenna wrote me about her Botswana trip; she **sees** new uranium mining.
  simple past tense   simple present tense

A CONSISTENT TENSE FOR WRITING ABOUT FICTION

When you summarize the plot or describe the actions in fiction, write as though the events happen in an eternal present: Put all descriptions in present tense.

In Colette's novels *Cheri* and *The Last of Cheri*, the character Léa works hard to appear and act young at the start; by the end she is gray-haired and stout.

BUT SOMETIMES YOU NEED TO CHANGE TENSES . . .

Because writing often involves describing relations among events that occured at different times, you sometimes need to change tenses, as this example shows:

A new study offers some relief to parents who worry that their children will never eat anything but chocolate milk, gummi vitamins, and the occasional grape. Researchers examined the eating habits of 5,390 pairs of twins between eight and eleven years old and found children's aversions to trying new foods are mostly inherited. The message to parents: It's not your cooking, it's your genes.

Present tense

The present tense verbs describe how a study can ease parental worries now.

Past tense

The past tense verbs describe the actions that had to have taken place before the study could be useful now, in the present.

Future tense

The future tense describes parents' fears about their children's future actions.

USING PRESENT PERFECT AND PAST PERFECT TO SHOW TIME DIFFERENCES

Writers can show relationships between actions or states by shifting from simple or progressive present tense to present perfect; they can also shift from simple or progressive past tense to past perfect. The perfect tenses signal that the action or state they describe occurred before the action or state in the other tense.

Present perfect maintains a present focus; past perfect maintains a past focus.

SWITCHING TENSES WHEN THE TIME FOCUS IS THE PRESENT

The homeless can be roughly divided into two groups: those who have had homelessness forced upon them and want nothing more than to escape it and those who have chosen it for themselves and now accept it or, in some cases, embrace it.

Present tense   **Present perfect tense**

This sentence focuses on a present distinction; for that distinction to be possible, however, the people being described had to have become homeless in the past.

SWITCHING TENSES WHEN THE TIME FOCUS IS THE PAST

In 1965, Thorazine was introduced. This drug is responsible for much of the homeless problem we see today. Before it was introduced, people diagnosed with mental illness, particularly schizophrenia, had been considered incurable and had been confined to mental institutions.

Past progressive tense

Past perfect tense

This sentence focuses on a distinction that occurred in the past. The writer uses the past progressive tense to describe how a drug was introduced in the past; the writer then uses the past perfect tense to show conditions that happened even further in the past than the drug's introduction.

→ See page 211 for a list of all verb tenses.

TIP: HOW TO EDIT FOR SHIFTS IN VERB TENSES

1 Using different colored pencils or pens, highlight each verb tense in its own color.

2 Where you see shifts, ask if readers will understand why the tense shifts.

3 If you need to clarify verb tense for readers, do one of the following:

- Add words or time expressions that signal a tense shift.
- Change one verb to present or past perfect to indicate that an action or state occurred prior to the other.
- Change the tense of the verb to maintain a consistent time focus.

USING VERB TENSES IN ACADEMIC WRITING

THE SIMPLE PRESENT is used to . . .

- describe the present situation.
  Conservationists at the Masai Mara work hard to protect the wildebeest from poachers.

- generalize.
  Studies show that chronic stress contributes to heart attacks and other diseases.

- describe the contents of a book, movie, or other text.
  In his thesis, "Intimate Relationships with Artificial Partners," Levy conjectures that robots will become so human-like that people will fall in love with them.

THE PRESENT PROGRESSIVE is used to . . .

- describe actions happening at the moment of speaking.
  Women are dying from complicated pregnancies and childbirth at almost the same rate as 1990.

- compare two present actions. One action is described in simple present, the other in present progressive.
  When strict parents are not watching, their children often engage in reckless actions.

THE PRESENT PERFECT is used to . . .

- describe actions begun in the past but not completed.
  The once vanished gray wolf has made a comeback in the Northern Rockies.

- describe actions begun at an unspecified past time.
  Over half of adolescents have tried alcohol and drugs at least once.

- introduce a topic.
  Once a disease of the Western world, breast cancer has become a global concern.

THE SIMPLE PAST is used to . . .

- describe completed events or states.
  Charles M. Schulz drew "Peanuts" for nearly half a century.

- report past research or events, summarize research results, and give narrative examples.
  Steven C. Amstrup of the United States Geological Survey led a recent study of polar bears.

THE PAST PERFECT is used to . . .

- compare two past events. The past perfect signals the event that happened first.
  The protesters were demanding the freedom and democracy for which their parents had fought.

FORMING THE TENSES OF ENGLISH VERBS

SIMPLE TENSES

Simple present: Describes actions taking place at the time a sentence is written or for actions that occur regularly.

Simple past: Describes actions completed in the past.

Simple future: Describes actions not yet begun.

PROGRESSIVE TENSES

Describe actions that continue—or will continue—over time.

PERFECT TENSES

Describe actions that have been (or will have been) completed.

PERFECT PROGRESSIVE TENSES

Present perfect progressive: Describes an action begun in the past, continuing in the present, and that may continue into the future.

Past perfect progressive: Describes a stretched-out action completed before some other past action; this tense usually appears in sentences that describe that other past action.

Future perfect progressive: Describes a stretched-out action that will occur before some specified future time.

THE PATTERN

	singular	plural
SIMPLE PRESENT		
Only the third person singular changes to the –s form.		
first	I ask.	We ask.
second	You ask.	You ask.
third	She/He/It asks.	They ask.
SIMPLE PAST		
All persons and numbers use the past form of the verb.		
	I/We/You/You/She/He/It/They asked.	
SIMPLE FUTURE		
All persons and numbers use *will* + the simple form of the verb.		
	I/We/You/You/She/He/It/They will ask.	
PRESENT PROGRESSIVE		
Use the appropriate simple present form of *be* + the present participle.		
first	I am asking.	We are asking.
second	You are asking.	You are asking.
third	She/He/It is asking.	They are asking.
PAST PROGRESSIVE		
Use the appropriate simple past form of *be* + the present participle.		
first	I was asking.	We were asking.
second	You were asking.	You were asking.
third	She/He/It was asking.	They were asking.
FUTURE PROGRESSIVE		
All persons and numbers use *will be* + the present participle.		
	I/We/You/You/She/He/It/They will be asking.	
PRESENT PERFECT		
Use the appropriate simple present form of *have* + the past participle.		
first	I have asked.	We have asked.
second	You have asked.	You have asked.
third	She/He/It has asked.	They have asked.
PAST PERFECT		
All persons and numbers use *had* + the past participle.		
	I/We/You/You/She/He/It/They had asked.	
FUTURE PERFECT		
All persons and numbers use *will have* + the past participle.		
	I/We/You/You/She/He/It/They will have asked.	
PRESENT PERFECT PROGRESSIVE		
All persons and numbers use *have been* + the present participle.		
	I/We/You/You/She/He/It/They have been asking.	
PAST PERFECT PROGRESSIVE		
All persons and numbers use *had been* + the present participle.		
	I/We/You/You/She/He/It/They had been asking.	
FUTURE PERFECT PROGRESSIVE		
All persons and numbers use *will have been* + the present participle.		
	I/We/You/You/She/He/It/They will have been asking.	

AVOIDING SHIFTS IN STYLE AND VOICE

PATTERN 1

SHIFTS BETWEEN DIRECT AND INDIRECT DISCOURSE IN VOICE

✓ **DIRECT DISCOURSE** "Are you going to the store without me?" Harriet's sister wanted to know. When you quote someone's words directly, you use **direct discourse**.

✓ **INDIRECT DISCOURSE** Harriet's sister wanted to know if we were going to the store without her. In **indirect discourse**, you report what someone else said.

✗ **MIXED** Harriet's sister wanted to know are we going to the store without her. A convention of formal written English is not to shift from one of these forms to another.

PATTERN 2

SHIFTS IN LEVELS OF FORMALITY

Even academic writing has levels of formality. Convention says to use only one level throughout a piece of writing.

✓ **FORMAL WRITING** Coltrane plays saxophone tenderly and searchingly, and this searching is perhaps the most salient characteristic of both his work and his life.

✓ **LESS FORMAL WRITING** Saxophones can whisper or shriek, breathe warmth or spit fire—and a quick listen to John Coltrane's 1965 album, *Transition*, will disabuse anyone of the misimpression that the saxophone is limited to that canned sound you heard during the credits of *L.A. Law*.

✗ **MIXED LEVELS** Coltrane plays saxophone tenderly, but there is a searching quality to it and sometimes his changes can really bug a listener.

TIP: PURPOSEFUL SHIFTS

Sometimes shifts make sentences do what you need them to. To be sure you use shifts only when necessary, follow this rule: *When you check your writing and find any of the shifts we describe here, remove the shift—unless you can give a solid reason why it is necessary.*

SHIFTS IN VOICE

Is the subject of a sentence performing an action or being acted upon? If the subject is performing an action, the sentence is in **active voice**; if the subject is being acted upon, the sentence is in **passive voice**.

ACTIVE VOICE   Amanda fed the macaw.
subject

We caught and ate the mice that came into our camp.
subject

PASSIVE VOICE   The macaw was fed by Amanda.
subject

Who ate the mice? The sentence doesn't say...!

Some of the mice that came into our camp were caught and eaten.
subject

✓ CONSISTENT VOICE   Jade fed the macaw even though David had fed it earlier.

When we had no food, we caught and ate the mice that came into our camp.

✗ MIXED VOICE   Jade fed the macaw even though it had been fed earlier by David.

When we had no food, the mice that came into our camp were caught and eaten.

Active voice uses action verbs, which convey movement and energy (→ see page 121). Passive voice uses forms of **be**; passive voice may also need a preposition before the noun that explains who performed the action—so passive sentences tend to be wordy and slower to read.

The passive voice is useful, however, when a writer wants to avoid naming who performed an action—as in the passively voiced sentence about the mice above. Scientific and technical writing often uses passive voice because it may seem fact-based and objective: Writers present their research and conclusions without attribution so that the writing appears to be unshaped by individual bias.

→ For more on uses of active and passive voices, see page 112.

AVOIDING SENTENCE FRAGMENTS

A sentence fragment is an incomplete sentence: Because Vered said so. • Where I watched.

A capital letter at the beginning and other conventional punctuation do not turn words into a sentence. A sentence, grammatically, is an independent clause (→ see page 253).

Vered said so. • In the hospital I watched my father sleep.

STEPS FOR DETERMINING IF YOU HAVE A SENTENCE—OR A FRAGMENT

Identify the phrase you think might be a fragment:	EXAMPLE 1 Danced in the streets.	EXAMPLE 2 The computer on the desk.	EXAMPLE 3 Unless there is old wiring in the house.	EXAMPLE 4 Nevertheless, they plotted.
1 Is there a subject? → See page 250.	**NO, there is no subject. This is a fragment.** To fix fragments lacking subjects, go to page 215.	**YES,** there is a subject: *The computer.* Move to the next step.	**YES,** there is a subject: *there.* Move to the next step.	**YES,** there is a subject: *they.* Move to the next step.
2 Is there a predicate? → See page 250.		**NO, there is no predicate. This is a fragment.** To fix fragments lacking predicates, go to page 216.	**YES,** there is a predicate: *is.* Move to the next step.	**YES,** there is a predicate: *plotted.* Move to the next step.
3 Do the words make up a dependent clause without an attached independent clause? → See page 217.			**YES, this is a dependent clause with no attached independent clause. THIS IS A FRAGMENT.** To fix dependent clause fragments, go to page 217.	**NO. THIS IS A SENTENCE.**

FIXING FRAGMENTS THAT LACK SUBJECTS

Fix fragments that lack subjects with one of the following two approaches:

1 ADD A SUBJECT TO THE FRAGMENT

These phrases are fragments because they lack subjects:

Danced in the street.

Sensing their delight in winning.

To add a subject, ask *Who is doing the action?* and then give that information:

Mary and Elaine danced in the street.

Christa was sensing their delight in winning. [OR] Christa sensed their delight in winning.

As with the second example, note that you may have to modify the verb when you add a subject.

2 ADD THE FRAGMENT TO A SENTENCE

Often people inadvertently write fragments in longer descriptions:

Mary and Elaine won the guitar contest last June. They were so happy they threw a party. Danced in the street.

The *danced in the street* fragment can be joined to the sentence before it with a coordinating conjunction:

Mary and Elaine won the guitar contest last June. They were so happy they threw a party and danced in the street.

→ We discuss coordinating conjunctions on pages 242 and 270–271.

Go to the next page to learn about fixing fragments missing predicates and fragments that are dependent clauses.

TIP: FINDING SENTENCE FRAGMENTS

If you are uncertain whether a phrase is a sentence or not, try saying it aloud with *I believe that . . .* in front of the phrase. If the result sounds odd to you, it probably is a fragment and worth checking with the steps to the right.

FIXING FRAGMENTS THAT LACK PREDICATES

Fix fragments that lack predicates with one of the following two approaches:

1 ADD A PREDICATE TO THE FRAGMENT

These phrases are fragments because they lack predicates:

The computer on the desk.

Only the lonely.

To add a predicate, ask *What is happening to the objects named in the fragment?*—and then give that information:

The computer on the desk was broken.

Only the lonely know how I feel tonight.

2 ADD THE FRAGMENT TO A SENTENCE

Just as with fragments that lack subjects, fragments without predicates often occur when people write descriptions:

Nobody was out walking after midnight. Only the lonely.

The *only the lonely* fragment can be joined to the sentence before it by making it into the subject:

Only the lonely were out walking after midnight.

Or you can use a conjunction to join the fragment to the end of the sentence:

Nobody was out walking after midnight, except for the lonely.

→ We discuss conjunctions on pages 242–245.

FIXING FRAGMENTS THAT ARE DEPENDENT CLAUSES WITHOUT ATTACHED INDEPENDENT CLAUSES

This fragment type is a common problem for those learning to write formal prose.

To identify dependent clauses, see the pattern below.

Fix fragments that are dependent clauses with one of the three approaches below.

1 JOIN DEPENDENT CLAUSE FRAGMENTS TO INDEPENDENT CLAUSES

Rather than build a road, they installed a tram over the trees.

Although my family lived under the Nazi regime for only one year, I will never forget the fear and humiliation I experienced that year in Vienna.

When the people of this part of Peru were building their cities, there was only one other urban complex on earth.

2 REMOVE THE SUBORDINATING CONJUNCTION TO MAKE A SENTENCE

We lived under the Nazi regime for only one year.

3 INSERT A DEPENDENT CLAUSE BEGINNING WITH A RELATIVE PRONOUN INTO AN INDEPENDENT CLAUSE

All the men who regularly sit in hot tubs showed signs of infertility.

Talib Kweli began recording with Mos Def, whom he met in high school.

THE PATTERN

IDENTIFYING DEPENDENT CLAUSES

Dependent clauses begin in one of two ways:

SUBORDINATING CONJUNCTIONS BEGIN DEPENDENT CLAUSES

rather than build a road

although we lived under the Nazi regime for only one year

when the people of this part of Peru were building their cities

→ See page 244 to learn about subordinating conjunctions.

RELATIVE PRONOUNS BEGIN DEPENDENT CLAUSES

who regularly sat in hot tubs • whom he had met in high school

→ See page 233 to learn about relative pronouns.

Anytime you see a phrase that begins with a subordinating conjunction or a relative pronoun, it cannot stand on its own as a sentence; each example above is a fragment.

AVOIDING COMMA SPLICES AND FUSED SENTENCES

Fused sentences and comma splices are examples of **run-on sentences**. Run-on sentences result when you join two independent clauses with unconventional or no punctuation.

JOINING TWO INDEPENDENT CLAUSES TO MAKE A SENTENCE

Imagine you wanted to join the two independent clauses below into one sentence.

Flower was one of the meerkats on the Animal Planet documentary series *Meerkat Manor*.

She died after being bitten by a cobra.

You have three options for joining the clauses, as we show below. We also show the two most common ways writers go awry when they join independent clauses.

→ See pages 254–255 to learn more about the conventions for joining independent clauses into compound sentences.

✓ WITH A SEMICOLON	Flower was one of the meerkats on the Animal Planet documentary series *Meerkat Manor*; she died after being bitten by a cobra.
✓ WITH A COMMA AND A COORDINATING CONJUNCTION	Flower was one of the meerkats on the Animal Planet documentary series *Meerkat Manor*, but she died after being bitten by a cobra.
✓ WITH A SEMICOLON AND A CONJUNCTIVE ADVERB	Flower was one of the meerkats on the Animal Planet documentary series *Meerkat Manor*; however, she died after being bitten by a cobra.
✗ FUSED SENTENCES	Flower was one of the meerkats on the Animal Planet documentary series *Meerkat Manor* she died after being bitten by a cobra. A fused sentence has no punctuation between its two independent clauses.
✗ COMMA SPLICES	Flower was one of the meerkats on the Animal Planet documentary series *Meerkat Manor*, she died after being bitten by a cobra. A comma splice puts a comma between its two independent clauses.

CONVERTING RUN-ON SENTENCES INTO CONVENTIONAL SENTENCES

1 **MAKE THE TWO INDEPENDENT CLAUSES INTO TWO SENTENCES**
Flower was one of the meerkats on the Animal Planet documentary series *Meerkat Manor*. She died after being bitten by a cobra in South Africa.

Put a period between the clauses; capitalize the first letter of the second sentence.

2 **JOIN THE INDEPENDENT CLAUSES WITH A SEMICOLON OR COLON**
Flower was one of the meerkats on the Animal Planet documentary series *Meerkat Manor*; she died after being bitten by a cobra.

In less formal writing, you can also join independent clauses with a dash.

→ See page 280 to learn about joining independent clauses with semicolons.

→ See page 279 to learn about joining independent clauses with colons.

3 **JOIN THE INDEPENDENT CLAUSES WITH A COMMA AND A COORDINATING CONJUNCTION**
Flower was one of the meerkats on the Animal Planet documentary series *Meerkat Manor*, but she died after being bitten by a cobra.

The coordinating conjunctions are *and*, *but*, *or*, *nor*, *for*, *so*, and *yet*.

→ See pages 242 and 270–271 to learn about coordinating conjunctions.

4 **MAKE ONE OF THE INDEPENDENT CLAUSES INTO A DEPENDENT CLAUSE**
Flower, who was a meerkat on *Meerkat Manor*, died after being bitten by a cobra.

→ Page 217 discusses dependent clauses.

5 **RESTRUCTURE THE TWO INDEPENDENT CLAUSES INTO ONE INDEPENDENT CLAUSE**
Flower, one of the meerkats on *Meerkat Manor*, died after being bitten by a cobra.

You might be able to turn one of the independent clauses into a phrase that you can then place next to the word it modifies.

TIP: FINDING COMMA SPLICES

Look for longer sentences that have a comma in the middle. When you find such a sentence, ask these two questions.

1 On either side of the comma, is there an independent clause? (→ See page 253.)

2 Is there a coordinating conjunction immediately after the comma? (→ See page 242.)

If you answer **YES** to #1 and **NO** to #2, then you have a comma splice.

WORKING WITH PRONOUN REFERENCE AND AGREEMENT

TO USE PRONOUNS CONVENTIONALLY, UNDERSTAND *ANTECEDENTS*

The person or thing to which a pronoun refers is its **antecedent**. In the sentences below, the antecedent is underlined.

The dog wasn't grey; it was black.

Marina came prepared: She brought a toolbox.

Computers change time: They speed it up.

Jamshed and I worked and then we ate lunch.

AVOID VAGUE PRONOUN REFERENCES

Check your writing for sentences in which a pronoun could have two antecedents. Revise the sentences to remove the ambiguity.

✗   Marisa told Tania that she had passed the class after all.

✓   Marisa told Tania, "I passed the class after all."

✗   After Lupita put the book in her bag, she couldn't find it.

✓   After Lupita put it in her bag, she couldn't find the book.

PRONOUN AGREEMENT

Conventionally, pronouns must agree in person, number, and gender with their antecedents.

AGREEMENT IN NUMBER

✗ If a person wants to be a good citizen, they should vote.
    singular   plural

✓ If people want to be good citizens, they should vote.
  plural   plural

AGREEMENT IN PERSON

✗ If people want to be good citizens, you should vote.
  third person   second person

✓ If people want to be good citizens, they should vote.
  third person   third person

AGREEMENT IN GENDER

✗ If Tamika wants to be a good citizen, he should vote.
  feminine   masculine

✓ If Tamika wants to be a good citizen, she should vote.
  feminine   feminine

FOR REFERENCE: PRONOUN PERSON AND NUMBER

	Singular Number	Plural Number
First Person	I, me, my	we, us, our
Second Person	you, your	you, your
Third Person	she, he, it, one, anyone	they
	her, his, him, its	them, their

TIP: HOW TO EDIT FOR PRONOUN REFERENCE AND AGREEMENT

Circle every pronoun in your paper and draw an arrow to each pronoun's antecedent.

1 If you *can't* find an antecedent, insert one beforehand or change the pronoun to a noun.

2 If the pronoun could have two different antecedents, edit the sentence to clarify the antecedent, as we show to the left.

3 If you *can* find an antecedent, be sure it agrees with your pronoun, as shown above.

AVOIDING DISRUPTIVE AND DANGLING MODIFIERS

Modifier is the collective name for adjectives, adjectival phrases, adverbs, and adverbial phrases. Modifiers make writing concrete and engaging—if readers can tell what words are being modified. Unfortunately, writers can easily put modifiers in odd places.

THE PATTERN

PUT MODIFIERS CLOSE TO THE WORDS THEY MODIFY

In this sentence—

✗ Covered in chocolate icing, my friends will love this cake.

—the friends sound like people we should approach with spoons in hand. When the adjectival phrase *covered in chocolate icing* is moved closer to the noun it is meant to modify, the result—

✓ My friends will love this cake covered in chocolate icing.

—is clearer about the icing's location.

You are most likely to make such slips when sentences contain several modifiers. The following sentence has two modifiers (*all over Europe* and *passing close to Earth*) placed to make it sound as though Europe passed close to Earth in 1577:

✗ The Great Comet of 1577 was viewed by people all over Europe passing close to Earth.

When *passing close to Earth* is moved closer to the noun phrase it should modify, the sentence is clearer:

✓ Passing close to Earth, the Great Comet of 1577 was viewed by people all over Europe.

TIP: HOW TO CHECK FOR DISRUPTIVE AND DANGLING MODIFIERS

Modification slips are easy to produce—and easy to fix. Fixing them requires finding them, however, and finding them takes time and careful reading. To check modifiers:

1 Underline every modifier in your writing; draw a line from each to the word it modifies.

2 Move modifiers that are far from the words they modify closer to those words.

3 If the underlined word is a limiting modifier (→ see page 223), is it placed so that the sentence means what you desire?

4 If you cannot find a noun to which the modifier refers, you have a dangling modifier. Choose one of the options on the facing page to fix it.

1 FIXING DISRUPTIVE MODIFIERS

Modifiers are disruptive when they disrupt a sentence's grammatical elements. In the first sentence below, a long phrase creates a distracting pause for readers between the sentence's subject and predicate:

Palenquero, although its grammar is so different that Spanish speakers cannot understand it, is thought to be the only Spanish-based Creole language in Latin America.

Moving the phrase makes the sentence easier to read:

Although its grammar is so different that Spanish speakers cannot understand it, *Palenquero* is thought to be the only Spanish-based Creole language in Latin America.

2 FIXING DANGLING MODIFIERS

A modifier **dangles** when it cannot logically modify anything in its sentence. For example, unless the writer of this sentence has an unusual dog—

While reading, my dog rested her head on my knee.

—the sentence describes an impossible situation: The position of the modifier *While reading* implies that the dog can read!

In addition, the person we assume is reading is not made explicit as a noun in the sentence. Because there is no such noun, the sentence cannot be fixed by moving the modifier closer to the (nonexistent) noun.

Because dangling modifiers cannot be fixed by being moved, two other options exist for fixing them:

1 Revise the dangling modifier to make explicit the noun to be modified:

As I was reading a book, my dog rested her head on my knee.

2 Revise the rest of the sentence so that the noun appears elsewhere:

While reading, I was warmed when my dog rested her head on my knee.

TIP: PAY PARTICULAR ATTENTION TO LIMITING MODIFIERS

Limiting modifiers are words such as *almost*, *even*, *hardly*, *just*, *nearly*, *not*, *only*, and *simply*. They can be placed almost anywhere in a sentence—and that makes them dangerous. Their placement can change a sentence's meaning.

For example, this sentence says Luther thought about donating his collection but didn't:

Luther almost donated his entire collection of LPs to the auction.

This sentence says that Luther *did* donate a large part of his collection:

Luther donated almost his entire collection of LPs to the auction.

Check each instance of limiting modifiers in your writing to be sure your sentences say what you want.

USING APOSTROPHES WITH POSSESSIVE FORMS (but not with plural forms)

Both plurals and possessives usually add an **-s** at the end of a noun. The difference is that possessives always have an apostrophe; plurals do not.

MAKING NOUNS POSSESSIVE

A possessive noun comes before another noun, and its possessive form—the addition of **-'s**—indicates possession of some other close association with the noun it precedes.

POSSESSIVES USING SINGULAR NOUNS

Add **-'s** to the end of the noun even if the noun ends in **-s**:

a cell's wall • my life's story • Luis's award • the grass's height • a potato's texture

POSSESSIVES USING PLURAL NOUNS

If the plural noun does not end in **-s**, add **-'s**.

the children's choir • the media's analysis • the deer's diseases

If the plural noun *does* end in **-s**, add only an apostrophe.

the boxes' interiors • the Kennedys' compound • the grasses' heights

POSSESSIVES USING COMPOUND NOUNS

The last word in a compound noun becomes possessive, following the above guidelines:

a NASCAR driver's car • the school nurse's office • some swimming pools' depths

POSSESSIVES USING TWO OR MORE NOUNS

If the object in question is owned jointly by the nouns, make the last noun possessive:

Abbott and Costello's "Who's on first?" routine was developed in the 1930s.

If each of the two nouns has possession, make both possessive:

Abbott's and Costello's lives had very different endings.

TIP: PROOFREADING FOR PLURALS AND POSSESSIVES

Circle every noun ending in **-s**. Ask yourself if the noun is possessive or plural; based on your decision, check that you have the conventional form.

If you have any questions about a noun's plural form, a dictionary will show it to you.

MAKING NOUNS PLURAL

In English, a noun's ending usually indicates whether it is singular or plural.

SINGULAR	PLURAL	
-s		
a boy	the boys	If a noun ends in an *-o* preceded by a *vowel*, it usually takes an *-s* to make it plural.
the site	many sites	
freedom	seven freedoms	
my radio	their radios	With compound hyphenated words, add *-s* to the main noun, even if that noun is not at the end of the word.
father-in-law	fathers-in-law	
-es		
a box	six boxes	Nouns that end in *-s*, *-sh*, *-ch*, and *-x* add *-es* to become plural.
my church	our churches	
one potato	two potatoes	If a noun ends in an *-o* preceded by a *consonant*, the plural forms usually ends in *-es*.
-ies		
the summary	several summaries	Nouns that end in *-y* lose the *-y* and add *-ies* to become plural.
a boundary	the boundaries	
-ves		
my life	our lives	With nouns that end in *-f* or *-fe*, replace the *-f* or *-fe* with *-ves* to become plural.
a calf	six calves	
other endings		
one medium	the media	Sometimes the plurals of words that derive from other languages take their plural form from the original language.
the analysis	the analyses	
one criterion	three criteria	
his child	his children	
changed form		
one man	many men	Words that have been in use since the beginning of language often change their forms to make plurals.
a mouse	three mice	
no change		
one moose	two moose	Many names for large animals keep the same form in both singular and plural.
one deer	many deer	

USING ARTICLES CONVENTIONALLY

TO USE ARTICLES CONVENTIONALLY, YOU NEED TO KNOW THE DIFFERENCE BETWEEN COUNT AND NONCOUNT NOUNS

Count nouns refer to objects that exist distinctly as countable units: *dogs, chairs, words, toes, plates, books, glances.* Count nouns refer to what you can perceive with your senses.

COUNT NOUN SINGULAR	a woman	the dog	his emotion
COUNT NOUN PLURAL	the women	the dogs	their emotions

Noncount nouns name what can't be cut into parts or counted: They name abstractions (*education, happiness*) and also collections of objects (*furniture, silverware, rice, coffee*).

NONCOUNT NOUN	justice	weather	anger

THE PATTERN

COUNT AND NONCOUNT NOUNS AND ARTICLES

Singular count nouns *always* need an article or another adjective (**this**, **that**, **my**, **each**) in front of them.

ARTICLE OR OTHER ADJECTIVE	SINGULAR COUNT NOUN

A snowstorm hit our town this week.

The teacher gave an apple to each child.

Plural count nouns do not need articles—but can have other adjectives.

PLURAL COUNT NOUN

or

ADJECTIVE	PLURAL COUNT NOUN

Dogs don't eat toys often, do they?

How did we come to associate teachers with apples?

Anger shows on bodies and faces.

Our winters have big snowstorms.

Of all the kinds of nouns, only **noncount nouns** can stand alone without an article. Because they cannot be counted, they cannot be used with quantifiers (**one**, **two**, **many**) or made plural. Use **much** (not *many*), **little** (not *few*), **amount of** (not *number of*) in front of these nouns.

NONCOUNT NOUN

Privacy is under attack online.

You can study anger in psychology.

PROOFREADING FOR ARTICLES

Here are two common mistakes in writing—and advice for proofreading for them.

MISSING *a* OR *an*

Underline all singular nouns that appear in your writing without an article or adjective. Decide whether the noun is countable or uncountable. (Many nouns can be either, depending on their contexts.)

❑ If what you've underlined is a noncount noun, it does not need *a*, *an*, or an adjective in front of it.

❑ If what you've underlined is a count noun, it must be marked in some way:

If the count noun refers to an indefinite or unspecified person, place, or thing, add *a* or *an*:

When I was young, I used an abacus instead of a calculator in math class.

If a noun is used as a representative of a class of nouns rather than of a particular individual member of that class, add *a* or *an*:

An abacus is a Chinese counting device.

If the noun refers to all members of the group or is general, make the noun plural and use no articles.

For some math problems, abacuses work as well as calculators.

IF YOU GREW UP SPEAKING A LANGUAGE OTHER THAN ENGLISH...

Count and noncount nouns are a feature of English that differs considerably from some other languages, so you may want to pay particular attention to how they work.

MISSING *the*

We use *the* when we know readers will understand exactly what object is meant by a noun we use (→ see page 235). To be sure you have used *the* when you should, underline all singular nouns that appear without an article or adjective. If the noun fits one of the three categories described below, it is "specific," so put *the* before it.

1 Shared knowledge. For example, because two people who live together can be expected to know that they have children, one could send this e-mail to the other:

Can you pick up the kids from school?

(Can you pick up kids would mean Pick up some kids, any kids...!)

2 Second mention. After a singular count noun is first used, readers will know what is meant by the second reference—and so *the* goes before its later uses:

Depo-Provera, a contraceptive, may cause serious side effects. Some drug companies, however, have promoted the contraceptive outside the U.S. with no warnings about its side effects.

> first mention

> second mention

3 If a noun is followed by a relative clause or a prepositional phrase that modifies it, and if there is a count noun in the clause or phrase, put *the* before the count noun:

He described the ways in which the sound of music calms him.

→ See pages 240–241 and 252 to learn more about prepositional phrases.

USING COMMAS WITH INTRODUCTORY PHRASES

To understand this particular use of commas, understand the difference between **a phrase** and **a clause**. Clauses contain subjects and predicates (➔ see pages 246 and 248–253); phrases do not.

(➔ see pages 246 and 248–253)

THE PATTERN

IF THE INTRODUCTORY PHRASE BEGINS WITH A PREPOSITION
Academic convention says to use a comma after any introductory phrase that begins with a preposition (➔ see page 273) and is longer than three or four words.

(➔ see page 273)

✓ In August, I returned to New Orleans to observe the changes following Hurricane Katrina.

✗ In August I returned to New Orleans to observe the changes following Hurricane Katrina.

✓ Out of desire not to be home alone on their computers, people come to this university library to work among others.

✗ Out of desire not to be home alone on their computers people come to this university library to work among others.

IF THE INTRODUCTORY PHRASE BEGINS WITH A PARTICIPLE OR INFINITIVE
Academic convention says to use a comma after any introductory phrase that begins with a participle or an infinitive (➔ see page 237).

(➔ see page 237)

✓ Vaulting and rolling over walls, Parkour practitioners propel themselves through cities.

✗ Vaulting and rolling over walls Parkour practitioners propel themselves through cities.

✓ To think like a computer scientist, you do not have to play Dungeons and Dragons.

✗ To think like a computer scientist you do not have to play Dungeons and Dragons.

PART 9
GRAMMAR, PUNCTUATION, AND MECHANICS

229

GRAMMAR

Using the grammar of academic English writing depends on understanding such writing's pieces and patterns. In this part, we look at the sentences' pieces and then at sentences.

THE PARTS OF SPEECH

The parts of speech, below, are the pieces out of which all sentences are built.

Words that describe the person, place, thing, or idea being discussed are **NOUNS**.

A certain kind of noun that refers back to an earlier mentioned noun is a **PRONOUN**.

Alice walks.

She walks.

Words that describe what the person, place, thing, or idea is doing are **VERBS**.

Words that give more details about nouns are **ADJECTIVES** and **ARTICLES**.

Words that give more detail about how an action is done (where, when, or in what manner) are **ADVERBS**.

The smiling woman walked happily yesterday.

Words to help us talk about more than one noun or action at a time are **CONJUNCTIONS**.

Alice and Omar walk and talk.

Words that allow us to describe how the actors and actions in a sentence are placed in space or time are **PREPOSITIONS**.

After saying goodbye, Alice walked into the store.

Prepositions are always the first words of phrases; those phrases can tell us more about nouns (in what shape was Alice?), in which case they are **ADJECTIVAL PREPOSITIONAL PHRASES** . . .

Out of breath, Alice leaned against the wall .

. . . or those phrases can tell us more about verbs (where did Alice lean?), in which case they are **ADVERBIAL PREPOSITIONAL PHRASES**.

NOUNS

Nouns name people, animals, places, things, and ideas or concepts.

THE PATTERN

any NOUN is . . .

SINGULAR	PLURAL		COMMON	PROPER
one	**many**		**just any thing**	**a specific one**
person	persons		person	Phillip Andrews
woman	women		woman	Tia Patrón
dog	dogs		dog	Lassie
city	cities		city	Milwaukee
tree	trees		tree	*Ficus benjamina*
religion	religions		religion	Buddhism

TIP: WORKING WITH PLURAL NOUNS

Most nouns make the plural form by adding an **–s** to the end of the singular form, but as you can see above not all do.

→ See page 225 to learn about irregular plural noun forms.

TIP: WORKING WITH PROPER NOUNS

Note above that proper nouns have their first letters capitalized.

IF YOU GREW UP SPEAKING A LANGUAGE OTHER THAN ENGLISH . . .

→ English differentiates between two kinds of nouns—count and noncount nouns—that challenge many writers. See page 226.

PRONOUNS

Pronouns take the place of nouns in many different ways.

PERSONAL PRONOUNS	I, me, he, him, she, her, it	we, our, they, their

Personal pronouns refer to specific people or things. In writing, you must first name the person or thing; then you can refer to the person or thing later with a pronoun:

Jenna came prepared: She brought her briefcase. (*She* and *her* are feminine.)

The dog wasn't gray; it was black. • Sara and Lia walked to the beach where they ate lunch.

Jamshed and I worked for a while, and then we ate lunch.

The person or thing to which the pronoun refers is called the pronoun's **antecedent**. (Note that *I* does not have an antecedent; readers will understand the person to whom *I* refers.)

→ In formal and academic English, a pronoun agrees in person, number, and gender with its antecedent. To learn more about this common problem for writers of formal English, see pages 220–221.

INTERROGATIVE PRONOUNS	who, which, what

We use interrogative pronouns to ask questions about people, places, things, or ideas. When we build such questions, there is a noun implied by the question.

Who climbed the stairs? (That is, someone climbed the stairs. *Who* was that someone?)

Which man spoke to you? • Which people were there?

POSSESSIVE PRONOUNS	my, mine, his, her, its	our, their

Possessive pronouns indicate close relationship or ownership. As with personal pronouns, you need to make clear to readers the person or thing for which the pronoun is standing in. (Again, as with **I**, the antecedent of **my** is understood.) Like adjectives, possessive pronouns tell us about the noun they precede: They tell us who **possesses** the noun.

Eva lost her backpack. • The dog leaned into my hand—its nose was cold! • My opinion is unsettled.

Jonathan and Mack got on the same train even though their destinations varied.

INDEFINITE PRONOUNS	one, each, every, another, anybody, none, no one, neither, either, both, few, some, many, most, all

Indefinite pronouns exist to help us communicate when we do not want to or cannot be specific about people or things. Indefinite pronouns function as adjectives, telling readers something about the noun they precede: They give readers a rough—indefinite—idea about the noun, not specifiying, for example, exactly which person or how many did something.

One could climb the stairs. • Each woman brought a book.

Few people complained. • Some dogs like to swim. • Most homes here are old.

RELATIVE PRONOUNS   who, whoever, whom, which, that, what, whatever

Relative pronouns allow us to combine sentences that are about the same person, place, thing, or idea. Using them, we can help readers see the connections between two sentences:

The man was tired. The man climbed all the stairs. • The man who climbed all the stairs was tired.

(The single sentence implies more strongly than the two separate sentences that the man was probably tired because he climbed the stairs. Note that **who** replaces **The man**.)

The buildings burned. The buildings were old. • The buildings that burned were old.

■ ■ ■

Relative pronouns function as the first words of clauses (→ page 246) that give additional information about a noun. Clauses made with relative pronouns are called **dependent clauses** (→ page 217) because they are not sentences by themselves; to make a sentence with such a dependent clause, join it to an **independent clause** (→ page 253).

DEPENDENT CLAUSE: who climbed all the stairs • INDEPENDENT CLAUSE: The man was tired.

SENTENCE: The man who climbed all the stairs was tired.

→ For more on using relative pronouns, see pages 217 and 256–257.

DEMONSTRATIVE PRONOUNS   this, that   these, those

These pronouns help us be specific about a person or object we want to discuss.

This woman is my friend. • That dog belongs to Mavis.

These people went to the museum. • Those buildings are on Washington Street.

In the examples above, the demonstrative pronouns function like adjectives, telling readers exactly what person or thing is meant. Below, the pronouns function like nouns:

This is the most important issue of our time: Are we running out of oil? • That is my best pen.

RECIPROCAL PRONOUNS   each other, one another

Use reciprocal pronouns when you want to show people or objects acting on each other.

The survivors helped one another. • The dogs chased each other.

GRAMMAR—PARTS OF SPEECH
ADJECTIVES
With adjectives, we can describe the specific qualities of people, places, objects, and ideas.

WHICH ONE? WHAT KIND?
Adjectives allow us to specify exactly which people, places, objects, or ideas we want to consider or discuss.

She wore red shoes. • The green ones are comfortable.

HOW MANY?
Adjectives help us say how many people, places, objects, or ideas are at stake.

Four of these potatoes will feed three people.

HOW DO THEY COMPARE?
Adjectives help us specify which people, places, objects, or ideas we mean by allowing us to make comparisons.

Please hand me the smallest book.

The larger of the two books contains less information than the smaller.

PLACEMENT OF ADJECTIVES

1 Adjectives usually come before the nouns they modify:

Use only the sharpest tools to prune your trees. • Last night we saw a brilliant green aurora.
There is no biological reason for this condition.
The jubilant procession danced through the narrow streets.

2 Adjectives come after the verbs *appear*, *be*, *feel*, *look*, *seem*, *smell*, *sound*, and *taste*:

She was not at her sharpest. • The frog looked a brilliant green in the sun.
The reason is purely biological. • The team sounded jubilant after their win.

→ See pages 222–223 to learn how to avoid some problems writers often have with placing adjectival phrases.

IF YOU GREW UP SPEAKING A LANGUAGE OTHER THAN ENGLISH . . .
→ Pages 266–267 offer help in using multiple adjectives.

ARTICLES

Articles are a special kind of adjective. There are three articles: *a*, *an*, and *the*.

THE INDEFINITE ARTICLES *a* AND *an*

A and **an** have the same function: They are used when a noun is not referring to a known or specific person, animal, place, thing, or idea.

■ ■ ■

Use indefinite articles before nouns when you are making general statements:

A computer is useful for homework.

A birthday happens only once a year.

Also use indefinite articles before nouns when you are not writing about a particular person or thing of its kind:

An hour passes quickly when you are focused on your work. *(It could be any hour of the day.)*

■ ■ ■

Use **a** before nouns (or adjectives placed before nouns) that begin with a consonant sound; use **an** before nouns (or adjectives placed before nouns) that begin with a vowel sound.

A knife is useful on a camping trip.

An octopus is an unusual pet.

Note that **h** and **u** can sometimes sound like vowels and sometimes like consonants at the beginning of words. Use the sound of the word following the article to determine whether to use **a** or **an**:

An honest person returned my wallet.

A history book was on the table.

THE DEFINITE ARTICLE *the*

The is used when your reader or listener will know or be able to figure out exactly which person, animal, place, thing, or idea you are describing.

■ ■ ■

To decide whether to use the definite or indefinite article, consider the context in which you are writing or speaking. If you know for sure that your readers or listeners will know the exact person or thing to which you refer, use **the**:

The rosebush needs water.

If you are standing in your yard speaking with neighbors and there is only one rosebush, everyone will know exactly which rosebush you mean.

GRAMMAR—PARTS OF SPEECH

VERBS

Verbs describe what the nouns of a sentence do in time. Verbs are about actions (whether of body or of mind) or about states of being in the present, past, or future.

AT THE PRESENT TIME: The man runs. • The man is running.

IN THE PAST: The man ran. • The man was running.

IN THE FUTURE: The man will run.

THE PATTERN

IN ENGLISH, VERBS CHANGE THEIR FORMS TO INDICATE:

TIME (OR TENSE: past, present, or future).
Some tenses are shown above. (➔ For more on English verb tenses, see pages 208–211.)

WHO IS DOING THE ACTION (OR BEING ACTED ON).
This is called the person of the verb.

first person:	I run.	I was thinking.	We will play.
second person:	You run.	You were thinking.	You will play.
third person:	She runs.	He was thinking.	It will play.

➔ The person of the verb has to agree with the verb form; see pages 204–207.

HOW MANY PEOPLE ARE DOING THE ACTION.
This is called the number of the verb.

singular:	I am thinking.	You, Kris, forgot.	She has run.
plural:	We are thinking.	You three forgot.	They have run.

➔ The number of the verb has to agree with the verb form; see pages 211 and 237.

VOICE.
There are two voices:

active: The person, animal, place, object, or idea named by the noun is performing the action described by the verb: You run. • She will play.

passive: The person, animal, place, object, or idea named by the noun has the action of the verb performed on it: The record was played. • The store was run by two sisters.

➔ For more on the voice of English verbs, see pages 112 and 213.

MOOD.
There are three moods:

indicative, for facts, opinions, and questions: The song plays for twenty minutes.

imperative, for commands and requests: Run! • Please think.

subjunctive, for wishes and hypothetical situations: I wish we could play.

FORMING THE TENSES OF ENGLISH VERBS
Except for the verb **be**, all English verbs have five forms.

	BASE FORM	-S FORM	PRESENT PARTICIPLE	PAST FORM	PAST PARTICIPLE
REGULAR VERB	walk	walks	walking	walked	walked
IRREGULAR VERB	sing	sings	singing	sang	sung
IRREGULAR VERB	ride	rides	riding	rode	ridden

THE BASE FORM
Use the base form to find a verb in a dictionary and to build all a verb's tenses. If you place **to** in front of the base form, you make what is called **the infinitive**.

THE -s FORM
This form is the third person singular present tense of any verb.

THE PRESENT PARTICIPLE
The present participle, made by adding **-ing** to the base form, is used with a helping verb to build any verb's progressive tenses. (If a verb's base form ends in **-e**, the **-e** is dropped before the **-ing**.) The present participle can be used as an adjective: Let sleeping dogs lie.

THE PAST FORM
The past form is used for the simple past tense. Because English has been formed from so many other languages, many frequently used verbs have irregular past forms. A dictionary will show you the past form of any verb.

THE PAST PARTICIPLE
With a helping verb, the past participle is used to construct the perfect tenses of any verb. For regular verbs, the past participle is the same as the past form; for irregular verbs, you will need to check a dictionary to learn the past participle.

→ See page 211 to see all the forms a verb can have.

INFINITIVES
Infinitives are made by putting the word **to** in front of the base form of a verb:

to walk • to talk • to eat • to dream • to argue

Infinitives can function as nouns, adjectives, or adverbs:

To walk is good. • To talk, one must have language. • He lives to eat. • He likes to argue.

MAIN VERBS AND HELPING VERBS

In the patterns on page 237, note that—except for the simple present and simple past—verb tenses are constructed from a main verb and a helping verb (➜ see page 211).

The main verb is one of the five forms of a verb described on the previous page; a helping verb is one of the forms of the irregular verbs **be**, **have**, and **do**.

THE FORMS OF HELPING VERBS

BASE FORM	PRESENT			PAST		
	SINGULAR	PLURAL	PARTICIPLE	SINGULAR	PLURAL	PARTICIPLE
be	I am You are He/She/It is	We are You are They are	being	I was You were He/She/It was	We were You were They were	been
have	I have You have He/She/It has	We have You have They have	having	I had You had He/She/It had	We had You had They had	had
do	I do You do He/She/It does	We do You do They do	doing	I did You did He/She/It did	We did You did They did	done

MODAL HELPING VERBS

Helping verbs also include the verbs called **modals**, whose form never changes: *can*, *could*, *may*, *might*, *must*, *ought to*, *shall*, *should*, *will*, *would*. Modals help us express abilities, possibilities, necessity, intentions, requests, or obligation.

ABILITY, POSSIBILITY, REQUEST: You could have gone running with us last night. • Can you play with our band this weekend?

POSSIBILITY, REQUEST: May I think a little longer about it? • Conrad might run in the race.

OBLIGATION: You must think about a vacation. • The senator ought to run harder in this election.

INTENTIONS: I shall play over the weekend. • You should run over to school. • Jamshed will practice his violin every day.

IF YOU GREW UP SPEAKING A LANGUAGE OTHER THAN ENGLISH . . .

How verb tenses change and how they are used differs considerably from language to language, so—no matter what your home language—pay particular attention to the information about verbs on these pages and on pages 204–211.

GRAMMAR—PARTS OF SPEECH
ADVERBS
Adverbs are most often used to show when, how, or where the action of a verb takes place. Adverbs can also modify adjectives or other adverbs.

ADVERBS OF TIME
Adverbs of time describe when something happened; they can also describe for how long and how often something happens.

She wants food now.   He slept all winter.   She plays sometimes.

ADVERBS OF MANNER
Adverbs of manner describe how something happened. They are usually formed by adding –ly to the end of an adjective.

He shook wildly.   He rolls the ball happily.   She rested lazily.   She waited patiently.

ADVERBS OF PLACE
Adverbs of place describe where or the direction in which something happened.

He walked forward.   She worked uphill.   She sat down.   He jumped high.

PLACEMENT OF ADVERBS
Adverbs generally follow the verb or the object.

She drives the car carefully.   The number of scholarships has dropped considerably.

CREATING EMPHASIS WITH PLACEMENT OF ADVERBS OF MANNER
Adverbs of manner generally go after the verb or object, as noted above—unless you want to emphasize the manner in which something is done. In such cases, you can place adverbs of manner before the verb.

The lion carefully approached the elephants.   The man repeatedly claimed his innocence.

For even more emphasis, you can start a sentence with an adverb of manner.

Belatedly the soldiers received their new protective bodywear.

PLACEMENT OF ADVERBS OF TIME
Adverbs of time that express how often something happens usually go before the verb.

Small refinements in energy production are rarely considered newsworthy.

When an adverb tells the exact number of times something happens, it usually goes at a sentence's end.

The city's alternative newspaper is published weekly.

GRAMMAR—PARTS OF SPEECH
PREPOSITIONS

Prepositions help us express a relationship in time or space between (usually) two nouns in a sentence.

PREPOSITIONS START PREPOSITIONAL PHRASES:

on the Web   in Asia and Europe

at almost the speed of light   to the first year of parenthood

PREPOSITIONAL PHRASES SERVE AS ADJECTIVES OR ADVERBS WITHIN SENTENCES

Would you put your health records on the Web? (In this sentence, *on the Web* is an adverbial prepositional phrase.)

My cellphone works in Asia and Europe. (In this sentence, *in Asia and Europe* is an adverbial prepositional phrase.)

Einstein's special theory of relativity describes the motion of particles at almost the speed of light. (In this sentence, *at almost the speed of light* is an adjectival prepositional phrase.)

Anna and Otto wrote a guide to the first year of parenthood. (In this sentence, *to the first year* is an adjectival prepositional phrase—and so is *of parenthood*.)

Prepositions functioning like adverbs can go anywhere in a sentence, depending on the emphasis you want to give. Prepositions that function like adjectives generally go right after the noun they modify.

IF YOU GREW UP SPEAKING A LANGUAGE OTHER THAN ENGLISH . . .

PREPOSITIONS ARE IDIOMATIC

Certain verbs are followed by certain prepositions: *He was listening to music. We rely on each other.* Checking a verb in the dictionary will tell you which prepositions follow it.

Similarly, certain nouns and adjectives are followed by certain prepositions: *He has an interest in anthropology. She puts emphasis on the importance of rules.* Again, checking nouns and adjectives in the dictionary will tell you which prepositions follow them.

PREPOSITIONS DESCRIBING RELATIONSHIPS IN TIME

The prepositions *at*, *on*, and *in* are conventionally used for certain time relations:

TIME WITH *at*

- exact time: at 3 p.m., at midnight
- meal times: at dinner, at breakfast
- parts of the day, when no article is used for the part of the day: at night, at daybreak, at noon (compare: in the morning, in the evening)
- age: At 21 you are legally considered a full adult.

TIME WITH *on*

- days of the week: on Monday, on Tuesdays
- parts of the day, when the day is named: on Friday evening, on Saturday morning
- dates: on July 28th, on September 22nd

TIME WITH *in*

- seasons: in spring, in summer
- months: in April, in March, in the third month
- years: in 2056, in 1956
- durations: in ten minutes, in one day, in a month

PREPOSITIONS DESCRIBING RELATIONSHIPS IN SPACE

at, by, in, on
show an object's settled position or position after it has moved

I arrived at the Baghdad airport.
In this town most people work at the call center.
They carry their children on their backs.

to, onto, into
show the direction of movement toward a point, surface, or area

They brought their babies to the clinic.
She placed the crown onto his head.
Walking into his office is like walking into a zoo.

by, along, through
show the direction of movement next to or past a point, surface, or area

We drove by the ocean.
From their castles along the Rhine River, German princes could regulate river traffic.
Omero Catan, a salesperson from New York, drove the first car through the Lincoln Tunnel after waiting in line for 30 hours.

from, out of
show the direction of movement away from a point, surface, or area

The *joropo* is a waltzy musical form from Venezuela.
After the airplane crashed, she had to walk out of the jungle.

CONJUNCTIONS

Conjunctions connect words or groups of words. There are four kinds of conjunctions, each of which helps you express different kinds of relations between the words you are connecting.

THE PATTERN

COORDINATING CONJUNCTIONS

Coordinating conjunctions can connect nouns (including pronouns), adjectives, adverbs, prepositions, clauses, and sentences.

Use a coordinating conjunction when you want a reader to see that the words you are connecting have equal—coordinate—emphasis. The coordinating conjunctions, together with the relations they show, are

and	addition	Jacob and Ali went to the store. Loretta cooked and ate dinner.
for	cause	The dog is wet, for she swam. I am hungry, for I forgot to eat.
but, yet	contrast	Jacob went to the store, but Ali stayed home. Loretta cooked dinner, yet she did not eat right away.
or	choice	Jacob or Ali can go. • Loretta can cook dinner or eat out.
so	effect	I am hungry, so I will eat. The dog is wet from the rain, so I will dry her.
nor	exclusion	José doesn't swim, nor do I.

To connect individual words—such as nouns (including pronouns), adjectives, adverbs, and prepositions—**or phrases,** use this pattern:

| WORD OR PHRASE | COORDINATING CONJUNCTION | WORD OR PHRASE |

To connect sentences, use this pattern:

| INDEPENDENT CLAUSE | , | COORDINATING CONJUNCTION | INDEPENDENT CLAUSE | . |

CORRELATIVE CONJUNCTIONS

Correlative conjunctions are like coordinating conjunctions in that they help you give equal emphasis to the words you are connecting—but correlative conjunctions come in two parts, and readers always expect to see both parts:

both . . . and, not only . . . but also
addition

Both Miguel and Rav are on vacation.
She did both her English and her math work.

either . . . or, whether . . . or
choice

I could hire either Paul or Shawna.
I want either to go out for dinner or to sleep.
Either you will eat at home, or you will go out.

just as . . . so
equality

Just as the air's smell brought back memories, so too
did the bread's taste.

neither . . . nor
exclusion

Neither this car nor that one is running.
Neither will Omi go out, nor will she stay in!

To connect **individual words**—such as nouns (including pronouns), adjectives, adverbs, and prepositions—**or phrases**, use this pattern:

WORD OR PHRASE	CORRELATIVE CONJUNCTION, PART 1	WORD OR PHRASE	CORRELATIVE CONJUNCTION, PART 2

To connect sentences, use this pattern:

CORRELATIVE CONJUNCTION, PART 1	INDEPENDENT CLAUSE	,	CORRELATIVE CONJUNCTION, PART 2	INDEPENDENT CLAUSE	.

SUBORDINATING CONJUNCTIONS

These conjunctions join two sentences. The sentence following the conjunction is subordinate to—less emphasized than—the other sentence.

as, because, since cause or reason	I am angry because she told lies. Since you left, our group has no women.
so that effect or result	He packs a lunch so that he can save money. So that you can travel, you must get a passport.
if, even if, provided that, unless condition	You couldn't get in even if you wanted. If you want, he can bake the cake.
although, even though, though contrast	He took the test even though he had not studied. Although she was tired, she went out.
where, wherever location	Nan sings wherever there is karaoke. Wherever Heather goes, laughter follows.
after, before, once, since, until, when, whenever, while time	She went to the movies after she had dinner. While it rains, the city cannot fix the road.

Putting a subordinating conjunction in front of a sentence turns the sentence into a dependent clause.

When you put the dependent clause at the beginning of a sentence, put a comma after it:

SUBORDINATING CONJUNCTION	INDEPENDENT CLAUSE	INDEPENDENT CLAUSE

When you join two sentences by putting a subordinating conjunction between them, you need no comma:

INDEPENDENT CLAUSE	SUBORDINATING CONJUNCTION	INDEPENDENT CLAUSE

CONJUNCTIVE ADVERBS

Independent clauses can be joined with a semicolon and conjunctive adverb to show the relationships listed here:

also, besides, furthermore, moreover	addition	We don't need a car; besides, we can't afford one. The city repaved our street; moreover, they put up a new sign.
however, instead, likewise, nevertheless, nonetheless, otherwise, similarly, still	comparison and contrast	We could eat; otherwise, we should go home. Their team went into the game with a three point advantage; nonetheless, they lost.
accordingly, consequently, hence, then, therefore, thus	result or summary	The jury found her not guilty; thus, she was freed. She went home with a migraine; consequently, she missed the lecture.
finally, meanwhile, next, now, then	time	The first expedition set out; meanwhile, the second expedition gathered its equipment.

When you use conjunctive adverbs, start with an independent clause followed by a semicolon; then, put the conjunction (followed by a comma) and then put the second independent clause.

INDEPENDENT CLAUSE **;** CONJUNCTIVE ADVERB **,** INDEPENDENT CLAUSE **.**

BUILDING SENTENCES

THE PARTS OF SPEECH (→ see pages 231–245)

NOUNS: Society, Diffusion, Knowledge, members, *Magazine*, *Cyclopedia*, practices, audience

PRONOUNS: its

ARTICLES: the

ADJECTIVES: nineteenth-century, Useful, working-class

ADVERBS: Really

CONJUNCTIONS: and

PREPOSITIONS: of

VERBS: published, distributed, worried

HELPING VERBS: were

ADVERBS: widely

CONJUNCTIONS: and

NOUN PHRASES

The nineteenth-century Society for the Diffusion of Really Useful Knowledge

The Penny Magazine and *The Penny Cyclopedia*

its members

the reading practices of its working-class audience

VERB PHRASES

published and distributed widely

were worried

SUBJECTS

The nineteenth-century Society for the Diffusion of Really Useful Knowledge

its members

PREDICATES

published and distributed widely *The Penny Magazine* and *The Penny Cyclopedia*

were worried about the reading practices of its working-class audience.

CLAUSES, of which there are two kinds, INDEPENDENT and DEPENDENT

The nineteenth-century Society for the Diffusion of Really Useful Knowledge published and distributed widely *The Penny Magazine* and *The Penny Cyclopedia*

because its members were worried about the reading practices of its working-class audience.

A SENTENCE

The nineteenth-century Society for the Diffusion of Really Useful Knowledge published and distributed widely *The Penny Magazine* and *The Penny Cyclopedia* because its members were worried about the reading practices of its working-class audience.

THERE ARE 4 SENTENCE FUNCTIONS.
With sentences, we can . . .

1 MAKE STATEMENTS
DECLARATIVE SENTENCES are the main kind of sentence you will see in all writing.
In the fifth and sixth centuries, Ireland was the center of high culture in Europe.

2 ASK QUESTIONS
INTERROGATIVE SENTENCES matter in all writing. In academic writing, authors often use questions to set up the problems they want to address.
How lethal was the flu of 1918? • What is it like to live in the most notorious prison in the country?

3 COMMAND
IMPERATIVE SENTENCES tell someone to do something. You find them in instruction sets and manuals. (They begin with the implied subject *You*.)
Watch out that the temperature of the beaker's contents does not rise above 275°.

4 BE EMOTIONAL
EXCLAMATORY SENTENCES express strong feeling and end with exclamation points.
If the electrons are not seen, we have interference!

THERE ARE 4 SENTENCE PATTERNS.
All American English sentences are built following one of the following patterns:

1 SIMPLE SENTENCES are used in all writing and are the building block for the other sentence patterns:
Dogs bark. • Children love robots. • They tracked the experiment and wrote their report.

2 COMPOUND SENTENCES join two simple sentences and are important in formal writing because they help you express relationships among the elements of your sentences.
An autumn wind gusts up to thirty miles an hour; a winter wind can gust up to fifty miles an hour.

3 COMPLEX SENTENCES allow you to express complicated relations among the elements you describe and so are important in academic and other formal writing.
In this chapter I examine the development of Piaget's thought, which has three main features.

4 COMPOUND-COMPLEX SENTENCES result when you combine a compound sentence with a complex sentence. These sentences tend to be long and are used almost exclusively in academic writing.
In the Sung and Yuan dynasties of the twelfth to fourteenth centuries A.D., the Chinese school led the world in solving equations; the triangle we call Pascal's was already old in China in 1300 A.D.

SIMPLE SENTENCES

Two words can make a sentence. The first word names a person, place, thing, or idea; the second word describes what that person, place, thing, or idea is, was, or will be doing.

THE BASIC PATTERN

PERSON, PLACE, THING, OR IDEA + ACTION = SIMPLEST SENTENCE

NOUN	VERB
Sylvia	swam.
Water	glistens.
Dogs	barked.
You	smile.
Happiness	is.
SUBJECT	**PREDICATE**
INDEPENDENT CLAUSE	

You can add descriptions to the nouns and verbs in the most basic sentences:

ADDING TO THE BASIC PATTERN

NOUN AND DESCRIPTION + VERB AND DESCRIPTION = SENTENCE

NOUN PHRASE	VERB PHRASE
The woman	swam slowly.
Blue water	glistens lightly.
A dog	barked loudly.
You	smile widely.
Our happiness	stays still.
SUBJECT	**PREDICATE**
INDEPENDENT CLAUSE	

To the nouns and verbs in the most basic sentences you can also add objects, which are the persons or things acted on by the subject.

ADDING TO THE BASIC PATTERN

NOUN PHRASE + VERB PHRASE + OBJECT (NOUN PHRASE) = SENTENCE

The woman	quickly walks	her barking dog.
An irritated man	slapped	a whiny mosquito.
The chair legs	dented	the floor.
The wind	easily moves	the lake water.
She	shifted	her weight.
You	warily watch	the changing weather.
I	make	the bed.
Our happiness	fills me.	

SUBJECT   PREDICATE

INDEPENDENT CLAUSE

→ To learn more about nouns, see pages 230 and 231.

→ To learn more about verbs, see pages 204–211 and 236–238.

→ To learn more about subjects, see pages 250–252. To learn more about predicates, see pages 250–252.

→ A subject and predicate together form a clause (page 246); when they can stand alone as a sentence, they are independent clauses (page 253).

→ The words that help us say descriptive things about nouns are called adjectives (page 234). Articles are the words *a, an,* and *the* and are a special kind of adjective (page 235).

→ The words that help us say descriptive things about verbs are called adverbs (page 239).

→ When nouns and verbs have descriptive words added to them, as above, they are called (respectively) noun phrases and verb phrases (page 246 in addition to this and the previous page).

GRAMMAR—SENTENCES
SUBJECTS & PREDICATES

To move from writing simple sentences to writing compound, complex, and compound-complex sentences, writers need to understand subjects and predicates.

SUBJECTS

Subjects are the word or words in a sentence that name who or what is performing some action. Subjects can be composed of one word (in which case it is always a noun) or multiple words (in which case they are some combination of nouns and articles, conjunctions, and/or adjectives).

Yang smiles.

Michael and the new student went to lunch together.

Their sad songs filled the valley and echoed in the air.

SUBJECT

→ To learn more about the kinds of words that make up subjects, see pages 231–233 for nouns and pronouns, page 234 for adjectives, page 235 for articles, and pages 242–245 for conjunctions.

SUBJECT-VERB AGREEMENT

→ In formal English, the subject of a sentence agrees with the verb in person and number. To learn how this works, see pages 204–207.

PREDICATES

Predicates are the words in a sentence that describe the action taken by the subject. Predicates can be made of one word (in which case it is always a verb) or multiple words (in which case they are some combination of verbs and adverbs, conjunctions, or noun phrases that are objects).

Yang smiles.

Michael and the new student went to lunch together.

Their sad songs filled the valley and echoed in the air.

PREDICATE

→ To learn more about the kinds of words that make up predicates, see pages 236–238 for verbs, page 239 for adverbs, page 249 for objects, pages 230 and 248–249 for noun phrases, and pages 242–245 for conjunctions.

COMPOUND SUBJECTS & PREDICATES

You can use the patterns on the preceding pages to build more detailed sentences. One way to do this is to use a kind of word called a **conjunction** to build:

SUBJECTS THAT DESCRIBE MORE THAN ONE PERSON, PLACE, THING, OR IDEA

You can substitute any of the following subjects for any of the noun phrases in the simple sentence patterns on the preceding pages (as long as you make the verb agree):

Sylvia and Luisa walk.

Neither the air nor my heart moved.

Dogs or coyotes barked last night outside my window.

Paul, Tonio, and I make the beds.

SUBJECT   PREDICATE

The subjects above are called **compound subjects** because they are compounded out of multiple nouns.

→ Note that the form of the verb sometimes has to change when you change the subject of a sentence; see pages 204–207 and 236–238.

PREDICATES THAT DESCRIBE MORE THAN ONE ACTION

You can substitute any of the following predicates for any of the verb phrases in the simple sentence patterns on the preceding pages (as long as the subject and predicate agree in number):

Sylvia walks or runs.

My heart jumped and stilled.

The dogs both barked and snored loudly.

Paul makes the bed and sweeps the floor.

SUBJECT   PREDICATE

The predicates above are called **compound predicates** because they are made of multiple predicates.

→ To learn more about conjunctions, see pages 242–245.

USING PREPOSITIONAL PHRASES TO MAKE MORE DESCRIPTIVE SUBJECTS AND PREDICATES

Prepositions are kinds of words that allow you to say more precisely where a noun is in space or time or where the action of a verb takes place. Prepositions do this by being the first word of **prepositional phrases**, which show where one noun is in relation to another or where the action of a verb takes place relative to some noun. Prepositional phrases thus allow you to make subjects and predicates that can be very descriptive.

MORE DESCRIPTIVE SUBJECTS

As parts of subjects, prepositional phrases function like adjectives, telling your readers more about the nouns you are using:

The dog on the sidewalk was barking.

The air in the tent shimmered.

Hiro, on the telephone, sounds less serious.

Children at school tend to be quieter.

SUBJECT   PREDICATE

MORE DESCRIPTIVE PREDICATES

As parts of predicates, prepositional phrases function like adverbs, telling your readers more about the action being described by the verb, such as where or when the action happens or happened:

Sylvia walks into the store.

My heart jumped at the sound of your voice.

The dogs hid underneath the table.

Peng makes the bed over the course of the day.

SUBJECT   PREDICATE

→ To learn more about prepositions, see pages 240–241.

→ To learn more about adverbs, see page 239.

INDEPENDENT CLAUSES

Consider what *independent* and *dependent* mean: Something that is independent can stand alone; something that is dependent cannot.

Independent clauses can be sentences, and dependent clauses cannot.

THE PATTERN

AN INDEPENDENT CLAUSE CAN STAND ALONE AS A SIMPLE SENTENCE

SUBJECT + PREDICATE = INDEPENDENT CLAUSE

Nazila bikes.

Dogs and coyotes bark in the lonely night.

The cell was large and unevenly shaped.

The fast growth of cities encumbers mapmakers.

When an independent clause stands by itself, it is a simple sentence. When it is combined with dependent clauses (as we show on the next pages), you build complex sentences.

→ See page 217 to learn more about dependent clauses.

COMPOUND SENTENCES

Compound sentences are made up of two or more simple sentences joined by punctuation or conjunctions—or both punctuation and conjunctions.

THE FUNCTIONS OF COMPOUND SENTENCES

When you write with compound sentences, your sentences can show readers more complex relations among events than simple sentences allow. Compound sentences show up frequently in academic writing.

Because compound sentences are made up of two independent clauses joined together, they show that the writer wants to give equal emphasis to both clauses.

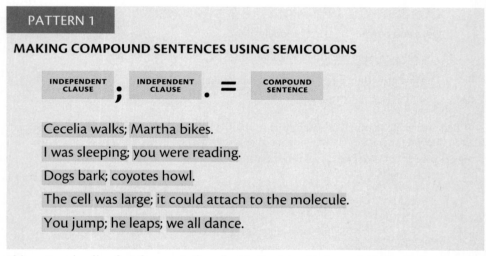

PATTERN 1

MAKING COMPOUND SENTENCES USING SEMICOLONS

INDEPENDENT CLAUSE **;** INDEPENDENT CLAUSE **. =** COMPOUND SENTENCE

Cecelia walks; Martha bikes.

I was sleeping; you were reading.

Dogs bark; coyotes howl.

The cell was large; it could attach to the molecule.

You jump; he leaps; we all dance.

This pattern implies that the events described in the joined independent clauses happened at the same time and are of equal importance.

→ To learn more about using semicolons to join two independent clauses, see page 280.

PATTERN 2

MAKING COMPOUND SENTENCES USING COMMAS AND COORDINATING CONJUNCTIONS

| INDEPENDENT CLAUSE | **,** | COORDINATING CONJUNCTION | INDEPENDENT CLAUSE | **.** | **=** | COMPOUND SENTENCE |

Cecelia walks, and Martha bikes.

I was sleeping, while you were reading.

Dogs bark, but coyotes howl.

The cell was large, but it could attach to the molecule.

This pattern uses **coordinating conjunctions**.

→ To learn more about coordinating conjunctions and the relations they can help you build between independent clauses, see page 242.

PATTERN 3

MAKING COMPOUND SENTENCES USING SEMICOLONS, CONJUNCTIVE ADVERBS, AND COMMAS

Some kinds of conjunctions take the following pattern for joining independent clauses (note the comma after the conjunction):

| INDEPENDENT CLAUSE | **;** | CONJUNCTIVE ADVERB | **,** | INDEPENDENT CLAUSE | **.** | **=** | COMPOUND SENTENCE |

Cecelia walks; meanwhile, Martha bikes.

I slept; instead, you read.

It rained while we were there; moreover, it was cold.

She was found innocent; accordingly, she will go free.

This pattern uses **conjunctive adverbs**.

→ To learn more about conjunctive adverbs, see page 245.

COMPLEX SENTENCES

Complex sentences combine one independent clause with at least one dependent clause.

THE FUNCTION OF COMPLEX SENTENCES

Complex sentences show readers more complex relations among events than simple sentences because complex sentences are made of two clauses, one of which—the independent clause—will always have more emphasis than the other.

PATTERN 1

COMPLEX SENTENCES WITH ADJECTIVE CLAUSES

RELATIVE PRONOUN + PREDICATE = ADJECTIVE CLAUSE

which was in the street

whose shape kept changing

Adjective clauses allow you to give additional information about subjects, and so they help you write expressive sentences. Adjective clauses are inserted into independent clauses to make **THE FIRST KIND OF COMPLEX SENTENCE**:

The bicycle, which was in the street, is missing.

The cell whose shape kept changing has been identified.

→ To learn more about relative pronouns, see page 233 (and also page 217).

→ To learn more about the punctuation of adjective phrases when you weave them into independent clauses, see pages 272–275. Pay close attention to this; punctuating adjective phrases can cause writers trouble.

Adjective clauses can look like independent clauses because they have a similar structure to sentences: There is a word and then a predicate. But, in formal English, relative pronouns cannot take the place of nouns—and so adjective clauses cannot stand alone as sentences.

NOT SENTENCES
which was in the street

whose shape kept changing

→ The phrases above are fragments of sentences that can be turned into sentences. To learn more about sentence fragments, see pages 214–217.

SENTENCES
If, in the adjective clauses above, you were to replace the relative pronouns with subjects, you would have sentences:

The bicycle was in the street.

The cell's shape kept changing.

SENTENCES
Sometimes, if you put a question mark on the end of an adjective clause—and you capitalize the first letter of the relative pronoun—you can make interrogatory sentences out of adjective clauses:

Whose shape kept changing?

When you do this, you are changing the function of the pronoun, and so you are changing the type of the pronoun, from a relative pronoun to an interrogative pronoun.

→ To learn more about interrogative pronouns, see page 232.

COMPLEX SENTENCES WITH ADVERB CLAUSES

SUBORDINATING CONJUNCTION + SUBJECT + PREDICATE = ADVERB CLAUSE

after it rains

while the cell's shape changed

Adverb clauses help writers express complex ideas and so are important in academic writing. Add adverb clauses to independent clauses to make **THE SECOND KIND OF COMPLEX SENTENCE**, which express subtle relationships.

After it rains, we will go for a bike ride.

While the cell's shape changed, it could not be identified.

→ To learn more about subordinating conjunctions, see page 244.

WATCH OUT FOR THIS!

Adverb clauses are not independent clauses, so they cannot stand alone as sentences.

NOT SENTENCES

after it rains

while the cell's shape changed

→ The phrases above are fragments of sentences that can be turned into sentences. To learn more about sentence fragments, see pages 214–217.

SENTENCES

If you remove the subordinating conjunctions or correlative adverbs, you have sentences:

It rains.

The cell's shape kept changing.

COMPOUND-COMPLEX SENTENCES

Compound-complex sentences are a sure sign of academic writing. Writers who know how to compose and mix compound and complex sentences into compound-complex sentences are writers who can build sentences for the widest range of contexts and purposes.

THE PATTERN

Compound-complex sentences consist of two or more independent clauses, at least one of which contains a dependent clause. The sentences can be joined in any of the ways compound sentences can be made.

Because compound-complex sentences are composed of many parts, they tend to be long:

> Young people who came of age during the Progressive Era years of 1910 to 1914 had grown up during a time of optimism and change, and they believed in a living wage for workers, reduced corporate power, and equitably distributed wealth.

Below you can see how this compound-complex sentence consists of:

- An independent clause, which is a complex sentence because it contains the dependent clause *who came of age in the Progressive Era years of 1910 to 1914*.
- A comma after the first independent clause.
- The conjunction *and*.
- A simple sentence.

> Young people who came of age during the Progressive Era years of 1910 to 1914 had grown up during a time of optimism and change, and they believed in a living wage for workers, reduced corporate power, and equitably distributed wealth.

PUNCTUATION

Before writing, there was no punctuation: People simply spoke, not thinking of what they said as being words, much less as being divided up by punctuation. People simply put sounds together in different orders, and they understood each other.

After the invention of writing, it was still many centuries before punctuation (or even spaces between words) was invented. What seems to have given rise to punctuation was the need for speakers to read printed words aloud to listeners, as in churches. Imagine reading this passage aloud if you hadn't had time to figure out the passage beforehand:

most punctuation marks are composed to be seen but not heard these subtle often understated devices are quite important however for they are the meter that determines the measure within the silent voice of typography punctuation directs tempo pitch volume and the separation of words periods signify full stops commas slow the reader down question marks change pitch quotation marks indicate references

Punctuation is thus an important part of writing to communicate: It shows readers how you are shaping your ideas, where you are putting emphasis, and when you are using others' words.

There is considerable room for you to choose how to punctuate in order to reach the audiences for whom you write—but the information in the following pages will help you make informed decisions.

THERE ARE TWO MAIN DIVISIONS OF PUNCTUATION MARKS:

PUNCTUATION THAT GOES WITHIN SENTENCES
- commas
- semicolons
- colons
- parentheses
- dashes
- brackets
- hyphens
- slashes
- quotation marks
- apostrophes

PUNCTUATION THAT GOES AT THE END OF SENTENCES
- periods
- exclamation points
- question marks

AND . . .

There is another form of punctuation that is not really a mark and that you might not think of as punctuation, but—like all punctuation—it is very important for helping readers understand where sentences begin and end:

CAPITALIZATION

COMMAS now have four main uses.

1
MAKING NUMBERS, PLACE-NAMES, AND DATES CLEAR

To learn how and when to use commas in sentences like the following—

Virginia's population was 1,000,000 in 1830.

If you visit Emily Dickinson's house in Amherst, Massachusetts, you won't see anything that truly belonged to Emily Dickinson.

Abraham Lincoln was shot the night of April 14, 1865, and died the following morning.

→ GO TO PAGE 262.

2
INDICATING WHEN YOU ARE QUOTING (EXACTLY) THE WORDS OF SOMEONE ELSE

To learn how and when to use commas in sentences like the following—

"The real problem with having a robot to dinner," argues Ellen Ullman, "is pleasure."

—or to learn about the following kinds of sentences (in which you aren't quoting someone else's words directly)—

Ellen Ullman argues that pleasure (or the lack of it) is why people don't have robots to dinner.

→ GO TO PAGE 263.

3
SEPARATING WORDS THAT ARE PARTS OF LISTS IN SENTENCES

To learn how and when to use commas in sentences like the following—

The stinking, reeking water roiled down the street.

She caught a cab, her breath, and then the flu.

He was livid, he was angry, and he was mad.

→ GO TO PAGE 264.

4
BUILDING SENTENCES THAT CONTAIN MULTIPLE PARTS

To learn how and when to use commas in sentences like the following—

Her father, who was born in Saudi Arabia, always longed for the hottest days in August.

Can you bring me the ladder, which is in the backyard?

He looked up at me, and he burst into tears.

→ GO TO PAGE 268.

COMMA USE 1
MAKING NUMBERS, PLACE-NAMES, AND DATES CLEAR

NUMBERS

When you are writing numbers, use commas to separate the digits in numbers higher than 999.

1,000 (but 999)   2,304,504 $87,000,000,000

Note that the commas separate the long numbers into groups of three, *moving from the right to the left*:

In 1889 more than 3,000,000 acres in the Indian Territory, now Oklahoma, were opened to non-Indian homesteaders; a territory that had held virtually no non-Indians in 1880 had 730,000 in 1900.

Large money amounts work the same way:

On the $65,000,000 bond sale, Morgan and Belmont made a perfectly legal profit somewhere between $1,500,000 and $16,000,000.

BUT!

In the examples above, notice that there are no commas in numbers that represent years. It is also conventional not to use commas in street addresses:

20419 West Second Street

DATES

Only one of the common formats for written dates in the United States requires a comma:

1 February 17, 1951

When you write a date in month-day-year order, put a comma after the day:

On January 26, 1950, the Constitution of India was adopted.

2 17 Feb. 1951

If you need to give a date in an MLA citation, a comma is not used within the date itself:

Sutliff, Amileah. "SXSW Explores Concept of Creative Safe Spaces." *Daily Cardinal*, 28 Mar. 2016, p. 7.

→ See pages 160–161 for more information on this use of dates.

3 February 1951

If you write only the month and year, you do not need a comma between them:

In February 1912 La Follette delivered an angry, rambling, and—according to some—drunken speech, extinguishing whatever chances he had had for the nomination.

PLACE-NAMES

In writing a location and a larger place of which it is part—such as a neighborhood in a city, a city in a state, a state or province in a country—separate the place-names with commas:

Neighborhood, city: Algiers, New Orleans   •   *City, state:* Houghton, Michigan

State, country: Oregon, United States   •   *Province, country:* Tangier, Morocco

In 1948, Adrian Piper, an artist and philosopher, was born in Harlem, New York City.

To finish his Ph.D. at the University of California, Davis, he had to figure out how to leash a rattlesnake.

To put a multiline address onto one line, put commas between the sections:

Please send your donations to Habitat for Humanity/Metro Jackson, P.O. Box 55634, Jackson, MS 39296.

COMMA USE 2
INDICATING WHEN YOU ARE QUOTE (EXACTLY) SOMEONE ELSE'S WORDS

When you embed someone else's spoken or written words into your own, use commas to separate the words you quote from the phrases that signal you are quoting:

"I've got to sing," he said, hoarsely.

WHEN YOU DON'T BREAK UP THE SENTENCES YOU QUOTE

You can put quoted words at the beginning or at the end of a sentence.

"Keep the hard hat on," she said to me.

As the poet W. H. Auden put it, "The chances are that, in the course of his lifetime, the major poet will write more bad poems than the minor."

In the first case, notice that the comma goes inside the quotation mark and before the *she said* phrase. In the second, the comma goes after the (equivalent of the) *she said* phrase, before and outside the quotation mark.

WHEN YOU DO BREAK UP THE SENTENCES YOU QUOTE

You can break up others' words for effect:

"Why," asks Jonathan Burt, "should the rat be such an apt figure for horror?"

Note the placement of the two commas.

→ See pages 55–59 for help in thinking about how and why to incorporate the words of others in your academic writing.

→ See pages 292–293 for more information on using quotation marks to punctuate quotations.

WHEN YOU DON'T QUOTE A WHOLE SENTENCE

Use no comma *before* the quoted words because the quoted words are not sentences.

In describing his cityscapes of Paris, Fox Talbot says that photography "chronicles whatever it sees," noting the complex and jumbled array of chimney pots and lightning rods.

WHEN YOU QUOTE SEVERAL SENTENCES

If the sentences all follow the signalling phrase, put a comma after the phrase:.

The cop observed, "In the older generations we didn't even drink a beer. If your mom and dad smelled a beer on you, oh my God, you might have to stay in for a year."

If you put the signalling phrase between the sentences, put a comma before the phrase:

"It was the sociological nadir of the American spirit," a Pepsi executive recalled. "Protests. Woodstock. Drugs. A surly and sullen generation occupying the dean's office, burning it down—whatever it was. It was all that sixties stuff."

WHEN YOU DON'T QUOTE WORDS EXACTLY

When you do not quote someone's exact words, you use indirect quotation. In indirect quotation, you do not use quotation marks or commas. Very often, *that* introduces the words that are being indirectly quoted.

INDIRECT QUOTATION:
Mr. Quiring told me that essays and stories come to a preordained ending out of a writer's control.

DIRECT QUOTATION:
In class, Mr. Quiring said, "Essays and stories come to a preordained ending organically—completely out of a writer's control!"

COMMA USE 3
SEPARATING WORDS THAT ARE PARTS OF LISTS IN SENTENCES

In official grammar-speak, a list of words—such as *dogs, tables, justice, snow,* and *imagination*— is referred to as a series.

1

If you are listing only two nouns, verbs, adjectives, phrases, or clauses in a sentence, here is the pattern to follow:

▭ **and** ▭

For example:

She ran and dove into the water.

or

The audience sing-along was flaccid and unenthusiastic.

2

If you are combining **three or more** nouns, verbs, adjectives, phrases, or clauses, here is the pattern to follow:

▭ **,** ▭ **, and** ▭

For example:

She grinned, ran, and dove into the water.

or

The audience sing-along was short, flaccid, and unenthusiastic.

This pattern can be expanded to include any number of items:

In the past week we had rain, hail, snow, and a desire for springtime.

USING COMMAS IN LISTS OF INDIVIDUAL NOUNS

When you list only two nouns in a sentence, no comma is necessary:

A hat and gloves are necessary for winter.

We find ourselves entering a realm of fantasy and paradox.

When you make a list of three or more nouns, put a comma after each item in the list—except the last:

A hat, gloves, and boots are necessary for winter.

After spending the bulk of the afternoon talking with patients who had no idea what year, month, or day it is, I myself felt rather disoriented.

Mr. Armstrong pleased most of the audience; he has timing, charisma, and plenty of eyeliner—and he's not afraid to sweat.

The player is then set loose in a huge, colorful fantasy world with cities, plains, oceans, mountains, forests, rivers, jungles, deserts, and (of course) dungeons.

Other writers who scholars have argued had temporal lobe epilepsy include Tennyson, Lear, Poe, Swinburne, Byron, de Maupassant, Molière, Pascal, Petrarch, Dante, Teresa of Avila, and Saint Paul.

USING COMMAS IN LISTS OF INDIVIDUAL VERBS

When you list only two verbs in a sentence, no comma is necessary:

The infant burped and grinned.

I learned to shovel coal and haul clinkers at an early age.

When you make a list of three or more verbs, put a comma after each item in the list—except the last:

On that rooftop, she sees, imagines, and remembers.

Lawrence North High School basketball center Greg Oden passes, blocks, shoots, scores, rebounds, and smiles.

→ The ability to use commas as we describe on these pages is important in building parallelism, which is a form of list building. See page 115 to learn about parallelism.

USING COMMAS IN LISTS OF PHRASES AND CLAUSES

As with nouns and verbs, when you list three or more phrases or clauses, use a comma between each.

Furious, Buffmeier walked through the front door, exited to the back, crossed the parking lot, and went into his shack.

Gilligan's work emphasizes relationships over rules, connection over isolation, caring over violence, and a web of relationships over hierarchy.

The Egyptians mummified their dead in a complex process that involved pulling the brain through the nostrils with an iron hook, washing the body with incense, and, in later dynasties, covering it with bitumen and linen.

BUT!

Use semicolons—and not commas—between a series of phrases that themselves contain commas:

The four common principles that ran through much of this thought through the end of the Cold War were a concern with democracy, human rights, and, more generally, the internal politics of states; a belief that American power can be used for moral purposes; a skepticism about the ability of international law and institutions to solve serious security problems; and, finally, a view that ambitious social engineering often leads to unexpected consequences and thereby undermines its own ends.

USING COMMAS IN LISTS OF INDIVIDUAL ADJECTIVES

When you put together two or more adjectives, you have to decide two things:

1	&	2
whether or not to use a comma between them		whether to use **and** between them.

WHEN TO USE A COMMA OR *and* IN LISTS OF ADJECTIVES

Use a comma or *and* to separate two adjectives if you can change their order without changing the meaning of the sentence. For example, the meaning of

He was a thin, dapper fellow who preferred a suit and vest to ordinary clothes.

isn't changed when it is written as

He was a dapper, thin fellow who preferred a suit and vest to ordinary clothes.

or as

He was a thin and dapper fellow who preferred a suit and vest to ordinary clothes.

In these examples, *thin* and *dapper* are called **coordinate adjectives**, the name for adjectives whose order can be changed without the meaning of the sentence changing.

WHEN TO USE NEITHER A COMMA NOR *and* IN LISTS OF ADJECTIVES

If you cannot rearrange the adjectives in a sentence without changing the meaning of the sentence, do not put a comma between them, *no matter how many adjectives you are using*:

The prize for my banana costume was a radio designed to look like a box of frozen niblets corn.

This sentence does not have a comma between *frozen* and *niblets* because, in the United States, we would not say *niblets frozen corn* or *niblets and frozen corn*.

Here is another example:

Three huge gray whales swam by.

Because *three* is describing how many huge gray whales this writer saw, *three* goes before the other adjectives.

Adjectives that cannot be rearranged are called **noncoordinate adjectives**, and they do not have commas between them.

WHEN TO USE A COMMA AND *and* IN LISTS OF ADJECTIVES

When you have three or more adjectives whose order can be changed without changing the meaning of the sentence, use the same pattern as with lists of nouns, verbs, phrases, and clauses. Put a comma after each of the adjectives except the last:

Reappropriate.com is a political, current-events, and personal blog written from the perspective of a loud and proud Asian American woman.

We have come to know zero intimately in its mathematical, physical, and psychological embodiments.

WHEN CAN YOU OMIT COMMAS?

Sometimes writers want to emphasize the length of time that goes into a series of actions, so they link the words or phrases of a series with *and* or *or*:

Instead, we arrange the platters of food and remove bread from the oven and fill cups with grape juice and wine.

The example at the left is correct, as is the example below (which creates a quicker sense of the time involved in all the actions):

Instead, we arrange the platters of food, remove bread from the oven, and fill cups with grape juice and wine.

COMMA USE 4
BUILDING SENTENCES THAT CONTAIN MULTIPLE PARTS

Here is a paragraph of simple sentences:

There was a racist bombing of a church in Alabama. This happened in 1963. *ID* magazine published an article about race in industrial design. The article discussed only one female African American designer. Her name is Madeleine Ward.

Here are those sentences joined into one:

In 1963, in response to a racist bombing of a church in Alabama, *ID* magazine published an article about race in industrial design, but they discussed only one female African American designer, Madeleine Ward.

The ideas are more tightly woven together in the single sentence, and (some would argue) they suggest more strongly than the individual sentences that something is wrong with the magazine article if it discusses only one female African American designer.

If you decide that the audience and purpose motivating your writing require using sentences like the single-sentence example, then your sentences will need commas. When you write such sentences, which complicate the basic subject-verb-object structure, commas set off the sentence's parts and help readers see and better understand how the sentence's parts relate to each other.

There are two patterns for building such sentences:

1

USING COMMAS TO ADD ONE SENTENCE ONTO THE END OF ANOTHER

To learn how and when to use commas in sentences like the following—

Her body seems distracted, but her mind is not.

Every limb was broken, and he ended up a triple amputee.

Music has got to be useful for survival, or we would have gotten rid of it years ago.

Will I get a second chance, or am I supposed to remain a suspect for the rest of my life?

One woman in each tent started dinner, and the other finished securing the tent and sleds for the night.

St. Sebastian was condemned to be shot by arrows, but a tradition says that he survived this torment only to be stoned to death.

→ GO TO PAGE 270 TO SEE THIS PATTERN.

2

USING COMMAS TO ADD ADDITIONAL INFORMATION TO THE MAIN IDEA OF A SENTENCE

To learn how and when to use commas in sentences like the following—

A parrot that cannot talk or sing is, we feel, an incomplete parrot.

Kudos are due to Dwyane Wade, who pretty much single-handedly won the NBA Finals.

Without raising his voice above a murmur, this artist-thinker gives the condition of exile an existential, universalist weight.

The freshwater vertebrates, originally found in the slow waters of East India, are fast replacing the lab rat as a prime model for studies in genetics and development.

→ GO TO PAGE 272 TO SEE THIS PATTERN.

→ The kinds of sentences we discuss here are part of the style of most academic writing; see page 113 to learn about other aspects of the style of academic writing.

USING COMMAS TO ADD ONE SENTENCE ONTO THE END OF ANOTHER

THE PATTERN

When you combine two sentences, one convention of written English is to put a comma and then a coordinating conjunction between the two:

INDEPENDENT CLAUSE	COORDINATING CONJUNCTION	INDEPENDENT CLAUSE

and
but
or
nor
for
so
yet

For example,

We passed them buckets of water , and they threw the water onto the fire.

or

He swung his arms wildly , but the mosquitoes still swarmed around him.

or

The molecules attach to this material , for they have proper affinity with it.

When you combine sentences in this way, be sure to put a comma before the coordinating conjunction.

Below are more examples. Note how each follows this pattern:

independent clause + + coordinating conjunction + independent clause •

I tried to draw him out, but it saddens Hugh to discuss his childhood monkey.

The sweaters I've made aren't impressive specimens, but they've taught me a lot.

Part of Goldstein's work was concerned with the effects of brain damage, and he found that, whenever there was extensive damage, there tended to be an impairment of abstract-categorical capacity.

Twenty years later there were 3,000 factory hands at Baldwin, and by 1900 there were more than 8,000.

You do not need a parachute to skydive, but you do need a parachute to skydive twice.

Several selective pressures may act similarly and simultaneously on trees, so it is difficult to tease apart the contributions those pressures make to tree evolution.

It sounds like something you'd read on a movie poster, but sometimes the sins you haven't committed are all you have to hold on to.

Like most Kenyans, I was not taught about my culture or about the things my parents learned from their parents in school, yet I was taught about the American Revolution, Niagara Falls, and the Second World War.

BE CAREFUL . . .

If you were to take these sentences—

In this section I focus on fluorescent biological samples.

The techniques may be applied to material science.

—and combine them with a comma but no coordinating conjunction—

In this section I focus on fluorescent biological samples, the techniques may be applied to material science.

—you would have **a comma splice**.

Writing teachers notice comma splices—so if you have been making this error without knowing it, now is the time to learn how to keep your writing teacher smiling at you.

Here is the version that will make a writing teacher put away the red pen:

In this section I focus on fluorescent biological samples, but the techniques may be applied to material science.

You can avoid comma splices by following the pattern shown on these pages, joining two sentences with a comma and a coordinating conjunction.

→ There are other strategies for mending comma splices; see pages 218–219.

→ For more on coordinating conjunctions, see page 242.

USING COMMAS TO ADD ADDITIONAL INFORMATION TO THE MAIN IDEA OF A SENTENCE

THE PATTERN

You can add additional information to a sentence at the beginning, middle, or end.

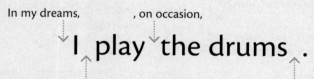

In my dreams,   , on occasion,

I play the drums .

, who have no musical sense,   , to the delight of my neighbor downstairs

You can add the suggested insertions (some of which are adjective phrases, some adverb phrases) to the sentence above to build the following:

In my dreams, I play the drums.

I, who have no musical sense, play the drums, to the delight of my neighbor downstairs.

I play, on occasion, the drums.

Notice the pattern of comma use around the inserted information:

- When you add information at the **beginning of a sentence**, put a single comma after what you add.
- When you add information in the **middle of a sentence**, put a comma before and a comma after what you add.
- When you add information at the **end of a sentence**, put a comma before what you add.

WHAT DO WE MEAN BY ADDITIONAL (OR "NONESSENTIAL") INFORMATION?

Each of the additions to the sentence *I play the drums* brings something new to the sentence, but if you took away all the additions, you would still understand the sentence's basic idea.

If you can remove information from a sentence without harming a reader's ability to understand the main point, then the information is additional, or **nonessential** (which is the grammatical term for such information).

If you can remove a phrase from a sentence without changing the basic meaning of the sentence, separate the phrase from the rest of the sentence with commas.

NONESSENTIAL INFORMATION AT THE BEGINNING OF A SENTENCE

These examples show ways you can start a sentence with a nonessential phrase. Notice the comma in each:

Unlike many other producers who step to the mic, Kanye is also an extremely talented emcee who flexes a relaxed but focused flow.

At the time of her husband's assassination, Mary Todd Lincoln had already buried two young sons.

Because data are always ambiguous, it can be years before physicists feel confident enough to publish potentially controversial results.

As unions waxed stronger after 1886, the number of strikes to enforce union rules grew steadily.

Once upon a time, I was one of those nerds who hung around Radio Shack and played with LEDs, resistors, and capacitors.

Even in the harsh penal environment of early America, some colonies had laws against feeding lobsters to inmates because it was thought to be cruel and unusual, like making people eat rats.

If you use only one or two introductory words, you can omit the comma:

On Wednesday we conduct the experiment.

NONESSENTIAL INFORMATION AT THE END OF A SENTENCE

These examples show some of the many ways you can end a sentence with a nonessential phrase. Notice where the comma is in these examples:

I used to play that song over and over in the dark when I was nine, the year I really became aware of my own existence.

Ray has exceptionally large glasses like an underwater mask, as if he never knows when he'll have to do some welding or shield himself from a solar eclipse.

Shani Davis stood out as a rare African American in a mostly white sport, supported by a single mother who helped bulldoze any barriers she sensed were in front of him.

Knitting is a skill that has come in handy throughout my life, mostly because I am so afflicted with the Protestant work ethic that I can't bear to watch television unless I am doing something productive with my hands.

Dogs are said to be the first domestic animals, displacing pigs for primal honors.

NONESSENTIAL INFORMATION IN THE MIDDLE OF A SENTENCE

Short interjections of words can add a conversational tone to writing; these interjections remind readers that a person wrote the words, so interjections can help writers build relations with their readers. Put a comma before and after such interjections:

Dirt, it seems, is an important ingredient in particle physics experiments.

Some sequels, as we all know, are better than the originals.

Let me clarify two points that will, I hope, make clear our disagreement.

■ ■ ■

When you use explanatory words and phrases such as *though* and *for example*, they should be set off by commas:

Once I'm awake, though, I tend to lie there wondering if I've made a terrible mistake.

Among Plains tribes, for example, certain forms of design knowledge, such as quill embroidery and beadwork, are sacred.

BUT!

Do not put a comma after *though* if the word introduces a phrase:

Though she had already been executed, Joan of Arc was acquitted on July 7, 1456.

■ ■ ■

The following sentences have phrases that come after nouns (nouns that are very often names) and that explain what the noun is; put a comma before and after all such phrases:

Aunty Lau, an accomplished weaver, teaches Hawaiian culture in the schools.

My son, who is eleven, has a memory like wet cement.

Lascelles Brown, an athletic Jamaican butcher who had briefly dabbled in boxing, first got interested in bobsledding after seeing the 1993 Disney film *Cool Runnings*, based on Jamaica's 1988 Olympic team.

Scissors, a mundane object to which we are introduced in kindergarten, are a sophisticated tool requiring opposable thumbs and some dexterity.

The Space Shuttle, on track and on schedule, came into view just after 5:53 Pacific time.

Nature, when abused, may react eventually like a tiger whose tail has been pulled.

We know from research that dogs, even kennel-raised puppies, do much better than generally more brilliant wolves or human-like chimpanzees in responding to human cues in a food-finding test.

STEPS FOR DECIDING IF INFORMATION IS ESSENTIAL OR NOT

1	EXAMPLE 1	EXAMPLE 2
For a sentence about which you are unsure, describe to yourself exactly what is most important to you in the sentence: *What exactly is it that you want your readers to take away from your sentence?*	Your sentence emphasizes some events that took place in New York City.	Your sentence focuses readers' attentions on society's responses to women who died in the Vietnam War.

2		
Identify in the sentence the information that may or may not be essential.	All of this took place in New York City, <u>which is cruelly, insanely expensive</u>.	This website is dedicated to women <u>who died in the Vietnam War</u>.

3		
Remove the information you identified in step 2.	All of this took place in New York City.	This website is dedicated to women.

4		
Ask yourself this question about the shortened sentence: *Does it give your readers exactly what you want them to take from the sentence?*	If you want to emphasize that the events you are describing took place in New York City and not to emphasize the cost of being in New York City, the answer is **yes**.	If you want to focus readers' attentions on society's responses to women who died in the Vietnam War—and not on all women—the answer is **no**.

5		
If the answer is **yes**, then the information you identified in step 2 is nonessential and should be separated from the rest of the sentence with commas. If the answer is **no**, then the information you identified in step 2 is essential and should not be separated with commas.	**YES?** Use commas: All of this took place in New York City, which is cruelly, insanely expensive.	**NO?** DON'T use commas: This website is dedicated to women who died in the Vietnam War.

WHEN NOT TO USE COMMAS

We list here kinds of sentences in which people are often tempted to use commas—but for which the conventions of formal writing say not to.

BEFORE INFORMATION ESSENTIAL TO A SENTENCE

delete

I am writing about the woman, who was nominated for president by the Republican Party in 1964.

I am writing about the woman who was nominated for president by the Republican Party in 1964.

Read the sentence without the part following the comma; if the sentence loses the meaning you want it to have, then you **do not** need the comma.

→ For more information on making this decision, see pages 273–275.

BETWEEN TWO CLAUSES THAT ARE NOT INDEPENDENT CLAUSES

delete

Some people look at war, and see nothing but violence and chaos.

Some people look at war and see nothing but violence and chaos.

→ If you need help determining whether you are writing independent clauses, see pages 217 and 253.

BEFORE "THAN"

Some scientists argue that there is no clearer indication of global warming, than Greenland's melting glaciers.

delete

Some scientists argue that there is no clearer indication of global warming than Greenland's melting glaciers.

BEFORE OR AFTER PARENTHESES

delete

A political career, (or a legal one) is the surest ticket to a historical legacy.

A political career (or a legal one) is the surest ticket to a historical legacy.

or

A political career, or a legal one, is the surest ticket to a historical legacy.

The convention is to use parentheses or commas around parenthetical comments, but not both.

AFTER A SUBORDINATING CONJUNCTION

Although, *delete* scientists no longer consider Pluto to be a planet, many still seek that little celestial body in their telescopes.

Although scientists no longer consider Pluto to be a planet, many still seek that little celestial body in their telescopes.

→ Page 244 lists and explains subordinating conjunctions.

BEFORE THE FIRST ITEM IN A LIST, OR AFTER THE LAST ITEM

E-mail spammers endure, *delete* legal harassment, exclusion from polite society, and the disgust of nearly every computer user.

E-mail spammers endure legal harassment, exclusion from polite society, and the disgust of nearly every computer user.

Many accidents of geography, history, and biology, *delete* created our lopsided world.

Many accidents of geography, history, and biology created our lopsided world.

→ See pages 264–267 for the conventional uses of commas with lists.

BETWEEN A SENTENCE'S VERB AND ITS SUBJECT OR OBJECT

Everything good, is bad for you. *delete*

Everything good is bad for you.

One of the dominant themes in American science policy this past year was, how we can maintain a competitive edge in a global economy. *delete*

One of the dominant themes in American science policy this past year was how we can maintain a competitive edge in a global economy.

If you include more than one word in a subject, it can be tempting to put a comma after it because you might read the sentence out loud with a pause after the subject—which can suggest that a comma should go there. The same temptation can happen with long objects: If you were reading it out loud, you would probably pause before the object. But in writing, the convention is not to put commas in these places.

COLONS have three main uses

USING COLONS IN CERTAIN CONVENTIONAL PATTERNS

SALUTATIONS
In formal or business letters, colons are used after the greeting at the beginning of the letter:

Dear Sir or Madam: • Dear Dr. Lucchesi:

MEMO HEADINGS
In workplaces, memos (less formal than letters) are used to inform others of project progress, meetings, or other events. The top of a memo will usually look like this:

To: The members of the Research Committee

From: Ralph Bunker

Re: Next Steps

(**Re:** means *regarding*; think of it as being like the subject heading of an e-mail.)

TIME
To write a time, use a colon between the hour, the minutes, and the seconds (if you include them):

12:32 P.M.   4:50:32 P.M.

I awoke just before the alarm went off, at 5:59:59 A.M.

She ran her first mile in 4:35 and her second in 4:50.

BETWEEN TITLE AND SUBTITLE
When you are writing the title of any communication—book, article, movie, television show—that has a subtitle, put the title, then a colon, then the subtitle:

Katherine Dunham: Dancing Queen

Wind: How the Flow of Air Has Shaped Life, Myth, and the Land

CITATIONS FROM THE BIBLE
Put a colon between the chapter and verse:

Matthew 6:5 • Deuteronomy 5:17 • Psalm 46:9

2

USING COLONS TO PREPARE READERS FOR INFORMATION AT THE END OF A SENTENCE

Use a colon at the end of a sentence to introduce an explanation:

If the three prongs of the suburban American dream are family, job, and house, there is a ghostly, underdiscussed consequence: yardwork.

The networked information economy holds out the possibility of reversing two trends in cultural production central to the project of control: concentration and commercialization.

Use a colon to introduce an example:

Writers ought to consider how the defense- and commercially tied history of computers shapes the thinking encouraged by the design of the software we use for writing: How many word-processing or webpage-composing software packages do you know that encourage scribbling, doodling, or writing outside the margins?

Use a colon to introduce a list:

I improvised with my equipment: fashioning together a hook and a line, making my own harpoons, or gathering up cast-off pieces of net from the fishermen.

→ When you put a list at the end of a sentence, punctuate it just as you would any other list; see pages 264–267.

3

USING COLONS TO LINK TWO SENTENCES

WHEN THE SECOND SENTENCE EXPLAINS OR SUMMARIZES THE FIRST

If you are joining two sentences where you could lead into the second sentence with *for example* or *that is*, use a colon between them:

Her illness confined her to a sofa, and so she did the one thing she could think to do on a sofa: She started writing.

There's a reason that freedom of the press was enumerated in the First Amendment: It's more fundamental to our liberty than even guns.

Some journals—and some teachers—request that the sentence following the colon start with a capital letter.

WHEN THE SECOND SENTENCE IS A QUOTATION

If you use a sentence to introduce a quotation, use a colon between them:

In order to write today's novel, movie, or song, I need to use and rework existing cultural forms, such as story lines and twists. This characteristic is known to economists as the "on the shoulders of giants" effect, recalling a statement attributed to Isaac Newton: "If I have seen farther it is because I stand on the shoulders of giants."

SEMICOLONS have two main uses ; those uses are:

1

JOINING SENTENCES

Be sure you have two complete sentences (that is, independent clauses), and then join them with a semicolon. The first letter of the word following the semicolon is not capitalized, unless it is a proper noun.

The father didn't move out; he just moved to a different bedroom.

The ceiling, freshly painted, was luminous as the sky; I almost thought I could smell the paint.

My fears were powerful and troubling and annoyingly vague; I couldn't establish exactly what it was that frightened me.

The highway went for miles between high mud walls and canebrakes; the black tracery of date palms rose above them, against the brilliant night sky.

You can use semicolons to join multiple sentences:

Work made people useful in a world of economic scarcity; it staved off the doubts and temptations that preyed on idleness; it opened the way to deserved wealth and status; it allowed one to put the impress of mind and skill on the material world.

→ To be sure you are joining complete sentences, read about independent and dependent clauses, pages 253 and 217.

2

USING SEMICOLONS TO JOIN LIST ELEMENTS THAT ARE COMPLICATED OR CONTAIN THEIR OWN PUNCTUATION

In complicated sentences, commas might not be enough to help readers see lists:

Istanbul's steep hills and harbor views remind you of San Francisco, its overcrowded streets recall Bombay, its transportation facilities evoke Venice, for you can go many places by boats, which are continually making stops.

Instead, with semicolons separating the items, it is easier to see the separate items:

Istanbul's steep hills and harbor views remind you of San Francisco; its overcrowded streets recall Bombay; its transportation facilities evoke Venice, for you can go many places by boats, which are continually making stops.

If you are building a list using items that contain their own punctuation, use semicolons to separate the items:

As the leech began to suck, it released several other substances into his ear: a powerful anticoagulant, which prevented his blood from clotting; a vasodilator, which opened his vessels, helping to increase blood flow; and a spreading factor, which moved these chemicals quickly into tissue farthest from the bite, liquefying any hardening blood.

ELLIPSES . . .
have two main uses.

1

USING ELLIPSES TO SHOW A PAUSE OR AN INTERRUPTION IN SPEECH THAT YOU ARE QUOTING

Because readers cannot hear words that you quote but can only see your transcription of them on a page, use ellipses to signal, visually, where someone you are quoting paused:

In an interview with Powells.com's Dave Weich, chef and writer Anthony Bourdain said: "I knew already that the best meal in the world, the perfect meal, is very rarely the most sophisticated or expensive one . . . Context and memory play powerful roles in all the truly great meals in one's life."

Put a space after the ellipsis.

■ ■ ■

In contexts less formal than the academic one, writers sometimes use ellipses to show hesitation or surprise; the following sentence, for example, comes from a science magazine for general audiences:

In the grand tradition of linking raunchy music with irresponsible sexual activity comes a new study touting a link between sexual risk taking and listening to . . . gospel music.

→ You can also use dashes to show hesitation in speech that you are quoting; see page 284.

2

USING ELLIPSES TO SHOW YOU HAVE OMITTED WORDS FROM A QUOTATION

IN A PROSE QUOTATION

If you need to drop words from a sentence you are quoting, use ellipses. Here are words from an interview with George Lucas, showing where words have been dropped:

When I was younger, I had a collection of history books that I was addicted to, a whole series about famous people in history . . . I collected a whole library.

Put a space before and after the ellipsis.

IN A QUOTATION OF POETRY

If you must drop one or more lines from poetry you quote, use a line of periods (with a space between each) to show where you have dropped lines; the line of periods should be as long as the poem's other lines.

William Butler Yeats often uses slight shifts in repeated sentence structure to build emotinal energy, as in these lines from "Maid Quiet":

> The winds that awakened the stars
> Are blowing through my blood.
>
> . . . .
>
> Now words that called up the lightning
> Are hurtling through my heart.

(PARENTHESES have four main uses.)

1

USING PARENTHESES TO EXPLAIN ABBREVIATIONS

Through use, long titles—of organizations, laws, and objects—often get abbreviated into acronyms. Acronyms are usually composed of the first letters of the title's main words, as **United States of America** is abbreviated **USA**.

If you are writing about something that has an acronym, don't assume that all your readers will know the acronym. The first time you mention the organization, law, or object, put the acronym in parentheses following the full name. After that, use the acronym:

The builders closely followed the Americans with Disabilities Act (ADA) when they constructed the entry to the building; the ADA requires that all buildings be accessible to people with a range of abilities.

San Francisco's Museum of the African Diaspora (MoAD) has a different goal than many other museums: The staff of MoAD work to put together exhibitions that represent the global impact of Africans—in South America, Central America, Europe, and Asia.

2

USING PARENTHESES FOR NUMBERS IN LISTS

If you are including a numbered list in your writing, use parentheses to indicate the steps:

The steps for checking writing that you think is done are (1) edit for readability, (2) check spelling, (3) check grammar, and (4) proofread.

The networked information economy improves the practical capacities of individuals along three dimensions: (1) It improves their capacity to do more for and by themselves; (2) it enhances their capacity to do more in loose commonality with others, without being constrained to organize their relationship through a price system or in traditional hierarchical models of social and economic organization; and (3) it improves the capacity of individuals to do more in formal organizations that operate outside the market sphere.

Note the punctuation above: If the steps are short, put a comma after each one; otherwise, put a semicolon.

3
USING PARENTHESES FOR IN-TEXT CITATIONS

Readers of academic research writing expect—whenever they find a source used in the writing—to also find information enabling them to check the source themselves. Conventionally, then, writers include the quoted author's name as well as the page number of the quoted words; readers can then look to the list of works cited at the essay's end to find the bibliographic information that enables them to find the cited work:

In Carruthers's argument, a sacred book is given a bejeweled cover to signify to readers that one's memory, growing out of the book, was "a storehouse, a treasure-chest, a vessel, into which the jewels, coins, fruits, and flowers of text are placed" (246). But, by the twelfth century, for those who could not afford treasure chests, the same books could also appear in "cheap and decorative binding" (Foot 118).

Notice that, if the author's name is included as part of a sentence, it is not noted in the parentheses; if the author's name is not included, then it is put in the parentheses along with the page number.

→ The example above is for MLA citation style, about which there is more on pages 124–165. For APA style, see pages 165–191.

4
USING PARENTHESES TO ADD INFORMATION

You can use parentheses to insert comments or additional information into a sentence. When you do this, you are adding **parenthetical remarks**. Many writers use this strategy to add humor to a sentence:

Sometimes in the morning Mrs. Murrow asks me if I heard the cobras singing during the night. I have never been able to answer in the affirmative, because in spite of her description ("like a silver coin falling against a rock"), I have no clear idea of what to listen for.

This afternoon, Johnny Depp is wearing a white undershirt tucked into gray tweed slacks hiked a tad too high (in the style of certain retirement-aged Italian gentlemen).

You can also use parenthetical information to add dates, definitions, a URL, or anything else you think will help readers understand:

Katherine Dunham's dance piece "Southland" (1951), which was a protest against lynching and depicted a lynching on stage, created a lot of controversy in America.

Traditionally, a hysterectomy (removal of the uterus) was the primary way to treat fibroids, and it remains the only permanent cure.

DASHES

and their four main uses.

1

USING A DASH TO EMPHASIZE INFORMATION AT THE END OF A SENTENCE

Sometimes writers want to put particular emphasis on a word or phrase. Should you choose to do this, using a dash to set off a word or phrase at the end of a sentence helps to emphasize that word or phrase:

I stood in my empty room. In place of the bed was—shame?

She danced by herself in the corner to a Brenda Lee record, but it was obvious she couldn't dance—she had the white girl's embarrassing habit of brandishing an invisible tambourine.

2

USING DASHES TO INDICATE A RESTATEMENT OR A CHANGE IN TONE

To make writing sound conversational and to add particular emphasis to phrases that might otherwise sound out of place because of the explanation or emotion they provide, writers will use dashes:

The wall-to-wall carpet—roughly the color of brains—was frayed and worn.

It dawned on him that he knew plenty of Americans—he was one himself—who held apparently contradictory beliefs, such as faith in both medicine and prayer.

3

USING DASHES TO SET OFF EXPLANATORY INFORMATION

Sometimes writers use dashes to put more emphasis on infomation, which could also be set off by commas:

A jay can store up to five acorns—depending on their size and his—in his throat.

4

USING DASHES TO SHOW HESITATION IN SPEECH

When writers are transcribing speech or are trying to emulate speech for readers, they use dashes to show where a speaker has hesitated or changed direction in mid-sentence:

On the witness stand, Michael Eisner responded to a lawyer's question by saying, "I think you're getting into an area that—that—I just want to say that this is ill-advised . . . ."

BRACKETS
have two main uses.

1

USING BRACKETS INSIDE PARENTHETICAL COMMENTS

Sometimes writers need to put parenthetical information inside other parenthetical information. When this is the case, the convention is to put the embedded information inside brackets instead of inside another set of parentheses:

(For further discussion, see Abdo [2000] and Burgat [2003].)

Khubz marquq (also called *lavash tannour* [mountain bread]) is a flat bread with a slightly tangy taste.

2

USING BRACKETS TO INSERT INFORMATION INTO A QUOTATION

Anytime writers use the words of someone else, the words are removed from their full context; sometimes, then, writers have to fill in information or change words so that readers can understand the quotation.

If writers need to do this in the middle of a quotation, the convention is to put the changed or added information inside brackets so that readers can see where the original has been changed. For example, here are words as they were originally spoken by Anthony B. Pinn, a professor of humanities and religion at Rice University in Houston:

What you get with mega-churches is a kind of caricature of the social gospel thrust. In terms of the hard issue of social justice, such churches tend to be theology-lite.

Here is how a magazine article quoted those words, in order to fit them to its needs:

What you get with mega-churches is a . . . caricature of the social gospel thrust. In terms of . . . social justice, [they] tend to be theology-lite.

→ If you need to leave words out of quotations, use ellipses, a punctuation mark explained on page 281, to show the omissions.

HY PHENS have two main uses.

1

USING HYPHENS FOR CLARITY

A precise reader sees considerable difference between these two sentences:

He was a big city man.

He was a big-city man.

The first is about a man from the city who is big; the second is about a man from a big city. When using two words as an adjective, put a hyphen between them if you wonder whether others will read your words as you intend.

■ ■ ■

When you use the prefixes *re-*, *anti-*, and *pre-* with verbs, use a hyphen between the prefix and the verb if, without the hyphen, a different meaning is made.

I resent her letter.

I re-sent her letter.

■ ■ ■

Use hyphens if the first word of a compound word you are making begins with the same letter as the second:

doll-like   non-native

2

USING HYPHENS IN COMPOUND WORDS

When writers put together two or more words to make one new word, the result is a compound word:

Operating on an off-the-shelf Linux-based computer, MooBella's fresh-on-the-spot system changes traditional ice-cream vending machines, which spit out months-old bars.

The longer a compound word has been in use, the more likely it won't have a hyphen in it (think of *bathtub*, *earthquake*, *bookshelf*, or *website*); conversely, the newest compound words most likely have hyphens.

Some compound words, however, do conventionally keep their hyphens:

Dr. Bonnez treated dairy cows, which grow grapefruit-sized warts. He still has a block of 20-year-old cow warts in his freezer.

When compound words are used as adjectives before nouns—such as *20-year-old* and *grapefruit-sized* above or in the term *nineteenth-century art*—they tend to be hyphenated.

To be safest, check a dictionary.

■ ■ ■

When you write out numbers between 21 and 99, a hyphen is conventional:

twenty-three • one hundred twenty-three

one thousand two hundred and ninety-four

SLASH / SLASHES have three main uses.

1

USING SLASHES IN PAIRED TERMS

Some terms in English are hard to separate:

on/off switch   and/or

a pass/fail class   an either/or situation

It is the preferred convention for writing in humanities disciplines **not** to use such terms, but sometimes a slash is the only way to give readers the sense you intend:

If all writing is a form of quotation—as blogs invariably include a mix of "original" text and text copied from other websites—we need to question the "original"/"copied" dichotomy.

If you need to use a slash in this way, do not put spaces on either side of the slash.

2

USING SLASHES TO INDICATE LINE BREAKS IN QUOTED POEMS

Because line breaks in poems indicate poets' rhetorical choices, be careful to reproduce line breaks when you quote poems.

These lines come from a poem by Charles Simic:

Like the sound of eyebrows
Raised by a villain
In a silent movie.

Here is a quotation using those lines:

Simic can create striking metaphors, as in these lines from "The Wooden Toy," where the toy is quiet, "Like the sound of eyebrows / Raised by a villain / In a silent movie."

Note that there is a space on either side of each slash.

3

USING SLASHES WITH DATES AND FRACTIONS

DATES

In informal and business writing in the United States, the convention is to write dates with slashes, giving the month, day, and year:

11/10/56   10/31/2009

Note that there are no spaces around the slashes and that you can use two or four digits for the year.

FRACTIONS

Put a slash between the two numbers of a fraction:

1/2   2/3   15/16

There are no spaces between the numbers and the slash.

" QUOTATION MARKS "
have six main uses.

1 **USING QUOTATION MARKS FOR TITLES OF SHORT WORKS**

For sentences like the following—

The radio is playing The Romantics' "That's What I Like About You."

→ GO TO PAGE 289.

2 **USING QUOTATION MARKS TO INDICATE YOU ARE USING A WORD AS A WORD**

For sentences like the following—

And by "malignant" and "addictive" I do not mean evil or hypnotizing.

→ GO TO PAGE 289.

3 **USING QUOTATION MARKS TO INDICATE TECHNICAL TERMS AND WORDS FROM OTHER LANGUAGES**

For sentences like the following—

"Malar" means relating to the cheek.

→ GO TO PAGE 290.

4 **USING QUOTATION MARKS TO SHOW IRONY**

For sentences like the following—

To quantify the "benefit" side of the equation, a dollar amount is assigned to each saved human's life.

→ GO TO PAGE 290.

5 **USING QUOTATION MARKS TO INDICATE DIRECT QUOTATION**

For sentences like the following—

David Foster Wallace believes that "fiction writers as a species tend to be oglers" (21).

→ GO TO PAGE 291.

6 **USING QUOTATION MARKS TO INDICATE SPEECH**

For sentences like the following—

The woman at Macy's asked me, "Would you be interested in full-time elf or evening and weekend elf?"
  I said, "Full-time elf."

→ GO TO PAGE 291.

QUOTATION MARKS USE 1

USING QUOTATION MARKS FOR TITLES OF SHORT WORKS

Use quotation marks to indicate the name of a show or exhibition—

"Goya's Last Works," at the Frick, isn't large, but neither are grenades.

—the titles of poems and musical pieces—

I had to study why Van Halen moved (certain) people as much as the Beatles, but, folks, they did, in the same way Whitman did. "Hot For Teacher" is "Song of Myself" with crappier words but much better lead guitar.

—and the titles of essays—

"The Making of Americans" was a work that Stein evidently had to get out of her system—almost like a person having to vomit—before she could become Gertrude Stein as we know her.

—or the titles of almost any work that is not book length.

→ Information on how to indicate the titles of book-length works is on page 298.

QUOTATION MARKS USE 2

USING QUOTATION MARKS TO INDICATE YOU ARE USING A WORD AS A WORD

Sometimes, writers need to refer to a word as a word. If ever you need to do this, put quotation marks around the word:

"Doctor" comes from the Latin word *docere*, "to teach."

The term "preservation" usually comes up in reference to buildings, not to the graffiti that covers them.

His student asked him how to use "until" according to English conventions.

Franziska often spews repetitive insults using the word "fool."

→ The use of quotation marks for this function goes back to the days of typewriters. With computers, italics can replace quotation marks; see page 298 on using italics.

→ Because quotation marks are almost always interwoven with other punctuation, it is tricky to use them as academic readers and readers of published works expect. On pages 292–293 we go over the little but important details of using quotation marks in expected ways.

QUOTATION MARKS USE 3
USING QUOTATION MARKS TO INDICATE TECHNICAL TERMS AND WORDS FROM OTHER LANGUAGES

Use quotation marks to indicate technical terms and words from other languages:

Ringed seals, ivory gulls, and other birds and mammals whose lives are ice-oriented are called "pagophylic."

During the thirteenth century, the Dutch instituted a "wind brief," a tax paid to the lord or king over whose fields the wind blew before reaching a mill.

Consider, for example, a form of creativity that seems strange to many Americans but that is inescapable within Japanese culture: "manga," or comics.

As I explain in the pages that follow, we come from a tradition of "free culture"—not "free" as in "free beer" (to borrow a phrase from the founder of the free software movement), but "free" as in "free speech," "free markets," "free trade," "free enterprise," "free will," and "free elections."

→ The use of quotation marks for this function goes back to the days of typewriters. With computers, italics can replace quotation marks; see page 298 on using italics.

→ Because quotation marks are almost always interwoven with other punctuation, it is tricky to use them as academic readers and readers of published works expect. On pages 292–293 we go over the little but important details of using quotation marks in expected ways.

QUOTATION MARKS USE 4
USING QUOTATION MARKS TO SHOW IRONY

Writers sometimes want to distance themselves from words: They need to use particular words, as in the examples below, but want to show that they don't agree with the word choice. In such cases, writers can put quotation marks around the words.

Look, for example, at how novelist Janet Frame, in her autobiography, uses quotation marks to let readers know how she feels about the sincerity of the women who visited her mother after her sister's death:

They sat patting and arranging their "permanent" waves.

Here are sentences from scientists commenting on how others have characterized scientific practice:

How can an experiment be "wrong"?

The problem I am posing here is not one of individual morality, of individual scientists doing "dirty" work or "clean" work; rather, the problem is institutional.

In each case, the quotation marks let readers know that the writers question the characterizations of experiments and other scientific work contained in the punctuated words.

→ Because quotation marks are almost always interwoven with other punctuation, it is tricky to use them as academic readers and readers of published works expect. On pages 292–293 we go over the little but important details of using quotation marks in expected ways.

QUOTATION MARKS USE 5
USING QUOTATION MARKS TO INDICATE DIRECT QUOTATION

Over the centuries, conventions have developed in different languages for indicating to readers that writers are quoting the words of others. In English, quotation marks—placed on either side of the words being quoted—have become the expected way of doing this, even if a writer is quoting only one word from someone else:

Fukasawa's approach to designing electronic gadgets, based on over 25 years' experience, has been called "anti-technical" because it dispenses with unnecessary buttons, displays, and other high-tech signifiers.

A comparison to make a point is Sarah Vowell's claim that "Going to Ford's Theatre to watch the play is like going to Hooter's for the food."

At the time the Wright brothers invented the airplane, American law held that a property owner owned not just the surface of his land, but all the land below, down to the center of the earth, and all the space above, to "an indefinite extent, upwards."

→ Because quotation marks are almost always interwoven with other punctuation, it is tricky to use them as academic readers expect. On pages 292–293 we go over the details of using quotation marks in expected ways.

QUOTATION MARKS USE 6
USING QUOTATION MARKS TO INDICATE SPEECH

When you wish to suggest to your readers that the words you are writing were spoken out loud by someone else, quotation marks are the customary strategy in English:

"He was going to write the definitive book on leeches," she says. "It was his primary ambition in life."

"Reading ability is a proxy for intelligence in American culture," said Dr. Sally E. Shaywitz of Yale University School of Medicine, a pediatrician who is an expert on dyslexia.

"You have to listen to music before you go out on a mission and get real hyped," says Sgt. Junelle Daniels, a twenty-five-year-old generator mechanic from Miami who is gearing up for a second deployment. "If not, you start thinking, 'What if? What if this happens? What if that happens?' You start to get the fear."

Note that indicating speech is sometimes the same as indicating a direct quotation.

→ Because quotation marks are almost always interwoven with other punctuation, it is tricky to use them as academic readers and readers of published works expect. On pages 292–293 we go over the little but important details of using quotation marks in expected ways.

→ In academic writing, any time you quote someone else, the expectation is that you will provide the source of the quotation; see pages 58–59 for how to do this.

USING QUOTATION MARKS AND OTHER PUNCTUATION WHEN YOU INCLUDE OTHERS' WORDS IN YOUR WRITING

To quote others' words in the patterns that readers of academic and other formal texts expect, pay close attention to these details in the examples below:

- The use of a comma or period at the end of the quotation. (Note also that, whether a comma or period is used, it is included inside the quotation mark.)
- The capitalization of the words at the beginning of the quotation.

THE PATTERN	QUOTING A COMPLETE SENTENCE
AT THE BEGINNING OF YOUR WRITING	"Most of what we teach is wrong," said Johndan Johnson-Eilola.
IN THE MIDDLE OF YOUR WRITING	Johndan Johnson-Eilola said, "Most of what we teach is wrong," while speaking at a recent conference.
AT THE END OF YOUR WRITING	Johndan Johnson-Eilola said, "Most of what we teach is wrong."
WITH IN-TEXT CITATION (MLA STYLE)	Johndan Johnson-Eilola said, "Most of what we teach is wrong" (77).

→ For more on in-text citations, see pages 136–139 for MLA style; pages 171–173 for APA style; page 194 for CSE style; page 197 for CMS style.

→ Quotations that will take up more than four lines in a paper are conventionally treated as **block quotations**; see page 59.

→ See page 59 for help with choosing the words to use to introduce or explain the words you are quoting.

QUOTING PARTS OF A SENTENCE

"A natural sense of geometry" is innate in babies, argues cognitive psychologist Elizabeth Spelke.

All babies have "a natural sense of geometry," argues cognitive psychologist Elizabeth Spelke.

Cognitive psychologist Elizabeth Spelke argues that all babies have "a natural sense of geometry."

All babies have "a natural sense of geometry," argues cognitive psychologist Elizabeth Spelke (qtd. in Talbot 92).

If you are quoting only part of a sentence, don't capitalize the first word, unless the quoted words start your sentence.

Note also that the quoted words in these examples do not have commas before them.

QUOTING A SENTENCE THAT ENDS WITH A QUESTION MARK OR EXCLAMATION POINT

"Why did wealth and power become distributed as they are now, rather than in some other way?" Jared Diamond asks at the beginning of his book.

Jared Diamond asks, "Why did wealth and power become distributed as they are now, rather than in some other way?" at the beginning of his book.

At the beginning of his book, Jared Diamond asks, "Why did wealth and power become distributed as they are now, rather than in some other way?"

"Why did wealth and power become distributed as they are now, rather than in some other way?" Jared Diamond asks at the beginning of his book (15).

NOTE: If you are quoting a sentence that ends with an exclamation point, the punctuation pattern is the same as when the sentence ends with a question mark.

Here are **APOSTROPHES'** three main uses.

1

USING APOSTROPHES TO MAKE PLURALS OF CERTAIN WORDS

Use apostrophes to make plurals of lowercase letters; otherwise, readers might confuse the plural with a word:

Is it "cross your is and dot your ts," or the reverse?

Is it "cross your i's and dot your t's," or the reverse?

Use an apostrophe to make plurals of uppercase letters if the addition of an **-s** without an apostrophe would make a word:

She earned As throughout school but could never rise above an entry-level position.

She earned A's throughout school but could never rise above an entry-level position.

But: He never earned higher than Cs or Ds in school, yet he's a well-known newscaster.

2

USING APOSTROPHES TO MAKE CONTRACTIONS

Apostrophes show where letters have been taken out of a contraction:

I am	= I'm	we are	= we're
I would	= I'd	we have	= we've
you are	= you're	they are	= they're
she is	= she's	do not	= don't
he is	= he's	did not	= didn't
it is	= it's	cannot	= can't

One odd pattern to learn:

will not = won't

I'm sure that we didn't leave the window open, but shouldn't we go back and check?

We've got time; he won't expect us until late.

3

USING APOSTROPHES TO MAKE POSSESSIVES

Seeing a word ending with an apostrophe and **-s**, readers assume the word is a possessive.

This blog's message is "Stop Buying Crap."

Uncovery Channel's new reality television show is *Could We Dream Some More, Please?*

→ To learn more about the possessive case, see page 224.

TIP: LEARN THE DIFFERENCE BETWEEN *it's* AND *its*

it's = it is   its = the possessive form of the pronoun *it*

It's going to rain. (It is going to rain.)

Democracy can be said to be its own biggest threat. (its is a stand-in for **democracy's**)

PERIODS have two main uses.

1

USING PERIODS WITH SOME ABBREVIATIONS

Abbreviations shorten words.

Company	→ Co.	Doctor	→ Dr.
etcetera	→ etc.	Incorporated	→ Inc.
Mister	→ Mr.	Monday	→ Mon.

These abbreviations are made of the first letter of the word and the last letter, or are truncated versions of the words (**Mon.** for **Monday** or **Co.** for **Company**). When an abbreviation is made this way, it will most likely have a period after it.

■ ■ ■

Name abbreviations customarily use periods:

John Fitzgerald Kennedy → John F. Kennedy

Mary Francis Kennedy Fisher → M. F. K. Fisher

Put a space after each period

■ ■ ■

Some abbreviations are the first letters of word series:

a.m.	→	**ante meridiem** (Latin for *before noon*)
r.s.v.p.	→	**respondez, s'il vous plait** (French for *Please respond*)
U.N.I.C.E.F.	→	United Nations International Children's Emergency Fund

The USPS requests that we abbreviate state names this way, without periods:

MI   CA   RI   AK

2

USING PERIODS TO END SENTENCES THAT MAKE STATEMENTS OR COMMANDS

Of the four kinds of sentences (→ page 247), two of them, declarative and imperative sentences, conventionally end with periods.

These are **declarative sentences**, which make statements:

Water buffalo do not exist in Africa.

Smaller species of exploding ants are more likely to combust than larger ones.

Neil Burger's movie *The Illusionist*, based on a short story by Steven Millhauser, is a delicate film, almost a fairy tale.

Though armed with a sharp, venom-coated barb on their tail, stingrays use the weapon only defensively, and attacks on humans are extremely rare.

These are **imperative sentences**, which make commands:

Mix the sliced pears and walnuts together.

Fasten your seat belt by sliding the metal notch into the buckle.

Use a period after most abbreviations.

> **TIP:** **USING PERIODS WITH QUOTATION MARKES**
>
> → Using periods with quotation marks requires careful attention. See pages 292–293.

Do you know the two main uses of
QUESTION MARKS

1

USING QUESTION MARKS TO END SENTENCES THAT ARE QUESTIONS

Of the four functions that sentences can have (➔ page 247), asking questions is one; sentences that ask questions are called interrogatory sentences:

What is education?

Have you ever browsed a sperm bank catalog?

You bought the CD or DVD, and that means you own it, right?

If prisons are meant to make troubled men and women into citizens, he wondered, might there be a social cost to bad prison design?

BUT!

The examples above are **direct questions**; there are also **indirect questions**, in which a writer describes someone else asking a question, without direct quotation. *These end with a period, not a question mark:*

I heard her ask whether the mail had arrived.

He asked how the test had gone.

2

USING QUESTION MARKS TO SHOW DOUBT ABOUT DATES AND NUMBERS

If you have doubts about a date or quantity, or if your sources describe doubt about a date or quantity, put **(?)** after the date or quantity.

In this photograph, Reynolds is seen with his mother in 1928 (?).

Witness reports put the number of people trapped in the building at 180 (?).

➔ Using question marks with quotation marks requires careful attention. See page 293.

EXCLAMATION POINTS!
have one main use, really and truly

1

USING EXCLAMATION POINTS TO INDICATE TO READERS THAT A SENTENCE CARRIES EMOTIONAL WEIGHT

It is customary in written American English to put a single exclamation point after a sentence when the sentence is an exclamation—

Yikes! Oh no!

—a strong command—

Help!

Don't touch that burner!

Don't go beyond the perimeter!

—or is meant by its writer to encourage a strong emotional response in a reader—

Each treehouse is built in two main pieces: the playhouse and the log. The log is a real, old, fallen tree that we hollow out using a chainsaw!

Age is absolutely no barrier in today's world. In fact, some 30 percent of students today are "non-traditional," meaning us, of course! Your age is not an issue unless you choose to make it one; don't!

In academic writing, exclamation points are almost nonexistent because such writing is meant to appeal primarily to reason. In most other kinds of writing, the exclamation point is also rare, because people who grow up speaking American English tend to think that exclamation points are a sign of youth or silliness—especially when several sentences in a row have them or when a single sentence ends in many of them.

There are exceptions: In blogs, for example, writers sometimes use them excessively, as a self-conscious indication that they know exclamation points are dangerous but still potent:

It's not that we know we aren't writing well—and so tack on some exclamations!!!—it's that we know what we're saying doesn't deserve to be written at all.

→ Using exclamation points with quotation marks requires careful attention. See page 293.

MECHANICS

USING ITALICS AND UNDERLINING

Italic type

Italic type was developed during the Italian Renaissance, and over time those who used printing presses developed specific uses for it.

Until computers were developed, those who did not have access to printing presses but who instead used typewriters—like most college students—could not use italic type. A convention developed to use underlining wherever a printer would use italics.

If you cannot use italics as we discuss below, use underlining.

FOR THE TITLES OF BOOKS AND OTHER LONG PUBLICATIONS

Use italics for the titles of books, magazines, journals, newspapers, websites, feature films, radio and television shows, book-length poems, comic strips, plays, operas and other musical performances, ballets and other dance performances, paintings, sculptures, pamphlets, and bulletins.

Marilyn's book will be titled *The Animal Who Writes*.

Little Nemo was a popular comic strip of the early twentieth century.

(Quotation marks are used for shorter publications; → see page 289.)

FOR FOREIGN TERMS

The environmental studies professor, who is from Pakistan, was first educated in a *madrassah*, or Muslim school.

China is shifting resources away from state-directed scientific research into initiatives designed to stimulate *zizhi chuangxin* (indigenous innovation).

You do not need to italicize commonly used foreign expressions and abbreviations:

cum laude	ex officio	et al.	e.g.
in vitro	vice versa	vis-à-vis	i.e.

FOR SCIENTIFIC NAMES IN LATIN

It is conventional to put the Latin names of organisms in italics.

Foot-and-mouth disease (*Aphtae epizooticae*) is a highly contagious and sometimes fatal viral disease of cattle and pigs.

The Bengal tiger is *Panthera tigris tigris* and the Siberian tiger is *Panthera tigris altaica*.

FOR REFERRING TO WORDS AS WORDS

When you need to discuss a word in its functions as a word, you can italicize it. (In this case, if you cannot italicize, use quotation marks.)

The English articles are *a, an,* and *the*.

FOR EMPHASIS

Do this sparingly. This kind of visual emphasis works only when it can stand out against large passages that receive no visual emphasis.

Sacks said, "I didn't just care for these patients. I *lived* with these patients."

SPELLING

It is now an expected sign of formal documents that the words are all spelled according to conventions that have developed over time and that are recorded in dictionaries.

CHECK A DICTIONARY

Spelling is the attempt to put spoken language into consistent patterns on the page, using just the twenty-six characters of the English alphabet. Because English developed out of many different languages, the spelling of a word often results from an attempt in the past to use the English alphabet to translate sounds made in other languages.

English spelling can therefore be vexing, even if your home language is English. There are some spelling rules for English, but all have considerable exceptions and variations, and many people find them confusing.

The best advice we can give you when you are trying to spell a word is to use a dictionary.

USING SPELL CHECKERS

Spell checkers only check spelling; they cannot tell if you are using the wrong word or have made other mistakes.

To use spell checkers well, follow these steps:

1 After you have a complete draft, use a spell checker to catch obvious spelling errors.

2 Use the items listed to the right under "*What spell checkers miss*" to find specific kinds of mistakes.

3 Proofread the whole text at least one more time.

WHAT SPELL CHECKERS MISS

- **Incorrect words that are spelled correctly.** In the sentence *He might loose his job,* all the words are spelled correctly, but *loose* should be *lose.* The Glossary (pages 304–306) shows words that are commonly confused.

- **Homonyms.** *Peace* and *piece* are homonyms: They are words that are spelled differently but sound the same. When writing quickly, it is easy to use a homonym in place of the word you want. The Glossary contains some common homonyms.

- **Possessives used as plurals—and vice versa.** If you are writing about more than one dress, it is easy to write *dress's* instead of *dresses.*

  → See page 224 to learn about possessives.

  → See page 225 to learn about plurals.

- **Pronouns that do not match their antecedents.**

  → See pages 220 and 232 to learn about pronouns and antecedents.

- **Words that are missing.** Spell checkers do not catch words left out of a sentence. Read your work out loud, slowly, so you hear if you have left out any words.

- **Misspelled names.** Spell checkers rarely check for proper nouns because there are so many. Misspelling the name of an author or major figure is not only embarrassing, but readers can also interpret this as a sign you were not paying close and careful attention while you were writing. Anytime you use a proper noun, check its spelling by looking up the name in a newspaper, magazine, biographical dictionary, or through an online search.

CAPITALIZING WORDS

Conventionally, capital letters are used in many ways:

THE FIRST WORDS OF SENTENCES

We must become spies on behalf of justice.

A combination of ego and gin stood between me and my ability to learn from my mistakes.

THE FIRST WORD IN A DIRECT QUOTATION

She said, simply, "No."

Chris Magnus, Chief of Police in Richmond, California, has said, "There's a mentality among some people that they're living some really violent video game."

DAYS, MONTHS, AND PUBLIC HOLIDAYS

On Tuesday, we'll be home late.

My family could celebrate Hanukkah, Christmas, and Kwanzaa.

NAMES OF PEOPLE

Capitalize first and last names, whether you use one or both.

Heidi worked until the early morning.

Thomas Pynchon begins his novel *Gravity's Rainbow* with the sentence, "A screaming comes across the sky."

NAMES OF CITIES, STATES, AND COUNTRIES

Capitalize these names when they are nouns and when they are adjectives.

Seattle has changed since I was born there.

The Waifs are an Australian band.

NAMES OF ORGANIZATIONS

My brother volunteered with Habitat for Humanity.

"Doctors Without Borders" is the English name for the organization started in France, *Médecins Sans Frontières*.

PROFESSIONAL TITLES

Whether they are spelled out or abbreviated, capitalize all professional titles when they come before a person's name.

It was Colonel Peacock in the kitchen with the knife.

Professor Yunus won the Nobel Prize.

Surgeon General Joycelyn Elders said, "When hope dies, moral decay can't be far behind."

TITLES OF ARTWORKS

The artworks can be paintings, sculptures, photographs, musical compositions, and songs.

Art historians do not know who posed for the *Mona Lisa*.

I wish I knew all the words to that Mose Allison song "Your Mind Is on Vacation, But Your Mouth Works Overtime."

TITLES OF BOOKS AND OTHER WRITINGS

Arundhati Roy's book, *The God of Small Things*, won the Booker Prize.

"The Moral Equivalent of War" is an essay by William James.

→ See page 289 to learn when to use quotation marks around titles; see page 298 to learn when to italicize titles.

NUMBERS

WRITING NUMBERS

In MLA style, spell out numbers that can be expressed in one or two words, using hyphens as in the examples below. Give the numerals for longer numbers.

seven	sixty-one	1,347
forty-one dollars	$77.17	ten miles
twenty-two years	250 years	352 miles

In APA style, use numerals for the numbers 10 and above; for numbers preceding a unit of measurement; and for dates, mathematical functions, and fractions:

seven	61	1,347
41 dollars	$77.17	10 miles
22 years	5 grams	3 times as many

Spell out numbers preceding other numbers expressed in numerals; otherwise readers might have trouble, as in the first sentence below, where it is possible to misread the two numbers as 10,250.

The game is run from 10 250 gigabyte servers.

The game is run from ten 250 gigabyte servers.

WRITE OUT NUMBERS THAT BEGIN SENTENCES

19% of survey respondents knew when the U.S. Constitution was written.

Nineteen percent of survey respondents knew when the U.S. Constitution was written.

USE NUMBERS CONSISTENTLY

If you spell numbers out or use numerals in a series, do so consistently.

League of Legends has twenty-seven million daily and 67 million monthly players.

League of Legends has 27 million daily and 67 million monthly players.

DATES AND TIMES

Use numerals for dates and times.

President John F. Kennedy was shot and killed on November 22, 1963, at 12:30 p.m.

PAGES AND OTHER PARTS OF BOOKS

Use numerals for pages, chapters, and other book divisions.

In his book *The Uses of Disorder,* Richard Sennett defines adulthood as the time when people "learn to tolerate painful ambiguity and uncertainty" (108).

ADDRESSES AND PHONE NUMBERS

Use numerals for addresses and phone numbers.

Grauman's Chinese Theatre is located at 6801 Hollywood Boulevard in Hollywood. For showtimes, call (323) 464-8111.

DECIMALS AND PERCENTAGES

Use numerals for percentages, and use the percentage sign (%).

By one estimate, 26% of all electric-cable breaks and 18% of all phone-cable disruptions are caused by rats.

(If the percentages come at the beginning of a sentence, however, use words for both the number and the percentage sign.)

SCORES AND STATISTICS

Use numerals for scores and statistics.

The average age of the most frequent game buyer is 38 years old. In 2007, 92% of computer game buyers and 80% of console game buyers were over the age of 18.

ABBREVIATIONS

TITLES

Dr. and *St.* (*Saint*) are abbreviated before a name but not after.

. . . said Dr. Robert Cantu.

. . . said Robert Cantu, a doctor specializing in neurosurgery.

Prof., *Sen.*, *Gen.*, *Capt.*, and other titles can be abbreviated when placed before a full name (i.e., first and last names, or initials and last name) but not before the last name when it is given alone:

Sen. Hattie Wyatt Caraway

Sen. H. W. Caraway

Senator Caraway

Put academic and professional titles—*Sr.*, *Jr.*, *J.D.*, *Ph.D.*, *M.F.A.*, *R.N.*, *C.P.A.*—after names. (The periods are often left out of abbreviated titles.)

Ralph Simmons, Ph.D., will speak.

Ralph Simmons, PhD, will speak.

COMPANY NAMES

If a company name contains an abbreviation, write the name as the company does:

Charlie and the Chocolate Factory, distributed by Warner Bros. Studios, is based on a novel by Roald Dahl.

MEASUREMENTS

In a paper's body, spell out measurement units such as *foot*, *percent*, *meter*—but abbreviate them in charts, tables, and graphs.

HMS Titanic was 883.75 feet long and 92.5 feet wide.

PLACE-NAMES

Spell out the names of continents, rivers, countries, states, cities, streets, and so on, except in these two cases:

1 You can use U.S. as an adjective, but not as a noun:

   U.S. soldiers

   soldiers from the United States

2 To put a full address in a sentence, write it as you would on an envelope, using the state's postal abbreviation.

   Please send your applications to Habitat for Humanity International, 121 Habitat St., Americus, GA 31709.

   Otherwise, spell out the state name:

   Habitat for Humanity International's head office is in Americus, Georgia.

DATES

Spell out months and days of the week.

"Statistically, you are more likely to have an accident on Monday, November 27, than any other day of the year," the insurance official said.

For dates, these abbreviations are customary:

399 BC	399 BCE
1215 CE	AD 1215

BC (*Before Christ*), **BCE** (*Before the Common Era*), and **CE** (*Common Era*) are placed after the year. **AD** (*Anno Domini*, "Year of Our Lord") goes before the year. *BCE* and *CE* are currently the most favored abbreviations.

TIMES

The conventional abbreviations for time of day are *A.M.* or *a.m.* for before noon and *P.M.* or *p.m.* for afternoon.

ACRONYMS

An acronym is a word formed by the initial letters of a phrase or title.

PC	personal computer
NPM	National Poetry Month
BBC	British Broadcasting Corporation

If you use an acronym that readers might not know, spell it out first, put the acronym in parentheses, and then use the acronym for all later references.

Folding At Home (FAH) is Stanford University's distributed computing project to study and understand protein folding, protein aggregation, and related diseases. So far, almost 500,000 users have donated processing time to FAH's projects.

LATIN EXPRESSIONS

Some Latin expressions, commonly used in academic writing, appear only as abbreviations:

cf.	compare	e.g.	for example
et al.	and others	etc.	and so forth
i.e.	that is	n.b.	note well

IN DOCUMENTING SOURCES

Different documentation styles use different abbreviations for words like *anonymous*, *editor*, or *no date*. Check your style manual for any abbreviations you need to use.

→ See page 295 for how to use periods with abbreviations.

TIP: MAKING ABBREVIATIONS PLURAL AND POSSESSIVE

To make an abbreviation plural, put **-s** after it.

Analysts estimate that more than 6,000 PCs become obsolete in California every day.

To make an abbreviation possessive, put **-'s** after it.

IBM's earning forecast was grim.

TIP: ABBREVIATIONS IN DIFFERENT DISCIPLINES

Different disciplines—from mathematics to the social sciences—use abbreviations differently. The advice we offer on these pages is general, so if you are writing for a specific discipline, ask someone familiar with the field (or a reference librarian) for help in learning the field's conventions.

GLOSSARY OF GRAMMATICAL TERMS

a/an **A** and **an** are indefinite articles because they indicate general objects (*a book, an apple*) rather than any specific object.

active voice In a sentence or clause in active voice, the subject of the clause or sentence performs the action. Also see **passive voice**. (See p. 112 and p. 213.)

adjective An adjective is a word that modifies a noun or pronoun. (See p. 234.)

adjective clause An adjective clause is a subordinate clause that modifies a noun or pronoun. Adjective clauses are also called relative clauses because they begin with a relative pronoun. (See pp. 256–257.)

adverb An adverb is a word that modifies a verb (*talk quietly*), another modifier (*very inexpensive*), or a whole clause or sentence (*Fortunately, we had an umbrella*). (See p. 239.)

adverb clause An adverb clause is a subordinate clause that modifies a verb, another modifier, or a whole clause or sentence. (See p. 258.)

agreement Agreement refers to the correspondence of one word to another in gender, number, or person. (See pp. 204–207 on subject-verb agreement, and pp. 220–221 on pronoun-antecedent agreement.)

an See **a/an**.

antecedent An antecedent is the noun or pronoun referred to by a pronoun. (See p. 220.)

article Articles are always followed by a noun. *A, an,* and *the* are articles. (See p. 235.)

auxiliary verb See **helping verb**.

case Case is the form of a noun or pronoun that indicates its function. Nouns change case only to show possession. (See p. 224.)

clause A clause is a group of words containing a subject and a verb. A **main** or **independent clause** can stand alone as a sentence (see p. 253), but a **subordinate** or **dependent clause** acts as a part of speech and cannot stand alone (see pp. 217 and 256–258).

comma splice A comma splice occurs when two independent clauses are joined unconventionally by a comma. (See pp. 218–219.)

common noun A common noun names a general person, place, or thing. Common nouns are not capitalized unless they are the first word of a sentence. (See p. 231.)

complex sentence A complex sentence is a sentence that contains at least one subordinate clause attached to an independent clause. (See pp. 256–258.)

compound sentence A compound sentence contains at least two main clauses. (See pp. 254–255.)

compound-complex sentence A compound-complex sentence contains at least two independent clauses and a subordinate clause. (See p. 259.)

conjunction A conjunction is a word that links and relates parts of a sentence. (See pp. 242–245.) See **coordinating conjunction**, **correlative conjunction**, and **subordinating conjunction**.

conjunctive adverb A conjunctive adverb is an adverb (such as *however, besides, consequently,* or *therefore*) that relates two main or independent clauses. (See p. 245.)

coordinating conjunction A coordinating conjunction is a word (such as *and, but, or, for, nor, yet,* and *so*) that links two grammatically equal parts of a sentence. (See pp. 242, 254, and 270–271.)

correlative conjunction Correlative conjunctions are two or more words (*neither...nor, either... or, not only...but also*) that work together to link parts of a sentence. (See p. 243.)

count noun A count noun names things that can be counted. (See pp. 226–227.)

dangling modifier A dangling modifier does not have a clear connection to the word it modifies. (See pp. 222–223.)

declarative   A declarative sentence is a statement. (See p. 247.) *The measurements were incorrect.*

dependent clause   See subordinate clause.

direct object   A direct object is the noun, pronoun, or noun clause naming the person or thing that takes the action of a transitive verb. (See p. 249.)

double negative   A double negative is the use of two negatives to convey one negative idea. It should be avoided in academic writing. (See p. 113.)

expletive   *There* and *it* are expletives, or "dummy subjects," that are used to fill a grammatical slot in a sentence. (See p. 114.)

fragment   A fragment is a group of words that is capitalized and punctuated like a sentence but lacks a subject and predicate. (See pp. 214–217.)

gender   Gender is the classification of nouns or pronouns as masculine and feminine. (See p. 221.)

he/she; s/he   Academic audiences prefer writing that is gender inclusive (unless a distinction of gender is necessary). (See p. 118.)

helping verb   Helping verbs are also known as auxiliary verbs. These verbs (forms of *be, do,* and *have*) join with other verbs to indicate tense and mood. Modal verbs can also be used as helping verbs. (See p. 238.)

herself/himself/myself/yourself   These *–self* pronouns refer to or intensify nouns or other pronouns. They are often used colloquially in place of personal pronouns, but not usually in academic writing.

imperative   An imperative sentence expresses a command. The subject of an imperative sentence is often implied. (See p. 247.) *Be quiet!*

independent clause   An independent—or main—clause is a group of words with a subject and predicate that can stand alone as a sentence. (See p. 253.)

indirect object   An indirect object is a noun, pronoun, or noun phrase that names the person or thing that is affected by the action of a transitive verb.

interjection   An interjection is a word that expresses strong emotion. *Ouch!*

interrogative   An interrogative sentence asks a question. (See p. 247.)

intransitive verb   An intransitive verb does not take an object. *I just wanted to participate.*

irregular verb   An irregular verb does not take *–ed* or *–d* to form its past tense or past participle. (See pp. 237–238.) *slept, swam*

its/it's   **Its** is the possessive form of **it** and does not take an apostrophe. **It's** is the contraction of **it** is. *As the fish swam, its fins undulated. It's a sad day when the Cubs lose.*

linking verb   A linking verb connects a subject to a complement.

main clause   See independent clause.

modifier   A modifier is a word, phrase, or clause that describes another word. Modifiers are adjectives (see p. 234), adverbs (see p. 239), adjective clauses (see pp. 256–257), and adverb clauses (see p. 258).

noncount noun   A noncount noun names things that cannot be counted. (See pp. 226–227.)

nonrestrictive modifier   A nonrestrictive modifier is not essential to the meaning of the word, phrase, or clause it modifies and should be set off by commas or other punctuation. (See pp. 272–275.)

noun   A noun names a person, place, or thing. (See p. 231.)

object   An object is the receiver of an action within a sentence, clause, or phrase. (See p. 249.)

parallelism   Parallelism is the practice of putting similar elements in a sentence in a similar grammatical pattern. (See p. 115.)

parts of speech   There are eight parts of speech, or groups of words classified by their grammatical functions and meanings: nouns, pronouns, verbs, adjectives, adverbs, prepositions, conjunctions, and interjections. (See pp. 230–242.)

passive voice   Passive voice is indicated by a clause with a transitive verb that is acting upon the subject. (See pp. 112 and 113.)

phrase   A phrase is a group of words that does not contain both a subject and a predicate. (See pp. 249–252.)

possessive case   The possessive case indicates ownership. (See p. 224.)

predicate   The predicate is the part of a clause that expresses the action or tells something about the subject. The predicate includes the verb and its complements, objects, and modifiers. (See pp. 248–252.)

preposition   A preposition is a part of speech that shows relationships or qualities. (See pp. 240–241.)

prepositional phrase   A prepositional phrase is a phrase formed by a preposition and its object. A prepositional phrase includes the modifiers of the object. (See p. 240.)

pronoun   A pronoun is a part of speech that stands for other nouns or pronouns. Classes of pronouns include: **possessive pronouns**, **personal pronouns**, **demonstrative pronouns**, **indefinite pronouns**, **relative pronouns**, **interrogative pronouns**, **reflexive pronouns**, and **reciprocal pronouns**. (See pp. 232–233.)

pronoun case   Pronouns that act as the subject of a sentence are in the **subjective case** (*I, you, he, she, it, we, they*). Pronouns that act as direct or indirect objects are in the **objective case** (*me, you, him, her, it, us, them*). Pronouns that indicate ownership are in the **possessive case** (*my, your, his, her, its, our, their*). (See pp. 232–233.)

proper noun   A proper noun is a noun that names a particular person, place, thing, or group. Proper nouns are capitalized. (See p. 231.)

relative pronoun   *That, which, what, who, whom,* and *whose* are relative pronouns. (See p. 233.)

restrictive modifier   A restrictive modifier is essential to the meaning of the word, phrase, or clause it modifies. Unlike a nonrestrictive modifier, it is not set off by punctuation. (See pp. 272–275.)

run-on sentence   A run-on sentence occurs when two main clauses are fused together without punctuation or a conjunction. (See pp. 218–219.)

sentence   A sentence is a grammatically independent group of words that contains at least one independent clause. (See pp. 247–259.)

subject   A subject is a noun, pronoun, or noun phrase that identifies what the clause is about and is connected to the predicate. (See pp. 248–252.)

subject-verb agreement   See **agreement**.

subjunctive mood   The subjunctive mood expresses a wish, a condition contrary to fact, a recommendation, or a request. (See p. 236.)

subordinate   A subordinate relationship is a relationship of unequal importance, in either grammar or meaning. (See pp. 116–117.)

subordinate clause   A subordinate clause, also called a dependent clause, is a clause that cannot stand alone but must be attached to a main clause. (See p. 217.)

subordinating conjunction   A subordinating conjunction is a word that introduces a subordinate clause. (See p. 244.)

their/there/they're   **Their** is a possessive pronoun (see p. 232); **there** is most commonly used as an expletive (see p. 114); and **they're** is a contraction of *they are* (see p. 294).

transition   A transition is a word or phrase that notes movement from one unit of writing to another. (See p. 85 and p. 111.)

transitive verb   A transitive verb is a verb that takes a direct object.

try and/try to   See **sure and/sure to**.

verb   A verb is a word that shows action or characterizes a subject in some way. (See pp. 204–211.)

who/whom   **Who** is the subject pronoun, while **whom** is the object pronoun. *Who is that in the yard? With whom did you dance?*

who's/whose   **Who's** is a contraction of *who is*, while **whose** is a possessive. *Who's there? Whose shoes are those?*

you   **You** is primarily used to directly address the reader, but it is often used informally to refer to people in general.

your/you're   **Your** and **you're** are not interchangeable. **Your** is the possessive form of *you. Your conscience will rest easier after you vote.* **You're** is the contraction of *you are. You're a citizen, and so you are expected to vote.*

INDEX

Q

Question(s)
  analyzing sources to ask. *See* Analyzing
    to ask questions
  for critical reading, 73
  for critical writing, 74
  direct and indirect, 296
  to guide research, 16–17
  in introductory paragraphs, 110
Question marks
  to end sentences that are questions, 296
  quoting sentences ending with, 293
  to show doubt about dates and
    numbers, 296
Quotation(s)
  block, 59, 292
  capitalization of first words in, 300
  commas with, 261, 263
  direct and indirect, 263
  ellipses to show pauses or omitted
    words in, 281
  in introductory paragraphs, 110
  MLA style for, 128, 138, 292–93
Quotation marks, 288–93
  to indicate direct quotations, 288, 291
  to indicate speech, 288, 291–93
  to indicate technical terms or words
    from other languages, 288, 290
  with other punctuation marks, 292, 295
  to refer to a word as a word, 288, 289
  to show irony, 288, 290
  for titles of short works, 288, 289
Quoting, 41, 55, 56, 58–59

R

Racism, avoiding, 118
Reading, critical, 72–73
Reasoning, critical, 78
Reciprocal pronouns, 233
Redundant words, 122
Reference books, 24–25. *See also*
  Dictionaries; Encyclopedias
  APA reference list style for, 185
  CMS style for, 200
Reference librarians, 30
Reference lists, 41. *See also* APA reference
  lists; bibliographies; MLA works-
  cited lists
  CSE style for, 8
Relative pronouns, 114, 233
Relevance, evaluating sources for, 34–35
Religious discrimination, avoiding, 119
Religious texts
  APA in-text citation style for, 173
  CMS style for, 200

colons in citations from Bible, 278
Repetition, for coherence in paragraphs, 86
Reports
  APA reference list style for, 178–79, 186
  CSE reference list style for, 196
Research, 11–32
  kinds of, 19
  in library, 29–31
  process for, 12
  questions to guide, 16–17, 20–21
  sources for. *See* Sources
  starting research papers, 32
  topics for, 13–15
Restatements, dashes to indicate, 284
Reviews
  APA reference list style for, 186
  MLA works-cited list example of, 155
Revised books, CSE reference list style, 195
Revising, 105–22, 202
  aspects of, 106
  developing a plan for, 107
  editing and proofreading compared
    with, 106
  styling paragraphs and, 108–12
  styling sentences and, 113–19
  styling words and, 120–22
Rhetoric, 3–4, 66–67, 79–101
  analyzing to understand, 70–71
Rhetorical situations, 3
Run-on sentences, 218–19

S

Salutations, colons in, 278
Scholarly journals. *See* Journal(s); Online
  databases
Scientific names, italics for, 298
Scientific writing, 8, 112
Scores, 301
Sculptures. *See* Artworks
Search engines. *See* Online databases
Secondary sources, 18
Semicolons, 280
  in compound sentences, 254, 255
  to join list elements that are
    complicated or contain their
    own punctuation, 266, 280
  to join sentences, 280
Sentence(s), 246–59
  academic, 113
  adding additional information to main
    idea of, 269, 272–75
  adding to the end of another sentence,
    269, 270–71
  beginning with numbers, 301
  capitalization of first words in, 300
  colons to link, 279

commas separating parts of lists in,
  261, 264–67, 277, 280
  complete, quoting, 292
  complex, 247, 256–58
  compound, 247, 254–55
  compound-complex, 247, 259
  containing multiple parts, commas in,
    268–75
  coordination and subordination in,
    116–17
  declarative, 247, 295
  easy-to-read, 114
  ending with question marks or excla-
    mation points, quoting, 293
  exclamatory, 247
  functions of, 247
  fused, 218, 219
  imperative, 247, 295
  inclusive language in, 118–19
  interrogative, 247. *See also* Question(s)
  omitting commas between verb and its
    subject or object in, 277
  parallelism in, 1115
  periods to end, 295
  question marks to end, 296
  quoting parts of, 293
  run-on, 218–19
  simple, 247, 248–49
  subject of. *See* Subjects (of sentences)
  varying order of, 108
  varying patterns of, 108
Sentence fragments, 214–17
Series
  semicolons to join elements that are
    complicated or contain their own
    punctuation, 266, 280
  of words, commas in, 261, 264–67, 277
Series, volumes in, CSE reference list style
  for, 196
Sexism, avoiding, 118
-s form of verbs, 237
Short stories, MLA works-cited list pat-
  tern for, 144–146
Signals for quotations, 59
Simple future tense, 211
Simple past tense, 210, 211
Simple present tense, 209, 210, 211
Simple sentences, 247, 248–49
Slashes
  with dates and fractions, 287
  to indicate line breaks in quoted
    poems, 287
  in paired terms, 287
Social sciences, writing in, 9
Software, APA reference list style for, 190
Sound recordings. *See* Audio recordings
Sources